D1570700

FLYING ON INSTRUMENTS
with Flight Simulator

Jonathan M. Stern

COMPUTE!™ Publications,Inc.abc
Part of ABC Consumer Magazines, Inc.
One of the ABC Publishing Companies
Greensboro, North Carolina

ISBN 0-87455-091-2

COMPUTE! Publications, Inc., Post Office Box 5406, Greensboro, NC 27403, (919) 275-9809, is part of ABC Consumer Magazines, Inc., one of the ABC Publishing Companies, and is not associated with any manufacturer of personal computers. Amiga is a trademark of Commodore-Amiga, Inc. Apple II is a trademark of Apple Computer, Inc. Atari and Atari ST are trademarks of Atari Corporation. Macintosh is a trademark of MacIntosh Laboratory, licensed to Apple Computer, Inc.

Flight Simulator is produced by Microsoft Corporation and copyright 1984 and 1986 by Bruce A. Artwick. Flight Simulator II is produced by SubLOGIC Corporation and copyright 1984 and 1986 by Bruce A. Artwick.

Contents

Foreword

You've flown *Flight Simulator* countless times, been sightseeing from Puget Sound to Martha's Vineyard, and can put your airplane down on the shortest landing strip. But unless you can fly in the worst conditions—through heavy clouds, in the dark of night, with low visibility—you're only a *fair-weather pilot*.

To fly in bad weather—just as every professional pilot does—you must use your airplane's instruments. You must know what each instrument is for, how to read it, and how to use those readings to navigate, fly, and land your aircraft.

Flying on Instruments with Flight Simulator is your tutor and guide to this new and challenging aspect of *Flight Simulator* and *Flight Simulator II*. Written by a pilot/instructor who is instrument rated (and who worked as an air traffic controller at Washington National Airport), this book will make you an *all-weather*, not just fair-weather, pilot.

You'll learn how your instruments operate, and what they're telling you. You'll learn how to climb, bank, and dive under complete control, with only instruments to guide you. And you'll learn how to navigate using the same kinds of charts real pilots use.

Then you'll delve into the instrument-rated pilot's world. You'll learn how to read and use Instrument Approach Procedure (IAP) charts—charts so vital to pilots that they're updated every 56 days by the Federal government. You'll execute actual instrument approaches, using actual charts, as you take off, fly, and land your airplane under less-than-perfect weather conditions.

Flight Simulator and *Flight Simulator II* provide three methods of navigating and landing with instruments. These three methods—VOR, NDB, and ILS—are thoroughly explained and illustrated. Then it's your turn as you fly VOR radials, read your ADF as you approach a nondirectional beacon (NDB), or stay on the ILS glideslope.

That's just the beginning. Once you've mastered flying on instruments in *Flight Simulator* (and you will have by the time you finish this book), you can use the more than 100 IAP charts to fly on instruments, on your own, into and out of most of the simulations airports.

Flying on Instruments with Flight Simulator can be used with any version of *Flight Simulator* or *Flight Simulator II*, with Atari, Atari ST, Apple, Amiga, Commodore 64/64C/128, IBM PC/PCjr, or Macintosh personal computers.

Learn to fly on instruments, not by the seat of your pants, with *Flying on Instruments*.

Dedication

To my wife, Joy, who has put up with my many hundreds of hours at the computer.

Introduction

Thousands of airplanes take off, fly to distant places, and land every day. There are many different types of airplanes and many different types of pilots. Some pilots fly to earn a living; some fly strictly for pleasure.

Perhaps more numerous than the daily airplane flights are the copies of *Flight Simulator*—the extremely popular flight simulation available on a host of microcomputers—which have been sold. People of all ages and all professions use *Flight Simulator*. For pilots, *Flight Simulator* is an opportunity to try things they wouldn't dare try in a real airplane. For nonpilots, *Flight Simulator* provides fantasy, education, and diversion.

No More Weekend Pilots

Pilots who fly for pleasure are sometimes called *weekend pilots*. As their name implies, they fly on fair-weather weekends. Most professional pilots, on the other hand, are licensed to fly on instruments, so that when the ceiling is low or the visibility is reduced, their flights aren't canceled.

Flying on Instruments with Flight Simulator can take you from being a weekend *Flight Simulator* pilot and turn you into a professional *Flight Simulator* pilot. You'll quickly see that instrument flying on *Flight Simulator* makes the simulation even more challenging and even more enjoyable.

Flying on Instruments with Flight Simulator lets you go a step further. The book teaches you how to take off, fly to another airport, and land when the clouds are only 200 feet above the ground. It teaches you how to read and fly the instrument approach procedure charts that instrument-rated pilots use daily. And it provides you with the actual instrument approach procedure charts for the geographic regions included on *Flight Simulator* software:

- Boston/New York
- Southern California
- Chicago
- Seattle
- San Francisco (not on all versions)

Flying on Instruments with Flight Simulator is *not* an instrument-flying training program. If you are not qualified
and licensed to fly an airplane in instrument conditions
before you read this book, you won't be when you finish.
The Federal Aviation Administration prescribes stringent
requirements for airplane pilots, and the *Flight Simulator*
software, with or without instruments, obviously does not
meet these requirements.

Before trying to learn instrument flying from this book,
you should be familiar with visual flight on your own version
of *Flight Simulator*. Know all of your controls, such as throttle,
aileron, flaps, and cloud-height adjustment.

Because this book may be used with any version of *Flight
Simulator* on any computer, references to specific controls
(function keys, joystick, or mouse, for instance) are not made.
Any reference to *Flight Simulator* includes *Flight Simulator*
and/or *Flight Simulator II*.

What's Here

Chapter 1 explains the function of the flight instruments.

Chapter 2 shows how to fly various maneuvers with reference
to your flight instruments. This is called *basic attitude instrument flying*.

Chapter 3 describes the charts that you'll use to fly on instruments with *Flight Simulator*.

Chapter 4 describes how you'll use the aircraft electronic
equipment (avionics) to begin an instrument flight, and then
lets you practice departing on instruments.

Chapters 5, 6, and **7** take you through VOR, NDB, and ILS instrument approaches.

Chapter 8 shows you some variations on the basic procedures
with which you will already be familiar. You'll learn how to
make approaches to land over water at night and what to do
when part of your instrument landing system fails and you're
in the clouds.

The **Appendices** contain the charts that will guide you down in the worst of weather, show you the procedure for taking off again before the weather clears, and plot your longest flights.

At the beginning of each chapter, if necessary, instructions are given on parameters to set up with *Flight Simulator*. As you go through the various maneuvers and procedures, you should pause the simulation whenever you find it necessary to read ahead. Then undo the pause and continue.

If you're ready to begin, sit down at your computer, strap in, and turn to Chapter 1. Get set to fly on instruments with *Flight Simulator*.

Chapter 1

Flight Instruments

Chapter 1
Flight Instruments

*Six flight instruments form the basis of flying on instruments.
Knowing what each does, and how, is important.*

Other than the need to know *where* you are, why do you need
instruments in the airplane? Believe it or not, the human abil-
ity to sense which way is up is easily deceived in an aircraft.
Balance control, other than through visual cues, comes from
your inner ears. When you fly in clouds or in areas of re-
stricted visibility, you depend on your inner ears to tell you
which way is up. Unfortunately, your inner ears can't handle
the job. That's why you need instruments.

Six flight instruments are found in almost every instrument-
equipped aircraft (Figure 1-1).

Figure 1-1. Flight Instruments

1. Airspeed Indicator
2. Altimeter
3. Vertical-Speed Indicator
4. Attitude Indicator
5. Turn Coordinator
6. Heading Indicator

Airspeed Indicator

The airspeed indicator shows the *indicated airspeed* of the airplane in nautical miles per hour, commonly called *knots*. The airspeed indicator, vertical-speed indicator, and altimeter are components of the Pitot-static system (Figure 1-2).

Figure 1-2. Pitot-Static System

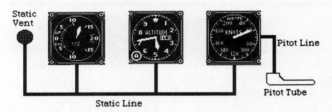

Three instruments—from left to right, the vertical-speed indicator, altimeter, and airspeed indicator—operate from the Pitot-static system.

The Pitot tube and static vent are mounted outside the airplane. The Pitot tube is positioned so that its front faces into the stream of air—the air rams into the opening. The static vent is usually flush-mounted on the side of the airplane so that there's no impact air measurement—in other words, the air doesn't rush into the vent. The airspeed indicator works by measuring the *difference* between the ram air pressure in the Pitot tube and the static air pressure in the vent.

To fully understand how these instruments operate, you have to understand some characteristics of air in the earth's atmosphere.

Air has weight: On a standard day at sea level when the temperature is 59° Fahrenheit, the atmosphere weighs 14.7 pounds per square inch (ppsi). Using a pressure measuring device called a barometer, this 14.7 ppsi equals 29.92 inches of mercury. Because air has weight, as you ascend from sea level, there is less air above you and, therefore, less weight on you. The rate at which the weight of the atmosphere changes isn't constant, but at the altitudes at which most single-engine airplanes fly, each 1000-foot increase in altitude results in a pressure decrease of approximately one inch of mercury.

Figure 1-3. Airspeed Indicator

When the airplane is parked on the ground, the Pitot tube senses the ambient air pressure (assuming no wind). Since the difference between the pressure in the Pitot tube and the pressure in the static vent is 0, the airspeed indicator indicates an airspeed of 0.

When the airplane is in flight, the pressure in the Pitot tube is greater than the ambient pressure measured by the static vent. This pressure difference is indicated as airspeed on the airspeed indicator.

If the airplane flies at sea level on a standard day (the pressure is 29.92 inches of mercury and the temperature is 59° Fahrenheit), the indicated airspeed accurately reports the speed at which the airplane is moving through the air. When the airplane is operated at other altitudes or in nonstandard atmospheric conditions, the indicated airspeed doesn't accurately reflect the *true airspeed*. But true airspeed can always be calculated if temperature, pressure, and indicated airspeed are known.

Measure True Airspeed

For *Flight Simulator* purposes, your true airspeed can be estimated by multiplying your indicated airspeed by 1 plus 1.5 percent for each 1000 feet above sea level that you're flying.

For example, if you're flying at 5000 feet with an indicated airspeed of 100 knots, your true airspeed is approximately 107.5 knots (100 * [1 + 5(.015)]).

True airspeed is *not* the speed at which the airplane moves over the ground. To compute *groundspeed*, any headwind must be subtracted from, or any tailwind must be added to, the true airspeed.

Altimeter

The altimeter is the only instrument which shows how high the airplane is above some level. The altimeter has two hands like those of a clock and a small indicator that appears near the numbers on the outer ring of the gauge. The large hand indicates hundreds of feet. The small hand shows thousands of feet. The small indicator indicates tens of thousands of feet. The altimeter in Figure 1-2 shows an altitude of 4720 feet.

The altimeter is an aneroid barometer that displays pressure in feet above sea level (mean sea level), not above ground level. The altimeter cannot work accurately unless the pilot sets it to the current altimeter setting, which is the pressure at sea level under existing atmospheric conditions. The Federal Aviation Regulations require pilots of radio-equipped airplanes to keep the altimeter set to the "current reported altimeter setting of a station along the route and within 100 nautical miles of the aircraft."

The altimeter measures the barometric pressure in the static vent.

Figure 1-4. Altimeter

Vertical Speed Indicator

The vertical speed indicator, like the altimeter, is connected only to the static vent. The vertical speed indicator shows whether the airplane is flying at a constant altitude, climbing, or descending, and if climbing or descending, at what rate. The face of the instrument is graduated in hundreds of feet per minute, with the top half showing climbs, and the bottom half, descents.

Figure 1-5. Vertical Speed Indicator

Attitude Indicator

The next three instruments—the attitude indicator, turn coordinator, and heading indicator—are gyroscopic instruments.
Each instrument uses a gyroscope to maintain its orientation
relative to one or more of the axes of the airplane.

The attitude indicator, as its name implies, indicates the
attitude of the airplane relative to the earth's surface. The instrument displays airplane *pitch* (whether its nose is up or
down) and airplane *bank* (the angle the wing forms with the
horizon). Marks around the top half of the instrument on
some versions of *Flight Simulator* indicate angles of bank of
10°, 20°, 30°, 60°, and 90°.

Figure 1-6. Attitude Indicator

Turn Coordinator

The turn coordinator is actually two instruments in one. The
airplane replica in the middle of the instrument rolls propor-
tionally to the roll rate of the airplane. When the bank angle is
maintained, the replica indicates the rate of turn. When the
right or left wing of the replica is aligned with the lower mark,
the airplane is turning at a rate of 3° per second (so a full
360° turn takes two minutes). This rate of turn is known as
standard rate.

The other instrument in the turn coordinator is called an
inclinometer. The inclinometer shows whether or not use of
rudder and aileron is coordinated. If the ball in the liquid-
filled glass tube moves outside of the center of the tube, the
rudder and ailerons are not coordinated. If the ball moves to
the outside of the turn, the airplane is skidding. If the ball
moves to the inside of the turn, the airplane is slipping.

Uncoordinated flight can always be corrected by applying
sufficient rudder pressure on the same side as the ball so that
it returns to the center of the tube. This is known to student
pilots as "stepping on the ball," because the rudder is con-
trolled by pedals; pressure on the left pedal coordinates the

turn if the ball is to the left of center, and pressure on the right pedal coordinates the turn if the ball is right of center.

Flight Simulator gives you the option of flying with auto-coordination. This lets you control the ailerons and have the proper amount of rudder automatically applied. I recommend that you use auto-coordination for learning to fly on instruments. Later, if you want, you can try what you've learned without auto-coordination.

Figure 1-7. Turn Coordinator

From left to right, these three turn coordinators show left standard rate turn slipping, coordinated, *and* skidding.

Heading Indicator

The third gyroscopic instrument is the heading indicator. The heading indicator is used because a magnetic compass only works accurately when the airplane is flying straight and level in unaccelerated flight. Any time the airplane is banked, pitched, accelerated, or decelerated, the magnetic compass gives a wrong reading. The heading indicator solves this problem by using a gyroscope instead of a magnet. The heading indicator has its own error, however. Bearing friction causes the heading indicator to creep from the heading to which it has been set. Therefore, the heading indicator should be reset to the magnetic compass every 10 or 15 minutes, but only when the airplane is straight and level in unaccelerated flight.

Figure 1-8. Heading Indicator

Chapter 2

Basic Attitude Instrument Flying

Chapter 2
Basic Attitude Instrument Flying

Learning how to scan the instruments—the right ones and in the right order—puts you on the right track for flying on instruments.

The basic formula for flying an airplane is

Attitude + Power = Performance

This formula simply states that for any given attitude (pitch and bank) and power setting, a certain performance will result. If you understand this formula, you'll understand what *instrument scanning* is all about.

Scanning

While flying in clouds, or when the ground isn't visible, pilots must constantly be aware of the attitude, power setting, and performance of their airplane. Since the sense of balance isn't adequate to keep an airplane flying right side up, the pilot must scan the instruments to make sure things are as they should be.

Although many different scan patterns may work, most instrument-flying authorities recommend a pattern that includes checking the attitude indicator between checks on every other instrument. Since attitude plus power equals performance, once you've set the power, it's imperative to set and maintain the desired attitude.

After checking the attitude indicator, scan the other instruments to verify that the desired performance actually occurs. If it does, then check the attitude indicator again to insure that the attitude is maintained. But if the performance is not what you want, use the attitude indicator to correct the attitude. This may sound complicated, but it's not—at least not when you're in the airplane looking at your instruments.

The exact scan pattern you use depends on the maneuver you're performing. All possible maneuvers of an airplane have only four fundamental components:

- Straight and level
- Climbs
- Descents
- Turns

These components—alone or in combination—cover all possible flying maneuvers. For each component, there's one instrument which gives the primary indication of pitch performance (PP), one instrument that gives the primary indication of bank performance (PB), and one instrument that gives the primary indication of power performance. The primary pitch and primary bank instruments vary with the maneuver component being performed. *But the primary power instrument is* always *the airspeed indicator.*

Straight and Level

Figure 2-1 shows the instruments of an airplane in straight and level flight. The aircraft is flying at 4980 feet, with an airspeed of 140 knots, and on a heading of 270°.

Figure 2-1. Straight and Level

In straight and level flight, the primary indicator of pitch performance (PP) is the altimeter. The primary indicator of bank performance (PB) is the heading indicator.

To maintain straight and level flight, the pilot might use this scan technique:

 Attitude indicator—wings level, pitch level

 Altimeter—20 feet below desired altitude

 Attitude indicator—pitch up slightly to climb to 5000 feet

 Heading indicator—right on heading

 Attitude indicator—maintain wings level

 Altimeter—approaching 5000 feet

 Attitude indicator—pitch down slightly to maintain 5000 feet

 Airspeed indicator—as desired

The scan should occasionally encompass the other instruments. For straight and level flight, the altimeter gives the primary indication of pitch performance and the heading indicator gives the primary bank-performance information. If the altimeter and heading indicator remain on the same marks, the airplane is flying straight and level.

The airspeed indicator is *always* the primary performance indicator for the power setting. The more power (throttle) applied, the faster the airspeed. Throttle back on the power and the airspeed drops.

In straight and level flight, it's useful to occasionally scan the vertical-speed indicator and the turn coordinator as backups to the primary instruments. If the vertical-speed indicator shows a 1000-foot-per-minute descent when the altitude is holding steady on the altimeter, there must be a problem with one of those two instruments. A third instrument can be checked to determine which of the two is malfunctioning. If the airspeed is normal for the throttle setting and level flight, then the pilot determines that the vertical-speed indicator is malfunctioning. On the other hand, if the airspeed is excessive, the pilot decides that the altimeter is not functioning.

Practice flying straight and level now. When the airplane is standing still on the ground, the instrument readings—with the exception of the airspeed indicator—will be similar to readings during straight and level flight. The attitude indicator will show wings level and level pitch; the altimeter will remain constant; the turn coordinator will be level; the heading indicator will remain constant; and the vertical speed indicator will be on 0.

Take off, climb to 5000 feet, and fly straight and level on a 270° heading. Try using the instrument-scan pattern described above. Look out the various windshield views to correlate what you see with the instrument readings. When you feel comfortable with straight and level flight, pause the simulation and continue reading.

Right Turn

Figure 2-2 shows the instrument panel of an airplane in a level right turn. As in straight and level flight, the altimeter is the primary pitch instrument in a level turn.

In this turn, the pilot is trying to maintain a standard rate turn. Therefore, the turn coordinator becomes the primary bank instrument and should take the place of the heading indicator in the scan pattern described for straight and level flight. If the pilot chose to make a 30° banked turn instead of a standard rate turn, then the attitude indicator would become the primary bank instrument (this is the only situation in which the attitude indicator is a primary performance instrument).

Figure 2-2. Right Turn

In a level-turn maneuver, the altimeter serves as the primary pitch (PP) instrument, while the turn coordinator becomes the primary bank (PB) instrument.

The scan pattern for this right turn might be

 Attitude indicator—shows approximately 20° right bank and level pitch. The bank angle necessary for a standard-rate turn can be estimated using the following formula:

Bank angle = Airspeed [Knots] / 10 + 7

 Altimeter—at desired altitude

Attitude indicator—same appearance as last scan

 Turn coordinator—shows standard-rate right turn

 Attitude indicator—same as last scan

 Airspeed indicator—at desired cruise speed

 Attitude indicator—same as last scan

 Heading indicator—are you approaching your desired heading? As a rule of thumb, rollout of the turn should begin when the airplane is within one-half of the bank angle of the desired heading. If a 20° bank is used in the turn, and the desired heading is 260°, begin your rollout when passing through heading 250°.

 Unpause *Flight Simulator* now and practice making turns to predetermined headings while maintaining 5000 feet. Practice both left and right turns.

As a general rule for flying on instruments, never use a turn steeper than standard rate or a bank angle greater than one-half the number of degrees to turn, whichever is less. Thus, if you want to turn through 40° of heading, don't use a bank angle steeper than 20°.

When you feel comfortable with both left and right turns, pause and keep reading.

Climb

Take a look at Figure 2-3, which shows the instruments of an airplane climbing at 500 feet per minute. Because a straight climb (without banks or turns) is being made, the heading indicator is the primary bank instrument. If the heading doesn't change, then the wings are level.

The vertical speed indicator is the primary pitch instrument for a *constant-rate* climb.

On the other hand, if you wanted to climb at a *constant airspeed*, not at a constant rate, the airspeed indicator would be the primary pitch instrument instead.

For a *constant rate, constant airspeed* climb, adjust the airplane pitch to establish the rate of climb (500 feet per minute, for instance); then adjust the throttle setting to maintain the desired airspeed. You may need to correct both the pitch and power setting to keep climbing at the same rate and with the same airspeed.

Figure 2-3. Climb

In a straight climb at a constant rate (as shown by these instruments), the heading indicator is the primary bank (PB) instrument, and the vertical speed indicator is the primary pitch (PP) instrument.

The instrument scan should include the secondary instruments—both as a backup and so that you know when to level off at the desired altitude. As a rule of thumb, the level-off should begin when the altitude is within 1/10 the rate of climb. For example, if the desired altitude is 6000 feet and the rate of climb is 500 feet per minute, begin leveling off as the airplane passes through 5950 feet.

Practice by climbing from 5000 feet to 6000 feet on a constant heading at 500 feet per minute while maintaining 80 knots. Keep trying to do it until you get everything right.

Descent

A constant-rate descent, as shown in Figure 2-4, is not much different from a constant-rate climb. The same primary instruments are used.

The major difference is that in the descent, earth's gravity is working for you rather than against you. Because of this, it's possible to build up excessive speed, speed that demands that you reduce the throttle setting.

Figure 2-4. Descent

The same primary instruments—the heading indicator and the vertical speed indicator—are used when conducting a constant-rate descent as when in a constant-rate climb.

Additionally—again because of gravity—the level-off should begin when the airplane is passing through an altitude 1/5 the rate of climb from the desired altitude. If the airplane whose instruments appear in Figure 2-4 is descending to 5000 feet, the pilot should begin leveling off when the airplane passes through 5080 feet (400 feet per minute divided by 5 equals 80 feet).

 Descend from 6000 feet to 4000 feet at 1000 feet per minute while maintaining 120 knots. If you do it just right, it will take you exactly two minutes and you'll travel four miles.

Climbing/Descending Turns

You've learned how to use your instruments to perform the four fundamental flight maneuvers. All that remains of basic attitude instrument flying are the two hybrids, *climbing* and *descending turns.*

These maneuvers are simply combinations of the components you've already seen demonstrated. If they appear more difficult, it may be due to the fact that more things are going on at the same time. In a climbing turn, for instance, not only is the heading changing, but the altitude is increasing. Therefore it's more important that you continue to scan the instruments and not fixate on any particular one. If you study only one instrument—say, the altimeter—it's likely you'll neglect to roll out on your desired heading.

Since the airplane shown in Figure 2-5 is making a standard-rate turn, the turn coordinator provides the primary indication of bank performance. And because a constant-rate climb is being carried out, the vertical speed indicator is the primary pitch performance instrument.

The heading indicator and altimeter serve as secondary pitch and bank instruments and provide the information you'll need to know in order to roll out of the turn and level off from the climb. As with all maneuvers, the airspeed indicator serves as the primary power performance indicator.

Begin the rollout from the turn when the heading is within 1/2 the bank angle of the desired heading, and start the level-off when the altitude is within 1/10 the rate of climb of the desired altitude.

Figure 2-5. Climbing Left Turn

This aircraft is in the middle of a constant rate, climbing, standard rate turn.

    Now try climbing from 4000 to 5000 feet at 500 feet per minute in a standard-rate left turn, finishing at the heading with which you began the turn. In other words, make a spiraling climb.

If you do this just right, you'll reach 5000 feet as you roll out at your initial heading.

Descend to 2000 feet at 1000 feet per minute while turning toward the departure airport. Land and proceed to Chapter 3.

Chapter 3

Navigation Charts

Chapter 3
Navigation Charts

En route and instrument approach procedure charts are vital to successful instrument flying in Flight Simulator.

Before you take off, it's always a good idea to know where you're going. That's especially true when you're flying on instruments, for without some navigational references, you'll quickly get lost. Fortunately, aeronautical navigation charts are available.

Such charts are published by the National Ocean Service, a division of the U.S. Department of Commerce's National Oceanic and Atmospheric Administration (NOAA). Some nongovernment publishers also produce and sell aeronautical charts.

The charts of primary concern to the instrument-rated single-engine airplane pilot are *en route low-altitude charts* and *instrument approach procedure* charts.

En Route Low-Altitude Charts

En route low-altitude charts provide information found on the charts included in the *Flight Simulator* owner's manual (VORs, NDBs, and airports, for instance). En route low-altitude charts also show *victor airways*, the highways in the sky used for airplane navigation.

Victor airways are nothing more than VOR radials. However, maximum and minimum altitudes are listed to insure that the airplane is at least 1000 feet above the highest obstacle along the route, and at an altitude that allows the airplane to receive the VOR signals. Unfortunately, the design of *Flight Simulator* makes en route low-altitude charts virtually unusable.

The transmission distance of a real VOR is often not duplicated on *Flight Simulator*, so that using the victor airways on the charts often does not work. Additionally, many of the VORs printed on the en route low-altitude charts aren't included in the *Flight Simulator* database.

That's why I recommend en route navigation be done using the charts included in the *Flight Simulator* owner's manual. These charts also appear, courtesy of SubLOGIC Corporation, in Appendix C of this book.

Using these en route charts may require some experimentation, and occasionally will result in a crash if the terrain is higher than you had anticipated. Generally, however, if you climb 5000 feet above the elevation of your departure or arrival airport, you can safely fly the route.

The Federal Aviation Regulations require that the airplane be operated at least "1,000 feet above the highest obstacle within a horizontal distance of five statute miles from the course to be flown." To comply with that regulation in *Flight Simulator*, you'll have to know the height of the highest obstacle within five statute miles of your path—a fact you're not likely to know. If you do know the height of the highest obstacle, however (maybe you're flying in a familiar area), you can choose your altitude accordingly.

Instrument Approach Procedure Charts

Instrument approach procedure (IAP) charts are the other important navigational aid for instrument-rated pilots. The IAP charts show the information you need to approach and land at an airport while flying on instruments.

IAP charts are published in bound regional volumes and distributed every 56 days. Twenty-eight days after they're released, a change notice is distributed. This change notice includes a new chart for each IAP that's altered or has been added since the previous round of publication. Pilots are told of notices to airmen (NOTAMs)—which include the most recent chart changes—when they get their weather briefing, done either in person or over the telephone.

> Because of the time-critical nature of IAP charts, it's vital that the charts reprinted in this book *not* be used for actual navigation. They will have expired long before this book is sold.

There are three primary types of instrument approach procedures—VOR, NDB, and ILS approaches. These will be discussed completely in Chapters 5–7.

In recent years, new types of approaches have been developed, including area navigation and microwave. These new types of approaches can't be used on *Flight Simulator*. In fact, most single-engine airplanes aren't equipped to use these approach methods.

Like the en route low-altitude charts, many of the IAP charts include some navigation aids which are not part of the *Flight Simulator* database. However, all IAPs reprinted in this book can be flown using *some* version of *Flight Simulator.*

Some versions of the program (Commodore, Atari, IBM, and Apple II) don't include the San Francisco database. The IBM version of *Flight Simulator* doesn't equip the airplane with an automatic direction finder (ADF). An ADF is necessary to use any of the NDB approaches. If your version of *Flight Simulator* doesn't include an ADF, you can't use the NDB approaches. There's also a restriction when you're using the Macintosh version of *Flight Simulator*—the ADF on the Macintosh isn't accurate. See Chapter 6 for details.

Around an IAP Chart
Appendix B includes over 125 IAP charts, reprinted from those published by the National Ocean Service. Though their function is explained in great detail in later chapters, let's take a look at the form of an IAP chart.

Margin. Information in the top and bottom margins provides the type of IAP (VORs, for instance), the runway or runways served by the IAP, the city and state of the airport, and the airport's name (which is in print larger than the city and state).

Planview. The planview depicts the navigation aids which are used to arrive at and conduct the instrument approach, including the procedure you should follow if you can't make a landing (called a *missed approach procedure*). The planview shows courses to be flown, communication frequencies, and other details. Most IAP charts include a solid ring which bounds the area within ten nautical miles of the facility on which the approach is based (the VOR for a VOR IAP, for example). If a dashed ring appears outside the ten-nautical-mile ring, only the area inside the solid ring is drawn to scale.

Profile. The profile depicts minimum, maximum, and mandatory altitudes to be flown for various segments of the instrument approach procedure. If an altitude is underlined, it's a minimum altitude. If the altitude is overlined, it's a maximum altitude. If the altitude is underlined *and* overlined, it's a mandatory altitude.

Figure 3-1. Instrument Approach Procedure Chart

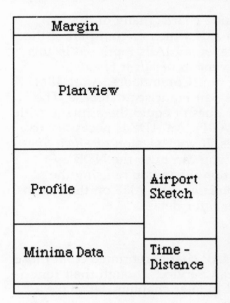

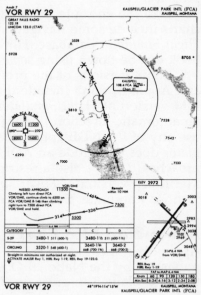

An IAP chart is divided into six sections, each of which provides the instrument-rated pilot with different information.

Airport Sketch. The airport sketch displays the runway pattern, runway numbers, lengths and widths of the runways, mean sea-level elevation of the airport, and lighting associated with each runway.

Minima Data. This provides the minimum altitudes to which you may descend and the minimum visibilities in which the IAP may be executed.

Time-Distance. This section of the chart is used on IAPs where the final-approach facility (say a VOR on a VOR IAP) is some distance from the missed approach point. Times are provided for various groundspeeds so that the pilot knows when to execute the missed approach procedure.

Instrument approach procedure charts and legends are reprinted in Appendix B for use with *Flight Simulator*. Learning how to read and use IAP charts requires practice. You'll get that practice as you work through Chapters 5–7.

Chapter 4

Instrument Departures and En Route Procedures

Chapter 4

Instrument Departures and En Route Procedures

Begin flying on instruments as you travel from Chicago's Meigs airport to Chicago Heights. Use the NAV radios and the Omni-Bearing Indicator as you fly through the cloud cover.

Begin this chapter with the following settings to *Flight Simulator*:

Cloud base:	1192
North position:	17189
East position:	16671
Altitude:	592
Season:	Winter

(Sometimes when you manually set the altitude in Flight Simulator, *then exit the environment editor, you'll find your aircraft at a height approximately* twice *what you entered. If this happens, simply set the altitude to 0; then exit the editor. Your airplane will appear on the ground at the location you specified.)*

It's a cloudy wintery morning at Chicago's Merrill C. Meigs airport. Snow is beginning to fall, and the clouds are only 600 feet above the ground. Your airplane is warmed up and ready to begin the journey from Meigs to Champaign, Illinois, with intermediate stops at Kankakee and Dwight.

Getting Clearance

Before taking off, you're required by the Federal Aviation Regulations to file a flight plan and receive clearance from air traffic control. Since *Flight Simulator* doesn't perform this function, make up your own clearance for the planned flight.

A typical clearance includes the following information:

- **A clearance limit.** Typically—and for *Flight Simulator* purposes, always—the destination airport.
- **A departure procedure.** The heading and altitude at which to depart the airport.
- **Route of flight.** The route to the destination airport. For simulation purposes, the flight route is defined by the names of VORs or NDBs along the flight path.
- **Altitude data.** The altitude to be flown along the route.

For the first leg of this morning's flight, your clearance is:

Cleared to the Greater Kankakee Airport via direct Chicago Heights direct Peotone direct, climb and maintain 6,000.

Before you take off, look at the IAP chart for Chicago/Lansing Municipal Airport, found in Appendix B on page 139.

See the white *T* in the black upside-down triangle near the bottom of the chart? This symbol means that there's a published departure procedure for this airport. (You'll find the departure procedure in Appendix A, under *Chicago, IL: Lansing Muni.*)

Now look at the IAP chart for Chicago/Merrill C. Meigs Airport. It's on page 140 of Appendix B. Note that the *T*-triangle symbol doesn't appear there. That indicates there's no published departure procedure for Merrill C. Meigs Airport. Where there's no published departure procedure, you must use good judgment in avoiding obstructions during takeoff.

Pre-Takeoff Avionics

Since your clearance directs you to fly direct to the Chicago Heights VOR, tune your NAV-1 radio to 114.2. Rotate the Omni-Bearing Selector (OBS) until the TO/FROM indicator displays *TO* and the course deviation indicator needle is centered.

While you're on the ground, tune your NAV-2 radio to Peotone on 113.2 and center the needle with a *TO* indication. (This saves you time when you're in the air.) Tune in the control tower by setting the COM radio to 121.3; then "listen" to the airport information.

Figure 4-1. Pre-Takeoff Avionics Settings

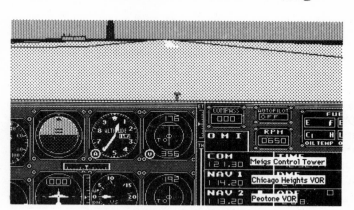

Your instrument panel should show these settings for COM, NAV 1, and NAV 2.

Cloud Quirks

To use *Flight Simulator* for instrument flying, you must be aware of one of its quirks. When air traffic controllers advise pilots of the weather, any reference to cloud heights is given as *height above ground level*.

With *Flight Simulator*, however, references to cloud heights are to *height above sea level*. To program cloud heights, then, you must add the height at which you want the clouds to appear to the airport elevation. Enter that sum in the environment editor. Remember that control tower reports of cloud heights will refer to mean sea level heights.

If you took off from Merrill C. Meigs with your environment editor showing the base of the clouds at 600 feet, you'd be inside those clouds immediately after takeoff (since Meigs' altitude is 592 feet above sea level). To prevent this, set the cloud base to 1192 feet (the airport elevation plus 600).

The flights in this chapter, and in the next three chapters, all use 1192 as a cloud base. You don't have to set the simulator's cloud tops if you don't want to. On some versions of *Flight Simulator*, setting only a cloud base has an important side effect—you'll fly through the cloud layer (it's not very thick) and once above it, there's a horizon line. This horizon can be especially helpful when you're just learning how to fly on instruments.

After you're more experienced, you may want to set cloud tops as well, so that you're flying in the midst of clouds during your entire flight. The view outside the aircraft should be completely white (or blank) when you're in clouds.

Takeoff

When you're ready, take off from Meigs. As you climb, bank right and turn to the heading shown on the Omni-Bearing Indicator (OBI). It should be close to 170°.

Figure 4-2. Needle Recentered

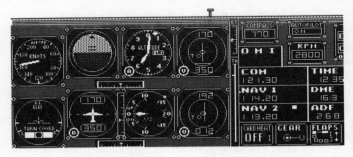

Centering the needle on the Omni-Bearing Indicator shows the course to the VOR station tuned in with the NAV 1 radio.

Continue climbing until you reach 6000 feet.

Reset the heading indicator to the magnetic compass when you level off at 6000 feet and are not accelerating. If the wind velocity is set to 0 in the environment editor, the needle should remain centered while you hold the heading shown on the OBI. If the wind velocity is greater than 0, though, you should use this procedure to track the VOR radial with a correction for wind.

Wind Compensation

- When the needle moves one dot or more either side of center, turn the airplane 20° toward the needle (Figure 4-3, airplane #2). The needle represents the course, and course corrections are made *toward* the needle. Remember, however, that if you're flying *to* the VOR with a *FROM* indication, or *from* the VOR with a *TO* indication, corrections must be made away from the needle.
- Fly the new heading until the needle approaches the center once again (Figure 4-3, airplane #3). If the needle continues to move away from the center, turn another 10° toward the needle and repeat this procedure up to a maximum correction of 90°.

Figure 4-3. VOR Tracking with Wind

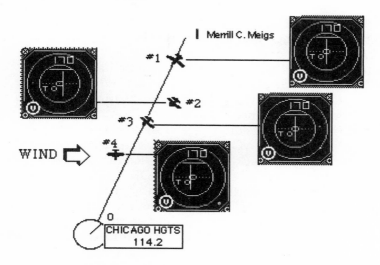

If wind is present in your simulation, you need to know how to conpensate for it as you fly on instruments.

- Take out one-half of the correction you used to recenter the needle (if you are tracking with the OBI set to 170°, and you turned 20° to the right to recenter the needle, turn left to heading 180° when the needle recenters). This establishes a correction angle of 10° to compensate for the wind's effect.
- If the needle stays centered, the wind correction angle is the proper amount of correction for the current wind conditions.
- If the needle begins to move to the opposite side, the wind correction angle is too great (see Figure 4-3, airplane #4). Turn the airplane so that its heading is the same as the Omni bearing selected, and when the needle recenters, turn so that you're using one-half of your previous wind correction angle.

The closer the airplane is to the VOR transmitter, the more sensitive the instrument becomes. When the airplane is within two miles of the transmitter, large needle deviations may occur. Don't chase the needle as it fluctuates when you're close to the transmitter.

Going On

As you pass over the Chicago Heights VOR transmitter, the *TO* indication automatically changes to a *FROM* indication. The distance-measuring equipment (DME) begins to show an increase rather than a decrease in its reading.

The most accurate way to tell you've passed a VOR station is when the TO/FROM indicator changes. When this occurs, center the needle on the NAV-2 Omni-Bearing Indicator and track directly to Peotone.

Chicago Heights and Peotone are close to one another. If you're navigating between VORs that are far apart, however, it might be necessary to track from one VOR until you're within transmission range of the second VOR. If this is necessary, use a ruler and the charts included in your *Flight Simulator* manual or in Appendix C to determine the outbound radial to track. Place the ruler on the chart so that it's on the center points of both VORs. Read the compass rose of the VOR you're receiving at the side closest to the distant VOR. The compass rose is graduated with 5° ticks. This is the radial that you should track outbound. Keep flying that radial (and that course if the VOR falls out of range) until you begin to receive the next VOR.

Now, turn the Omni-Bearing Selector (OBS) of the NAV-2 OBI until the needle is centered and a *TO* indication shows. Track that radial. (It should be close to what you read from the chart-and-ruler exercise.)

Figure 4-4 illustrates the procedure.

Figure 4-4. Flying Between Distant VORs

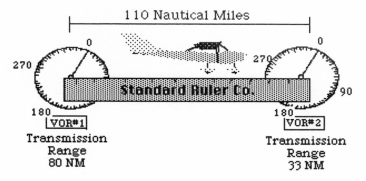

Eastbound: Track the 060 radial from
VOR #1 for 77NM
Westbound: Track the 240 radial from
VOR #2 for 30NM

Use a ruler and one of the en route charts to track from one VOR until you're within range of a second, distant VOR.

Chapter 5

VOR Approaches

Chapter 5
VOR Approaches

Tackle your first instrument approach procedure as you use VOR radials to guide you to Kankakee.

You've just passed over the Chicago Heights VOR at 6000 feet. Your NAV-2 Omni-Bearing Selector (OBS) should be set to approximately 216° with a *TO* indication to guide you directly to the Peotone VOR. While the airplane is flying toward Peotone, tune 111.6, the Kankakee VOR frequency, into NAV-1. Until you get within a few miles of Peotone, the Kankakee VOR will be out of range.

Note: The database on at least one early version of *Flight Simulator* was missing the Kankakee VOR.

If, by the time you pass the Peotone VOR (as shown by the *FROM* indication), you've not been able to receive the Kankakee VOR, use the Chicago Heights VOR instead of Kankakee. Read through this chapter, but substitute the Chicago Heights VOR for all instances of the Kankakee VOR.

Proceed directly to Chicago Heights while descending to 2300 feet. You'll not be able to use the Peotone VOR to identify the AROMA intersection. Instead, substitute 4.8 DME for AROMA. When you complete the approach (there won't be an airport in sight), pause the simulation and begin Chapter 6.

Descending Time

It's time to start thinking about a descent. Tune in the Greater Kankakee control tower on 123.0 to find out which runway is in use. The control tower reported runway 22 in use when I made the flight. Look in Appendix B, page 169, for the VOR RWY 22 approach to Greater Kankakee.

See the short, thin line extending from Peotone toward the Kankakee VOR in the planview? That line is called a *terminal route* and indicates that you can descend to 2300 feet

Chapter 5

and follow the 191° radial for 12 nautical miles to the Kankakee VOR. *Flight Simulator* only provides even-numbered radials, so use 190° or 192°. (The Atari ST and Commodore Amiga versions of *Flight Simulator* are exceptions to this last statement. You can set the OBI to any radial. If you're using one of these versions, you can use the actual radial described, not just an even-numbered one.)

But you're at (or should be at) 6000 feet now. Time to start down.

To calculate how many miles in advance you should begin your descent, use this formula:

groundspeed/60 * (feet to descend/rate of descent) = miles

In this case, if your groundspeed is 120 knots and you want to descend at 500 feet per minute, you'll need 14.8 nautical miles (120/60 * (3700/500) =14.8).

Figure 5-1. Descending

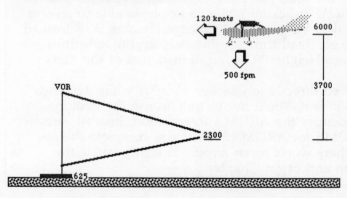

To descend from 6000 to 2300 feet at a rate of 500 feet per minute while flying with a groundspeed of 120 knots, you need to begin the descent about 14.8 miles from the Kankakee VOR.

Don't worry if you're not down to 2300 feet by the time you reach the Kankakee VOR. You can fly at least another ten nautical miles after reaching the VOR before a descent below 2300 feet is authorized. However, if you want to minimize the time required to fly the approach, you won't want to be very high above the minimum altitude when you cross the VOR.

If you find that you don't have enough distance remaining to make your descent at 500 feet per minute, you can compute the necessary rate of descent using this second formula:

feet to descend * (groundspeed/(60 * miles)) = required rate of descent

After crossing the Peotone VOR, establish yourself on the radial (190° or 192°), pause the simulation, and familiarize yourself with the Kankakee VOR RWY 22 IAP chart.

The Kankakee IAP

Take a look at this reduced version of the VOR RWY 22 IAP chart for Kankakee.

Figure 5-2. Kankakee

Not for use in Navigation

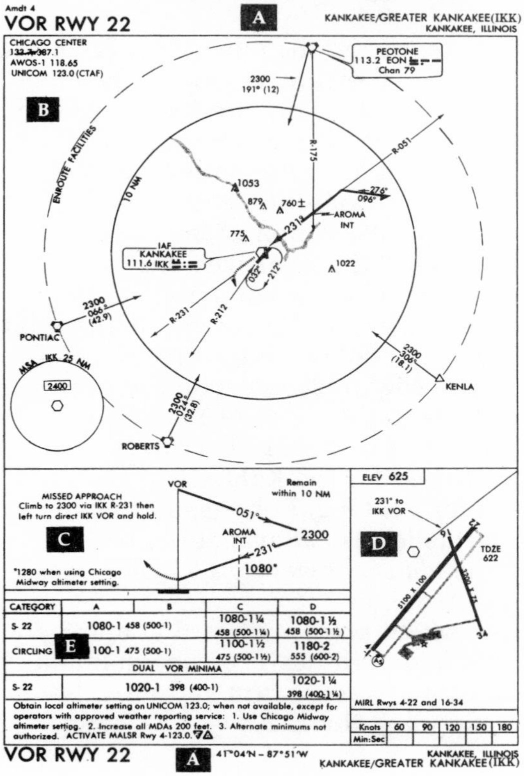

Margins (A). These tell you that this is the VOR RWY 22 IAP to Greater Kankakee Airport in Kankakee, Illinois. The latitude and longitude at the bottom center are provided for aircraft with inertial navigation systems.

The amendment number in the upper left-hand margin identifies how many times the IAP has been amended since it was first published. In this case—*Amdt 4*—the IAP has been amended four times.

Planview (B). The upper left corner of the planview contains communication frequencies used by aircraft landing at Kankakee. Frequency 123.0, labeled UNICOM, is available for traffic advisories.

The solid ring labeled *10 NM* bounds the area ten nautical miles around the Kankakee VOR. Everything inside this ring is drawn to scale. Note that certain topographical features—the river, for instance—appear only inside this ring. The dashed ring outside the 10-NM ring tells you that things outside the 10-NM ring are not drawn to scale.

Four en route facilities appear on the outer ring. From the top and going counterclockwise, they are as follows: Peotone VOR, Pontiac VOR, Roberts VOR, and the intersection of two VOR radials at KENLA intersection. There is a terminal route from each of these en route facilities to the Kankakee VOR.

The second radial, extending from the Peotone VOR (the 175° radial) identifies AROMA intersection at the point where the Peotone 175° radial intersects the Kankakee 051° radial.

Obstacles which meet certain height criteria are charted inside the 10-NM ring. The 1053-foot obstacle north and a bit west of the Kankakee VOR is the tallest on the chart, and is shown by an obstacle symbol slightly larger than the others.

The height of the obstacle to the north of Kankakee VOR—the one marked 760 ± —is of doubtful accuracy.

Notice that the symbol used for the Kankakee VOR is different from the three used for Peotone, Roberts, and Pontiac. This means that DME information is *not* available from the Kankakee VOR. In *Flight Simulator*, however, all VORs transmit distance information.

Find the barbed arrow which points outward at a 45° angle from the Kankakee 051° radial (it has 276° above it and 096° below it). This is called a *procedure turn* and provides a way to reverse course in executing the IAP.

The scalloped arrow extending from the Kankakee 231°
radial and the racetrack-shaped holding pattern (both near the
airport symbol) show the missed approach procedure you'd
use if you couldn't make a landing.

The final item on the planview is the Minimum Safe Altitude (MSA) circle in the lower left corner. The MSA will show
an altitude or altitudes which assure the pilot of at least 1000
feet of vertical obstacle clearance within 25 nautical miles of
the VOR or NDB on which the IAP is based. Here, an altitude
of 2400 feet assures the pilot of at least 1000 feet between that
altitude and the tallest obstacle within 25 nautical miles of the
Kankakee VOR. The MSA is to be used for emergencies only.

Profile (C). The underlined *2300* indicates that an aircraft
executing the approach can descend to a minimum altitude of
2300 feet while established on the Kankakee 051° radial. The
notation *Remain within 10 NM* restricts the outbound leg and
the procedure turn to an area within ten nautical miles of the
Kankakee VOR. Once the aircraft has become established on
the inbound course, descent to a minimum altitude of 1080
feet is permitted, as shown by the underlined *1080*. (The aster-
isk note is irrelevant when you're using *Flight Simulator*.)

Once the aircraft passes the AROMA intersection while
inbound, you can descend to the minimum descent altitude—
1020 feet. The scalloped arrow and text provide the missed
approach procedure.

Airport sketch (D). The airport elevation is listed as 625
feet mean sea level. The notation *TDZE 622* means that the
touchdown zone elevation (the highest point in the first 3000
feet of the runway) is 622 feet above sea level. Runway
lengths and widths are also listed. The star shows the position
of the airport rotating beacon.

The thin arrow details the relationship between the final
approach course and runway 22.

Minima data (E). In reality, an airplane's approach category is based on its stall speed when it's getting ready to land.

Generally speaking, use the minima category below that's
associated with the speed at which you're flying the final
approach.

Approach Category	A	B	C	D
Speed (Knots)	0–90	91–120	121–140	141–165

Thus if you fly the final approach at 100 knots, use the minima set for category B.

S-22 minima are for straight-in approaches (the VOR RWY 22 IAP is executed and landing is planned on runway 22). If the VOR RWY 22 IAP is made with a landing planned on another runway, then the *Circling* minima should be used.

If a straight-in approach is planned with a final approach speed of 100 knots and using both VOR receivers, the applicable minima are a minimum descent altitude (MDA) of 1020 feet and a minimum visibility of one mile (*1020-1*).

The *398* is the *height above touchdown* (HAT) when you're at the MDA. The *475* shown in the same location for the Circling approach is the *height above airport* (HAA). The difference between the two numbers is that one (HAT) is referenced to the touchdown zone elevation (the highest point in the first 3000 feet of the runway). The other (HAA) is referenced to the airport elevation.

The figures inside parentheses are for military use only.

Note that a lower MDA is allowed when the airplane is equipped with two VOR receivers—that's because the AROMA intersection can be identified.

If you look at either the planview or the profile for the VOR RWY 22 IAP, you will see that the VOR is located on the airport. This IAP is called a *terminal VOR approach*. When you execute a terminal VOR approach, use the missed approach procedure when the airplane is *over* the VOR.

Figure 5-3. Go Ahead and Descend

Runway in sight; in position from which I can make a normal landing; visibility above minimum. I can descend

MDA

Every condition must be met before a landing can be undertaken.

Federal Aviation Regulations prohibit descent below the minimum descent altitude unless the airplane is "continuously in a position from which a descent to a landing on the intended runway can be made at a normal rate of descent using normal maneuvers..., the flight visibility is not less than the visibility prescribed in the standard instrument approach procedure being used," and the pilot distinctly sees the runway of intended landing (or specified lights or markings associated with that runway). If any of these conditions aren't met, the pilot is required to execute the missed approach procedure.

Shoot the Procedure

Unpause *Flight Simulator* now and give the VOR RWY 22 IAP a try.

All IAPs begin at an initial approach fix (IAF), except for those where the aircraft must be given headings by an air traffic controller (called radar vectors) to intercept the final approach course. The VOR RWY 22 approach has only one IAF. Some approaches have many.

The VOR is the IAF for the VOR RWY 22 IAP. Notice that *IAF* is printed above the nav-aid box in the planview (to the left of the Kankakee VOR symbol).

Follow these instructions, using Figure 5-4 as a guide.

Figure 5-4. Shooting the Procedure

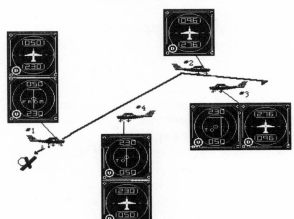

This illustration outlines the turns and OBI course indications for flying the VOR RWY 22 approach at Kankakee.

To VOR, turn and establish on 51° radial. Fly over the VOR; then make a left turn and fly away from the airport on the 051° radial, as shown in both the planview and the profile view. Since *Flight Simulator* provides even-numbered radials in most versions (exceptions are the Atari ST and Commodore Amiga versions), you'll have to modify the approach by flying either the 050° or 052° radial. Fly outbound from the VOR with a *FROM* indication and the OBS set to 050° (Figure 5-4, airplane #1). Fly far enough to give yourself room to reestablish yourself on the inbound course and descend to 1080 feet, but in no case fly more than ten nautical miles from the VOR. While you're doing this, reduce your speed to approach speed (90–110 knots in most single-engine airplanes).

Procedure turn. Try beginning the procedure turn when you're five miles from the VOR. Turn right to 096° and fly that heading for one minute (Figure 5-4, airplane #2). Reset the NAV-1 OBI to the inbound radial (either 230° or 232°), and set the NAV-2 OBI to 174° or 176° so that you'll be able to identify the AROMA intersection.

Turn left to 276°. After one minute, turn left to 276°, and fly that heading until the NAV-1 needle approaches the center (Figure 5-4, airplane #3).

Turn to inbound course of 231°. When the NAV-1 needle approaches center, turn to the inbound course of 231° and track the VOR inbound (Figure 5-4, airplane #4). Once the needle is centered and you're established on the inbound radial, begin a descent to 1080 feet.

When you pass the AROMA intersection, you may descend to 1020 feet. You'll know that you're past the intersection when the NAV-2 OBI needle shifts to the left of center.

Descend to 1020 feet. When you descend below 1192 feet, you should break out of the clouds and be able to see the airport. If you're in a position from which a normal landing can be made and you have the airport in sight, you may descend below the MDA and land the airplane.

On the other hand, if you never break out of the clouds, or if, when you do, you find that you aren't in a position from which a normal landing can be made, follow the missed approach instructions back to the VOR and try the approach again when the TO/FROM indicator changes to *FROM*. An alternative is to fly to another destination.

Figure 5-5. Land It

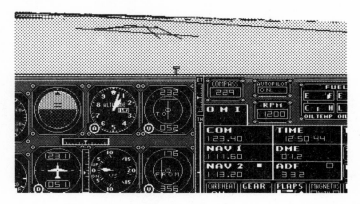

You're past the AROMA intersection (as shown by the needle left-of-center on the NAV-2 OBI), at an altitude of 1020 feet, and have the airport in sight. Land the airplane.

If you want to practice more VOR approaches before trying other types of approaches, skip ahead to Chapter 8. If you're ready to try NDB approaches, move on to Chapter 6. If your version of *Flight Simulator* is not equipped with an ADF, read Chapter 6 before proceeding to Chapter 7 and begin Chapter 7 after positioning your airplane at Dwight Airport.

Note: The ADF on version 1.0 of Microsoft Flight Simulator *for the Macintosh doesn't function properly and cannot be accurately used for NDB approaches.*

Chapter 6

NDB
Approaches

Chapter 6
NDB Approaches

Fly to airports using the automatic direction finder (ADF) and nondirectional beacons (NDB). Take off from Kankakee and make for Dwight.

Begin this chapter with the following settings to *Flight Simulator*:

Cloud base	1192
North position	16846
East position	16597
Altitude	625
Season	Winter

Assuming everything went right during your approach and landing at Greater Kankakee, you're now safe and sound on the ground, near the fueling area. The weather hasn't changed since you left Chicago, but it's time to begin the next leg of your trip to Dwight, Illinois.

Unlike Chicago Meigs Airport, there's a *T* in an upside-down triangle in the bottom margin of each of the Greater Kankakee IAP charts. Earlier, you learned this symbol means there is a published departure procedure for the airport. In fact, the *T* means that either there's a published departure procedure or that the minimum weather conditions for takeoff are nonstandard. Takeoff-weather minima, however, apply only to commercial aircraft operators.

The standard takeoff minima are one statute mile visibility for aircraft with two engines or less, and one-half statute mile visibility for aircraft with three engines or more.

If you look under *Kankakee* in Appendix A, you'll find only a nonstandard takeoff minimum listed. For commercial operators which operate under Federal Aviation Regulations (FAR) Part 135, the takeoff minimum on runway 4 is reduced for single- and twin-engine aircraft to one-half mile.

This doesn't apply to your flight, for two reasons. First, you'll depart on runway 22, the same runway you landed on.

Second, unless today's fantasy trip includes being a Part 135 commercial operator, the nonstandard minimum has no application to your flight.

Pre-Flight

Before you take off from Kankakee, turn to page 152 of Appendix B—the NDB RWY 27 IAP chart for Dwight. Notice that there's a terminal route from the Peotone VOR to the Dwight nondirectional beacon (NDB). The terminal route is the Peotone 253° radial at 2300 feet. Your clearance for this flight might be something like

Cleared to the Dwight Airport via the Peotone two-five-three radial, climb and maintain 2,300.

Set up your aircraft for departure by tuning the NAV-1 radio to the Peotone VOR, the ADF to Dwight's NDB frequency, and the COM radio to the Kankakee CT. Figure 6-1 shows you what your instruments should read.

Figure 6-1. Pre-Takeoff Avionics Settings

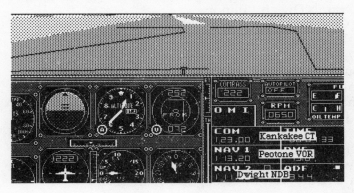

Tune your NAV-1 radio, ADF, and COM to these settings before taking off from Kankakee.

Look at the Chicago Area Chart in your *Flight Simulator* manual, or in Appendix C. Try to visualize the Peotone 253° radial extending from the VOR. If it's helpful, place a pencil or a ruler along the radial. Now look at runway 22 at Greater Kankakee. You'll fly from runway 22 to intercept the Peotone 253° radial.

Intercepting the 253° Radial

 Take off from Greater Kankakee's runway 22 and immediately use this procedure to intercept the Peotone 253° radial.

 Turn the airplane to parallel the desired course (253°).

 Rotate the OBS to center the needle with a *FROM* indication since you'll be tracking from Peotone.

 Calculate the difference between the desired radial and the radial that you're presently on (if you're currently flying on the 216° radial, you're 37° off the desired radial).

 Reset the OBS to the desired course of 252° or 254° (or 253° on the Amiga or Atari ST versions of *Flight Simulator*).

 Turn *toward* the needle, *past* the desired course by two times the number of degrees you're off course, but never more than 90°. Thus, if you're on the 216° radial, you're 37° off course and should turn right to 327° [253° + (2 * 37)]).

 When the needle moves toward the center, turn to 253° and make any necessary corrections for wind, using the procedures discussed in Chapter 4.

By using this procedure, you'll intercept and follow the terminal route that will take you directly to the Dwight NDB. When Dwight NDB is within range, the needle on your ADF should point to Dwight NDB and be within a few degrees of 0.

Automatic Direction Finder

An automatic direction finder (ADF) is a relatively simple radio receiver that points directly *at* the transmitter to which it's tuned. In this respect it's far simpler than a VOR receiver. Many pilots, however, are confused by the use of an ADF.

The ADF display is a single needle on top of a compass rose. Unlike a VOR, ADF guidance is relative to the heading of the aircraft. The *0* on the compass rose represents the nose of the airplane, and the *18* represents the tail. If the needle points to the *6*, the NDB to which the ADF is tuned is 60° to the right of the airplane's nose. This 60° is referred to as the *relative bearing* of the NDB.

> On some versions of *Flight Simulator*, the ADF display uses a square box with marks at the four cardinal headings in lieu of a compass rose. On these displays, the relative bearing is displayed digitally at the top of the instrument.

The heading that will point the airplane right at the NDB is called the *magnetic bearing.* The magnetic bearing is found by adding the relative bearing to the airplane's current heading. For instance, if the airplane's current heading is 085° and the relative bearing is 60°, then the magnetic bearing is 145° (Figure 6-2).

Figure 6-2. Magnetic Bearing of 145°

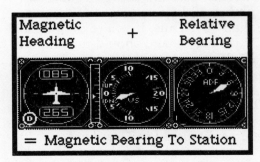

Add the airplane's current heading (85°) to the relative bearing shown on the ADF (60°) to find the magnetic bearing to the ADF station (145°).

If the sum of the magnetic heading and the relative bearing exceeds 360°, an additional step is needed to calculate the magnetic bearing. For example, assume the relative bearing is 300° and the magnetic heading is 205°. Since headings, bearings, and courses range from 0° to 360°, the magnetic bearing could not be 505°. Simply subtract 360° from the sum to find the magnetic bearing. In this example, the magnetic bearing is 505° − 360°, or 145° (Figure 6-3).

Figure 6-3. Magnetic Bearing of 145° Again

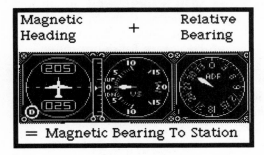

Magnetic Heading	+	Relative Bearing

= Magnetic Bearing To Station

When the sum of the magnetic heading and the relative bearing is greater than 360°, you need to subtract that amount to arrive at the true magnetic bearing to the ADF station.

Don't be surprised that the result was the same in both examples. The airplane used in this example stayed in the same position when it turned from a heading of 85° to 205°. As the airplane turned, the ADF needle turned at the same rate. Since the airplane was in the same position both times, it only makes sense that the same heading now points the airplane toward the NDB.

Knowing what you now know, you could figure out how to use the ADF to track NDB bearings, with or without wind. To make it easier, though, the procedures for tracking NDB bearings are outlined below within the discussion of the NDB RWY 27 IAP to Dwight.

On to Dwight

Since the ADF needle always points *toward* the transmitter, you can recognize the moment you pass over the NDB when the needle moves from a relative bearing of 0° to a relative bearing of 180° (or thereabouts). The speed at which the needle moves from nose to tail depends on how close you are to being right over the top of the transmitter. If you're exactly on course, the needle snaps around to the tail. More likely, you're slightly off course and the needle makes the change somewhat more leisurely. If you're significantly off course, the needle revolves slowly and may never move all the way to a relative bearing of 180°.

The NDB RWY 27 IAP is not significantly different from the VOR IAP you made at Greater Kankakee. Again, the IAP is of the terminal type since the NDB is located on the airport and the missed approach procedure begins at the NDB. There's only one initial approach fix (IAF), the Dwight NDB. There are three terminal routes, one of which you're following now.

Again, the procedure turn must be made within ten nautical miles of the NDB. The minima section reveals that the minimum descent altitude (MDA) does not differ if you circle to land on another runway, nor does it depend on which approach category your aircraft is in.

Procedure at Dwight

Since 2300 feet is the initial approach altitude (as you can see from the underlined *2300* in the the profile view), you're already at the appropriate altitude. When the ADF needle swings toward the tail, you've passed over the NDB. Turn left to 096°, the outbound heading shown in the planview. As you make the turn to 096°, the ADF needle will move toward the nose. Once again you'll pass over the NDB, this time heading away from it, or outbound.

It's necessary to calculate your distance from the NDB to make sure you remain within ten nautical miles. The only way to do this is to time your outbound leg. You should leave yourself at least three miles for the procedure turn, so start the outbound portion of the procedure turn no more than seven miles from the NDB. If your groundspeed is 120 knots, your airplane travels two miles per minute, and you should begin the procedure turn within 3½ minutes of crossing the NDB the second time.

After you've passed the NDB, you may need to make a course correction. If the relative bearing is not 180°, turn *toward* the needle twice the number of degrees that the relative

bearing varies from 180°. Figure 6-4 shows the airplane 20°
off course (a 160° relative bearing on the outbound heading).

Figure 6-4. Twenty Degrees Off Course

*The ADF reading shows that the aircraft is 20° off course while on
the outbound leg of the Dwight procedure.*

The airplane should be turned 40° to the right (toward
the ADF needle) to a heading of 136°. When the airplane is
heading 136°, the relative bearing will be 120° (Figure 6-5).

Figure 6-5. Twenty Degrees Off Course with a
40-Degree Correction

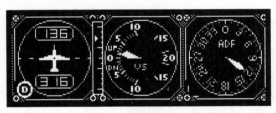

*When you correct your course by 40°, the relative bearing seems to
show that you're even more off course than before. Don't worry—
you're not.*

Keep the airplane on the 136° heading until the relative
bearing is 140° (that's the amount of the course correction
away from the tail [180 − 40]). At that point, the airplane is
back on the outbound course, *but not on the outbound heading.*
(The relative bearing of 140° plus the magnetic heading of
136° equals the inbound course of 276°.)

Assuming there's no wind, once you're back on the outbound course, you'll want to return to the outbound heading
of 96°.

Wind

Once you've established the airplane on the outbound course, course corrections will be necessary if the wind isn't calm. Use this procedure to track the NDB bearing:

- If the needle moves 5° or more from the nose or tail (Figure 6-6, #1A), depending on whether you're inbound or outbound, turn the airplane 20° *toward* the needle (Figure 6-6, #1B).
- Fly the new heading until the needle is 20° away from the nose or tail, as appropriate. You're back on course (Figure 6-6, #2).
- Establish a wind correction angle by turning 10° toward your original heading (Figure 6-6, #3). The needle will now point 10° from the nose *opposite the direction* of your wind correction angle if you're inbound to the NDB, or 10° from the tail in the *same direction* as your wind correction angle if you're outbound from the NDB.
- If the needle drifts closer to the nose or further away from the tail, the wind correction angle is insufficient. If this happens, repeat the first three steps above, except use a 15° wind correction angle instead of 10° (Figure 6-6, #4).

Figure 6-6. Wind Correction

Follow this procedure to make course corrections while tracking the NDB bearing.

If you're traveling over the ground at 120 knots or less, you should begin the procedure turn 3½ minutes after passing over the NDB the second time. Once you've completed the procedure turn and have established yourself on the inbound course, you'll need to descend from 2300 feet to 1380 feet, and then from 1380 feet to 632 feet, the airport elevation. At a descent rate of 500 feet per minute, you'll need almost 3½ minutes of flying time if you're traveling at 120 knots.

Procedure Turn

Make the procedure turn by turning right to a heading of 141° for one minute, followed by a left turn to a heading of 321° until you're established on the inbound course. The procedure turn is at a 45° angle to the inbound course, so when the ADF needle is 45° to the left of the nose (a relative bearing of 315°), the airplane is on the inbound course and must be turned to the inbound heading.

Once you're on the inbound course, you may begin your descent to the minimum descent altitude (MDA), which for this IAP is 1380 feet. When you reach that altitude, level off the airplane and maintain 1380 feet until you have the runway in sight and are in a position from which a normal landing can be made (in which case you may descend below the MDA and land), or until you pass the Dwight NDB (in which case you must follow the missed approach procedure instructions printed in the profile).

Tracking Inbound

The same procedures used for tracking outbound are used for tracking inbound. Figure 6-7 shows an airplane on the inbound heading. Its ADF needle has drifted 10° to the left of the nose, meaning that the airplane is 10° right of course.

Figure 6-7. Ten Degrees Right of Course

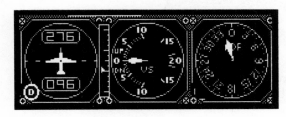

This airplane is off course while inbound. The heading is correct, but the ADF shows that the aircraft is 10° right of the correct course.

Using the NDB tracking procedures, turn the airplane 20° to the left (toward the needle). As the airplane turns, the ADF needles also turns 20°, though in the opposite direction (Figure 6-8).

Figure 6-8. Ten Degrees Right of Course with a 20-Degree-Left Correction

Correcting the course by changing the heading 20° also changes the ADF needle's position. Note, however, that the ADF needle turns 20° in the opposite direction of the course correction.

When the needle is 20° to the right of the nose, the airplane is back on course (Figure 6-9).

Figure 6-9. Back On Course

The airplane is back on course when the ADF needle reads 20° right of the nose.

Now, turn the airplane 10° to the right. The airplane will remain on course if 10° is the appropriate wind-correction angle.

Missing Dwight

If you followed all the instructions, you should now be executing the missed approach procedure. That's because the cloud base was set to 1192 feet—as you flew at 1380 feet, you never saw the runway.

Return to 2300 feet and head back to the Dwight NDB. Since the cloud ceiling is too low to let you land at Dwight, continue on to your final destination—Champaign, Illinois.

If you descended below the MDA *before* you had the runway in sight, remember one thing—there are **old** pilots, and there are **bold** pilots, but there are no **old bold** pilots.

Chapter 7

ILS
Approaches

Chapter 7
ILS Approaches

Learn how to use the ILS (Instrument Landing System) to execute precision instrument approaches—and land in the nastiest of weather conditions.

Begin this chapter with the following settings to *Flight Simulator*:

Cloud base	1192
North position	16874
East position	16404
Altitude	630
Season	Winter

Up to now, you've practiced nonprecision instrument approach procedures using VORs and NDBs. The ILS (Instrument Landing System) approach procedure adds a new dimension to instrument flying.

ILS approaches are precision approaches in that they provide electronic glidepath information. In addition to a course guidance system which uses the NAV-1 radio in a similar way to that used by a VOR approach, the ILS provides glidepath guidance (more on that term later). Because of their precision, most ILS IAPs allow a pilot to descend to a mere 200 feet above the touchdown zone elevation before committing to the landing.

The Instrument Landing System

The ILS is made up of a localizer, glideslope, marker beacons (outer, middle, and inner), and DME.

Localizer. The *localizer* is a ground-based transmitter which provides course guidance for the pilot. Unlike a VOR, the localizer has only one fixed course, and it will not vary if you turn the OBS. The width of the localizer is one-fourth the width of a VOR radial. That means the needle on the indicator is much more precise in its reading. When you're tracking a VOR radial, for instance, and the needle on the indicator is fully to one side, it means you're 10° off course. Using the ILS and seeing the same reading, however, means that you're only 2½° off course.

When you're tracking inbound on an ILS IAP, you make course corrections in the direction of the needle. If the needle appears to the right of center, you turn the airplane in that direction. When you're tracking outbound, however, course corrections are made *away* from the needle, just as you would with a VOR if you were tracking inbound with a *FROM* indication.

Although the OBS has no effect on the ILS, I recommend you set the OBS to the inbound course as a reminder of the inbound heading. Additionally, if you ever use your NAV-2 radio for localizer tracking, a quirk in the programming, at least on some versions of *Flight Simulator*, requires that you select the inbound course on the OBS.

Unlike flying over a VOR, when you fly over the localizer transmitter, there will be no indication that you've passed it other than the fact that when you're very close to the transmitter it's very sensitive.

Glideslope. The *glideslope* is easy to understand if you imagine a localizer transmitter turned on its side and transmitting a single course upward at a 3° angle. The glideslope is shown in the cockpit by a horizontal needle on the NAV-1 display (Figure 7-1).

Figure 7-1. Horizontal Needle Shows on Glideslope Indication

Glideslope indication appears on the NAV-1 display.

If the glideslope needle moves above center, you're too low. If the glideslope needle moves below center, you're too high.

Appendix B includes a Rate of Descent Table, which shows the rate of descent you must maintain for a given speed and glideslope angle to keep within the glideslope. The glideslope angle is listed in the profile section of an ILS IAP chart next to the letters *GS*.

DME and Marker Beacons. Distance information is provided by DME and *marker beacons*. Marker beacons are ground-based radio transmitters which transmit an elliptical pattern that's displayed in the cockpit as the airplane passes over the antenna. Most ILS IAPs employ an outer marker and a middle marker. The outer marker marks the approximate position where an aircraft at the initial approach altitude will intercept the glideslope.

An ILS IAP

Take a look at the profile of the ILS RWY 32 IAP to Champaign-Urbana Airport. It's on page 131 in Appendix B. The initial approach altitude is 2600 feet, indicated by the underlined *2600*. The glideslope intercept point is marked by *2573*, which is the exact altitude of the glideslope over the outer marker. The middle marker (MM on the profile) indicates the position at which an aircraft on glideslope is required to continue descent for landing or execute the missed approach procedure.

Inner markers are associated with a special type of ILS IAP that's not found on *Flight Simulator*. On some ILS IAPs, there's no outer marker (ILS RWY 24 IAP to Martha's Vineyard, Massachusetts, for instance). If that's the case, DME may be substituted for the outer marker if it's shown on the IAP chart (on the Martha's Vineyard ILS RWY 24 IAP chart profile and planview, *I-MVY 5 DME* is printed at the glideslope intercept point, BORST intersection).

No Minimum Descent Altitude

A significant difference between precision and nonprecision IAPs is that precision approaches do not have minimum descent altitudes (MDAs). Instead, precision approaches are made along the glideslope to a decision height (DH). When the airplane reaches the decision height, the pilot must immediately decide whether the requirements to continue the

approach have been met or whether the missed approach procedure must be executed.

The requirements for continuing the approach below the
decision height are the same as for descending below an MDA
on a nonprecision approach—the pilot must have the runway
or certain elements of the runway environment (such as its
lights) in sight and be in a position from which a normal landing can be made.

Give ILS a Try

You should either be on the ground at Dwight Airport or flying nearby at 2300 feet. Your clearance for the last leg of today's flight is:

*Cleared to the Champaign-Urbana Airport via direct Rob-
erts direct, climb and maintain 2,600.*

You should set up your radios just as you have for the previous two legs of today's flight. Set the NAV-1 radio to the
Roberts VOR frequency, 116.8. Set the NAV-2 radio to the Champaign VOR frequency, 110.0. Turn the OBS on both to center
the needles with a *TO* indication. Since Dwight Airport doesn't
have a control tower, you can go ahead and set the Champaign
ATIS frequency, 124.85, in the COM radio (Figure 7-2).

Figure 7-2. Pre-Takeoff Avionics Settings

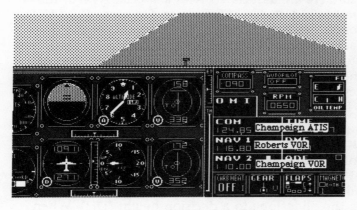

*This is what your NAV-1, NAV-2, and COM radios should show
before you begin the last leg of your trip.*

If you're on the ground at Dwight, take off and proceed direct to Roberts while climbing to 2600 feet. Since the Dwight NDB RWY 27 IAP chart doesn't contain a *T* in an upside-down triangle, you know there's no published departure procedure for Dwight Airport.

If you're already airborne, climb to 2600 and proceed as cleared.

While en route to Champaign-Urbana, locate the ILS RWY 32 IAP chart in Appendix B and study it. You'll notice that there's only one initial approach fix (IAF)—the VEALS LOM, near the center of the planview. LOM, or Locater Outer Marker, is the name given to an NDB that's co-located with an outer marker. If your airplane is equipped with a functioning ADF, use VEALS as the IAF.

> Note: On some versions of *Flight Simulator*, VEALS was incorrectly co-located with the middle marker. You can still use it as the IAF, but you should ignore your ADF after getting established on the outbound course.

If your ADF isn't functioning, you'll have to improvise a little. Use the Champaign VOR as an IAF.

Flying In

Whatever you're using as an IAF, track from Roberts VOR to Champaign VOR. If you're using VEALS as the IAF, proceed directly to VEALS once you've received it.

After passing Roberts VOR, set your NAV-1 radio to 109.1, the Champaign localizer frequency. Remember to set the OBS to the inbound course of 316°. You're still reading the needle of the NAV-2 radio to track to the Champaign VOR, however.

When the localizer needle begins to center, turn left to track the localizer outbound on a 136° heading. Remember that the localizer needle now has reverse sensing—that is, make course corrections *away* from the needle rather than toward it (Figure 7-3).

Again, the IAP instructs you to remain within ten nautical miles, though this time it means within ten nautical miles of the outer marker. Since your DME is measured from the runway, you can add the distance from the runway to the outer marker (six miles) and allow yourself to go no further than 16 DME from the runway.

Figure 7-3. Tracking the Localizer

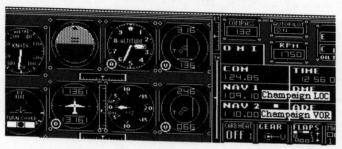

As you fly outbound on the localizer, your airplane has drifted slightly to the right of the proper course, as shown by the needle. To correct course, you need to turn slightly to the left.

Try starting the procedure turn at approximately 10 DME. Fly a 091° heading for one minute. After one minute, turn right to 271° and hold that heading until the needle begins to center.

As the needle centers, turn right to the inbound course of 316°. Because the localizer is more sensitive than a VOR, use small corrections—no more than 2 or 3 degrees at a time.

As you approach 6 DME, the glideslope needle (the horizontal needle) begins to move downward from the top of the NAV-1 display. As the glideslope needle approaches the center, reduce the throttle setting so that you maintain both your desired approach speed and the rate of descent necessary to stay on the glideslope at that approach speed. You can find the correct rate of descent from the Rate of Descent Table in Appendix B. Turn to it now.

The angle of descent for this IAP is 3.0°—shown by the 3.00° beside the GS in the profile. Assuming 90 knots groundspeed, and using the 3.0 row on the Table, you can see that the necessary rate of descent is 480 feet per minute.

At 6.0 DME, you should pass over the outer marker. The IAP (in the profile) shows that you should be at 2573 feet when you fly over the marker. As you continue the approach, try to keep both the localizer and the glideslope needle centered. Make whatever small corrections toward the needles are necessary.

Figure 7-4. Intercepting the Glideslope

The instruments show that this aircraft is right on the glideslope as it passes over the outer marker.

If you look at the minima section of the IAP chart, you'll see that the decision height (DH) for this approach is 949 feet (as indicated by *949/24*), exactly 200 feet above the touch-down zone elevation of runway 32. As the airplane descends below 1192 feet, you should break out of the clouds and see the runway. When the airplane reaches 949 feet, you must immediately decide whether to continue the approach below the DH or execute the missed approach procedure. The middle marker should be a second reminder of when you must make that decision.

Make sure you're familiar with the method your version of *Flight Simulator* uses to tell you that you've passed an outer, middle, or inner marker.

On the Macintosh, for instance, a light appears beneath the *O, M,* or *I* located immediately above the COM radio frequency. (Contrary to the documentation, there is no audio signal.)

If the runway is in sight and you're in a position from which a normal landing can be made, land at Champaign-Urbana Airport and complete the day's flight.

Figure 7-5. Descending Below the Decision Height

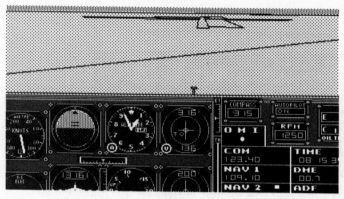

You're below the decision height and ready to make a normal landing.

You may be wondering why you executed the ILS RWY 32 IAP and then landed on runway 31. Did you land on the wrong runway? At the wrong airport?

No. Runways are numbered by their magnetic headings. The relationship between true north and magnetic north varies in different parts of the country. This variation changes over time. When the database for *Flight Simulator* was being designed, what is now runway 32 at Champaign-Urbana Airport *was* runway 31. When the magnetic heading of the runway became 315°, the runway number was changed to 32.

You may find other IAPs where there's a discrepancy between the chart and the database in *Flight Simulator*. In most cases a little improvisation will easily correct the situation.

Chapter 8

Variations

Chapter 8
Variations

This last chapter offers variations on the approaches you've already learned and practiced. After you've mastered these approaches, you'll be well prepared to delve into the many instrument approach procedures which await you in Appendix B.

Night ILS Approach

Begin this section with the following settings to *Flight Simulator*:

Cloud base	275
North position	17490
East position	22043
Altitude	68
Time	23:45

You're on the ground at Martha's Vineyard Airport in Massachusetts. It's almost midnight, and the clouds are just 207 feet above the ground. You're about to take off, fly the ILS RWY 24 IAP, and land. Turn to page 173, Appendix B, and study the IAP chart.

Taxi your airplane out to the end of runway 6 and set up your avionics for the flight. Tune your NAV-1 radio to the localizer frequency (108.7), your NAV-2 radio to the Martha's Vineyard VOR (108.2), and your COM radio to the control tower (121.4). Set your NAV-1 OBS to the inbound course of 236°. After you've looked carefully at the IAP chart, start your takeoff roll.

 As you lift off from runway 6, track outbound along the localizer while climbing to 1500 feet. You should be flying at a heading of 56°. When you enter the clouds, the windshield turns pitch-black. It's just you and the instruments this time.

Remember that the localizer needle has *reverse* sensing while you're outbound.

There's no procedure turn on this IAP. When you see a boldface racetrack-like pattern on the planview—as you do here—it means that you use the holding pattern for your course reversal instead of a procedure turn.

It's really quite easy. When the DME reads 5.0, turn right 30° to an 86° heading, and fly that heading for one minute. Then turn left at standard rate to the inbound course heading of 236° and re-intercept the localizer course inbound.

As you approach the 5.0 DME mark, the glideslope needle will begin to descend from the top of the localizer display. As the glideslope needle approaches center, reduce the throttle and begin your descent along the glideslope. Just before you get to the decision height (DH), which is 263 feet, you should break out of the clouds and see the runway lights. If you land safely, you've just completed your first overwater instrument approach at night with the weather near minimums. Congratulations!

Figure 8-1. At Decision Height at Night

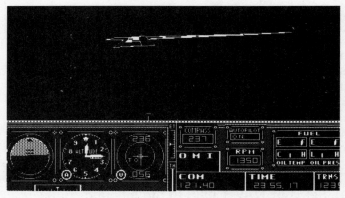

Just before you reach the decision height of 263 feet, you should break out of the clouds and see the runway lights in front of you.

VOR/DME Approaches

Begin this section with the following settings to *Flight Simulator*:

Cloud base	800
North position	17733
East position	21543
Altitude	697

You're on the ground at Southbridge Municipal Airport, which is between Hartford, Connecticut and Boston, Massachusetts.

 Take off to the north and track direct to Gardner VOR (110.6) at 4000 feet. When you arrive at Gardner, you're cleared for the VOR/DME RWY 15R IAP to Boston/General Edward Lawrence Logan International.

There are only two significant differences between this approach and others that you've already flown. First, there are three stepdown fixes along the approach in addition to the final approach fix. Look at the profile view of the VOR/DME RWY 15R IAP chart on page 122 of Appendix B. At the 15, 10.5, and 8 DME fixes, you can descend to lower published altitudes of 3000, 2300, and 1400 feet, respectively. At 5 DME, you descend to the minimum descent altitude (780 feet).

Second, the missed approach point is at the 1.4 DME fix instead of at the VOR (again, look at the chart's profile section).

Enjoy the approach, and don't land in the sea.

Figure 8-2. Too High for a Normal Landing

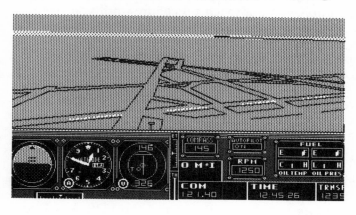

This airplane is obviously too high for a normal landing. Its pilot should execute the missed approach procedure and then try again.

Circling Approaches

> Begin this section with the following settings to *Flight Simulator*:
>
> | | |
> |---|---|
> | **Cloud base** | 900 |
> | **North position** | 14974 |
> | **East position** | 6095 |
> | **Altitude** | 28 |

Circling approaches were discussed briefly in Chapter 5. A circling approach is made when the executed IAP serves a runway *other* than the landing runway. Because such a procedure involves maneuvering from the final approach course to another runway, the minima for a circling approach are usually higher than those for a straight-in approach.

Approaches that don't meet specified criteria for runway alignment are designed as circling approaches only and are designated by the type of approach (VOR or NDB, for example) and a single letter (such as *B*). Each such approach to an airport is given a different letter, beginning with *A* and moving up the alphabet.

When you execute a circling approach, you may not depart from the published approach procedure until you have the runway in sight and are in a position from which a normal landing can be made.

You should maneuver the airplane as close as possible to the airport. If, during the circling procedure, you lose sight of the airport, you must immediately execute the missed approach procedure. Because you have maneuvered off of the approach course, executing the missed approach procedure may require a left turn when a right is called for, or vice versa.

 In this scenario, you're on the ground at Oceanside Municipal Airport in Southern California. After setting up your avionics for the published departure procedure (see Appendix A) and the VOR-A IAP to Carlsbad/McClellan-Palomar Airport (see Appendix B), take off and follow the published departure procedure.

Continue your climb to 3000 feet. When you cross the Oceanside VOR, turn left to 270°, and hold that heading for one minute. Then turn left at standard rate and re-intercept the 270° radial inbound (on a 90° course). When you cross the VOR, track the 120° radial outbound while descending to 1300 feet.

At the 7 DME fix, you can continue your descent to the circling minimum, 860 feet. As you descend through 900 feet, you should break out of the clouds and have the airport in sight. Choose the runway that you'll land on; then maneuver as close to the airport as possible to land on that runway.

Figure 8-3. At Circling Minimums—Airport in Sight

These instruments show an airplane at the circling minimums for Oceanside. The airport is barely visible in the distance (it may be more easily seen in your version of Flight Simulator*).*

DME Arcs

Begin this section with the following settings to *Flight Simulator*:

Cloud base	2500
North position	16471
East position	16685
Altitude	695

Some IAPs use a curved path instead of a straight course to lead into the final approach. One example of this can be found at the Danville Airport in Danville, Illinois.

That's where your airplane is sitting right now. If you look at the VOR/DME RWY 3 IAP chart to Danville (page 151 in Appendix B), you'll see that there are three IAFs. One is SOREZ intersection. The other two are at the ends of the 16 DME arc. If you begin the IAP from SOREZ, you must execute the procedure turn. If you begin on either end of the arc, however, you don't execute a procedure turn.

 Take off from runway 3 and fly the runway heading until you intercept the Danville 085° radial. Climb and maintain 2300 feet. The clouds will be above you during the approach.

Track the 085° radial outbound. When you get to approximately 15.5 DME, turn right to 185°. Because you continue to travel eastward as you turn, you need the one-half-mile lead. By turning 100° to the right, you should stay within one mile of the arc.

Rotate the OBS all the way around until the needle centers with a *TO* indication. Keep the needle centered so that you can keep track of which radial you're on—turn the airplane every time you've traveled 10° to keep the airplane's heading 100° to the right of the radial you're passing. Remember that the radial you're passing is the reciprocal of the OBS setting when you have a *TO* indication. The reciprocal is the number on the bottom of the Omni-Bearing Indicator. In other words, your heading should be 100 greater than the radial shown on the bottom of the OBI—if the radial reads 195, for instance, then your heading should be 295°.

If the DME reading is greater than 16, make a correction to the right to get back on the arc. If the DME readout is less than 16, make a correction to the left.

As you approach the inbound course of 16°, time your turn so that you roll out on the inbound heading as the needle centers with the OBS set to 016°. When you're established on the inbound course, you're authorized to descend to 2200 feet. At SOREZ (DME 11), you can descend to 1300 feet. At 8.5 DME, you may descend to the MDA. The missed approach point is the Danville 6.3 DME.

ILS Approaches After Glideslope Fails

Begin this section with the following settings to *Flight Simulator*:

Cloud base	1000
North position	21525
East position	6665
Altitude	603

Occasionally, the glideslope transmitter on the ground isn't working, or the glideslope receiver in the aircraft fails. In such a situation, a localizer approach may be made in lieu of a full ILS IAP.

To simulate this situation, you have a choice. Either use your NAV-2 radio—which has no glideslope receiver—for the localizer, or use the NAV-1 radio and pretend that the glideslope is inoperative.

 You're sitting on the ground at Snohomish County Airport in Everett, Washington. Study the ILS RWY 16 IAP to Everett. When you're ready, take off from runway 34 and track the localizer outbound while climbing to 3000 feet.

Track outbound past the outer marker and execute the procedure turn. When you're established on the inbound course, maintain 3000 feet until you cross the outer marker. Note the time that you cross the outer marker.

The missed approach point is determined by elapsed time on a localizer-only approach. The time-distance table at the bottom right of the IAP chart provides the times it will take to fly from the outer marker to the missed approach point at various groundspeeds. If your groundspeed is 90 knots, for example, it will take you 5 minutes and 12 seconds.

After crossing the outer marker, descend to 980 feet, the minimum descent altitude (not DH, since there's no glideslope) for localizer-only approaches (*S-LOC 16* in the minima section of the chart stands for straight-in localizer approach to runway 16).

Maintain 980 feet until you have the runway in sight and are in a position from which a normal landing can be made, or until your approach time runs out. Time should run out at about the same time you pass over the middle marker.

Figure 8-4. Failed Glideslope Receiver

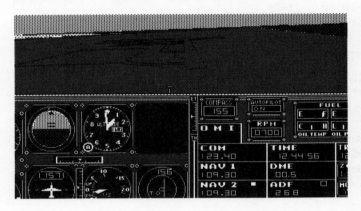

You're at minimum descent altitude (MDA), but your glideslope receiver isn't working.

Radar Vectors to the Final Approach Course

Begin this section with the following settings to *Flight Simulator*:

Cloud base	900
North position	17089
East position	21177
Altitude	81

Some IAPs require an air traffic controller to provide radar vectors (or headings) to the final approach course. One example of this is the VOR RWY 31L to New York/John F. Kennedy International Airport.

Notice the *RADAR REQUIRED* note in the planview. There are no IAFs, because the only way to execute the approach is to receive radar vectors to the final approach course.

Unfortunately, *Flight Simulator* doesn't provide air traffic control services (other than the information provided on ATIS or on control tower frequencies). Fortunately, there is a way that you can play the role of a radar air traffic controller.

After you take off from Republic Airport, you can use the overhead, or map view, to view your airplane relative to the airport at which you're landing. Try assigning yourself headings that will place you on the final approach course outside the final approach fix. Ideally, your intercept heading should be within 30° of the final approach course.

 To get yourself started, take off from Republic and intercept the 220° radial from Deer Park. Follow the radial with the map view selected until you can see the runway layout at Kennedy Airport. Begin giving yourself radar vectors.

Good luck in your new career as an air traffic controller!

Figure 8-5. Vectoring Yourself

This map (or overhead) view shows an airplane on a heading to join the final approach course into Kennedy.

Appendices

Appendix A

IFR Takeoff Minimums and Departure Procedures

These procedures are copied from publications produced by the U.S. Department of Commerce.

Changes, omissions, and format changes have been made for easier comprehension and compatibility with *Flight Simulator*.

These procedures *cannot* be used for actual navigation. They *do not* insure terrain or obstruction clearance in actual navigation.

> Do not use for actual navigation. These materials are outdated and modified for use with *Flight Simulator*. Terrain and obstruction clearance are *not* insured.

Avalon, CA
Catalina

Rwys 4 and 22: Climb straight ahead to 2300'; then proceed on course.

Block Island State, RI
Rwy 10: 300-1
Rwy 28: 300-1

Boston, MA
General Edward Lawrence Logan Intl

Rwy 27: 900-1
Rwy 15R: RVR/40*
Rwy 4R: 300-1 or standard (RVR/18 FAR 135) with minimum climb of 320' per NM to 300'.

Appendix A

Rwy 4L: 300-1 or standard with a minimum climb of 340' per NM to 300'.

Rwy 9: 300-1 or standard with a minimum climb of 230' per NM to 300'.

Rwy 22R: 400-1 or 300-1 with minimum climb of 310' per NM to 400'.

Rwy 22L: 300-1 or standard when control tower reports no tall vessels in departure area.

Rwy 33L: 500-1 or standard RVR/18 (Federal Air Regulation 135) with minimum climb of 250' per NM to 500'.

* *Federal Air Regulation 135*

IFR Departure Procedure
Rwys 22L and 22R: Climb on runway heading to 700' before turning right.
Rwy 33L: Climb runway heading to 700' before turning left.

Bremerton National, WA
Rwys 1 and 34: Turn right; intercept and climb on 187° bearing from Kitsap NDB within 10 NM to cross Kitsap NDB northbound at 2000'.

Bridgeport, CT
Igor I. Sikorsky Memorial

Rwys 11, 16, and 34: 300-1
Rwy 29: 500-1

Carlsbad, CA
McClellan-Palomar

Rwy 6: 400-1 or standard with a minimum climb of 320' per NM to 800'.

IFR Departure Procedure
Rwy 6: Climbing left turn heading 240°.
Rwy 24: Climb straight ahead.
Both departures climb to 1900' before proceeding on course.

Chicago, IL
Chicago Midway

Rwys 4L, 4R, and 22R: 300-1
Rwy 13L: 300-1 or standard with minimum climb of 324' per NM to 700'.
Rwy 13R: 300-1 or standard with minimum climb of 212' per NM to 700'.
Rwy 31L: 300-1 or standard with minimum climb of 273' per NM to 700'.
Rwy 22L: 300-1 or standard with minimum climb of 213' per NM to 700'.

IFR Departure Procedure
Rwys 22L, 22R, 31L, and 31R: Climb runway heading to 1300' before turning east.
Rwys 4L and 4R: Climb to 2400' on heading 090° before turning north.
Rwys 13L/13R: Climb runway heading to 1300' before turning.

Chicago-O'Hare Intl

Rwy 18: NA
Rwy 36: 500-1

IFR Departure Procedure
Rwy 32L: Climb runway heading to 1500' before turning left when weather is below 1000-3.

Lansing Muni

Rwys 9 and 36: 300-1

IFR Departure Procedure
Rwys 9, 27, and 36: Climb runway heading to 2000' before turning.

Chicago (West Chicago), IL
Du Page

IFR Departure Procedure
Rwys 4, 10, 15, 22, 28, and 33: Climb on runway heading to 1200' before turning.

Appendix A

Chico Muni, CA
Rwy 13L: ¾ mile*

* *Federal Air Regulation 135*

IFR Departure Procedure
Rwy 13L/R: Turn right.
Rwy 31L/R: Turn left.
Climb to 3000' or above on the Chico R-202. Then proceed on course.

Chino, CA
Rwy 3: 300-1
Rwy 21: 1200-2
Rwy 26 (northbound and eastbound): standard
Rwy 26 (westbound and southbound): 2700-2 or standard with a minimum climb of 220' per NM to 4000'.

IFR Departure Procedure
Northbound and eastbound
  Rwys 3 and 8: Turn right.
  Rwys 26 and 21: Turn left.
  Direct to Paradise VORTAC; cross Paradise VORTAC at or above 4000'.
Westbound and southbound
  Rwy 3: Turn left.
  Rwys 8, 21, and 26: Turn right.
  Direct Pomona VORTAC; cross Pomona VORTAC at or above 5000'.

Columbia, CA
Rwy 17: 400-2 or standard with minimum climb of 210' per NM to 3000'.
Rwy 35: 800-1½ or standard with minimum climb of 442' per NM to 3000'.

IFR Departure Procedure
Rwy 17: Climb on 175° bearing from Columbia NDB to 3000'. Continue climbing right turn to 5000' or above direct Columbia NDB.
Rwy 35: Climb on 355° bearing from Columbia NDB to 3000'. Continue climbing left turn to 5000' or above direct Columbia NDB.

Concord, CA
Buchanan Field

Rwys 14L/R and 19L/R: 500-1. Climb direct Concord VOR.
Minimum climb rate of 350' per NM to 1000' required.

Corona Muni, CA
Rwy 7: 1000-2
Rwy 25: 800-2

IFR Departure Procedure
Rwy 7: Turn left.
Rwy 25: Turn right.
Both to intercept Paradise VORTAC R-256 direct Paradise
VORTAC. Cross Paradise VORTAC at or above 4000'.

Danbury Muni, CT
All Rwys: 700-1½

Danielson, CT
Rwy 13: 500-1
Rwy 31: 400-1

El Monte, CA
Rwy 1: 400-1
Rwy 19: 1100-2 or 400-1 with minimum climb of 250' per NM
to 1700'.

IFR Departure Procedure
Rwy 1: Climbing right turn; intercept Paradise R-276 to Para-
dise VORTAC.
Rwy 19: Climb runway heading to 800'; then climbing left
turn to 4000' intercept Paradise R-276 to Paradise VORTAC.
All aircraft cross Paradise VORTAC at or above 4000'.

Everett, WA
Snohomish County (Paine Field)

Rwy 16: RVR/24*

* Federal Air Regulation 135

Farmingdale, NY
Republic

Rwy 1: 200-1

IFR Departure Procedure
Rwy 1: Climb runway heading to 600' before proceeding on course.
Rwy 32: Climb runway heading to 600' before proceeding on course.

Frankfort, IL
Rwy 27: 300-1

IFR Departure Procedure
Rwy 9: Climb runway heading to 1200' before turning northbound.

Fresno, CA
Fresno Air Terminal

Rwy 29R: RVR/24*

IFR Departure Procedure
Climb direct to Fresno VORTAC.

* *Federal Air Regulation 135*

Fresno-Chandler Downtown

Rwys 12L/R: Climb heading 165°.
Rwys 30L/R: Climb heading 345°.
Both to 1000' before proceeding on course.

Hartford-Brainard, CT
Rwys 2, 11, and 20: 300-1

IFR Departure Procedure
Rwy 2: Climb to 800' via runway heading before turning westbound.
Rwy 20: Climb to 1900' via runway heading before turning westbound.
Rwy 11: Climb to 600' via runway heading before turning westbound.

Rwy 29: Climbing left turn to 2100' direct Hartford VORTAC before proceeding west or northwest bound.

Hawthorne Muni, CA
Rwy 7: 400-1
Rwy 25: 400-1 or standard with minimum climb of 280' per NM to 400'.

IFR Departure Procedure
Rwy 7: Turn right; climb heading 240°.
Rwy 25: Turn left; climb heading 210°.
To 3000' via Los Angeles R-170 to Los Angeles 10 DME. Then proceed on course.

Joliet Park District, IL
Rwy 12: 500-1
Rwy 22: 300-1

IFR Departure Procedure
Rwy 4: Climb to 1000' before turning right.
Rwy 30: Climb to 1000' before turning left.
Rwy 22: When ceiling is below 500', climb to 1100' before turning left.

Kankakee, IL
Greater Kankakee

Rwy 4: ½ mile*

* *Federal Air Regulation 135*

Lodi, CA
Rwys 8, 12, 26, and 30: 300-1. Climb direct to Linden VORTAC.

Los Angeles Intl, CA
IFR Departure Procedure
Rwys 6L/R and 7L/R: Climb to 2000' heading 070°; then turn right direct Seal Beach VORTAC.
Rwys 24L/R and 25L/R: Climb to 3000' heading 250°; then turn left direct Seal Beach VORTAC.

Marysville, CA
Yuba County

IFR Departure Procedure
All rwys: Climb direct Williams VORTAC.

Merced Muni, CA
Rwy 30: ½ mile*

IFR Departure Procedure
Rwys 12 and 30: Climb to 2000' direct Merced VOR.

* *Federal Air Regulation 135*

Meriden Markham Muni, CT
Rwy 36: 1200-1 or standard with minimum climb of 420' per
  NM to 1300'.

IFR Departure Procedure
Rwy 18: Climb runway heading to 700' before proceeding
  west or northbound.
Rwy 36: Climbing left turn to 1800' via 325° bearing from
  Meriden NDB before proceeding on course.
Caution: Rapidly rising terrain 2.4 NM north of airport.

Modesto City-County Airport—Harry Sham Field, CA
Rwys 10L and 28L: 100-1 or standard with minimum climb of
  300' per NM to 300'.
Rwy 10R: 100-1 or standard with minimum climb of 350' per
  NM to 300'.

IFR Departure Procedure
All rwys: Climb to 1000' on runway heading before proceeding on course.

Napa County, CA
Rwys 6 and 36L/R: 700-1

IFR Departure Procedure
Rwy 6 and Rwys 18L/R: right turn
Rwy 24 and Rwy 36L/R: left turn
Direct to Scaggs Island VORTAC.

New Haven, CT
Tweed–New Haven

Rwys 2 and 20: 300-1
Rwy 32: 400-1
Rwy 14: 300-1

New York, NY
John F. Kennedy Intl

Rwy 13R: 300-1

La Guardia

Rwys 4 and 13: 400-1
Rwy 31: 400-1
Caution: Tall buildings and towers to 1749' at 5.0 NM southwest of airport. Plan departure to avoid this area.

Oakland, CA
Metropolitan Oakland Intl

Rwy 11: RVR/24*
Rwy 29: RVR/18*

* Federal Air Regulation 135

IFR Departure Procedure
Rwys 9R, 9L, 11, 15, and 29: Turn right.
Rwy 33: Turn left.
Rwys 27L and 27R: Maintain runway heading.
Climb to 3000' via Oakland R-288 to Oakland 15.5 DME.
    Then proceed on course.

Oceanside Muni, CA
Rwys 6 and 24: 400-1

IFR Departure Procedure
Rwy 6: Turn right.
Rwy 24: Turn left.
Climb to 1500' heading 235°; then climbing right turn direct
    Oceanside VORTAC. Cross Oceanside VORTAC at or above
    2500'.

Olympia, WA

Rwys 8, 26, and 35: 300-1
Rwy 17: 300-1

IFR Departure Procedure
Rwy 8: Turn left.
Rwys 17 and 26: Turn right.
Climb on Olympia VORTAC R-348 within 10 miles to cross
   Olympia VORTAC at or above 5400'.

Ontario Intl, CA

Rwys 8L/R: 1300-2 or standard with minimum climb of 230'
   per NM to 2600'.
Rwys 3 and 21: 400-1

IFR Departure Procedure
Rwys 3 and 8L/R: Turn right as soon as practical.
Rwys 21 and 26L/R: Turn left.
All departures climb direct Paradise VORTAC. Departures on
   Paradise VORTAC R-105 CW R-140 or R-215 CW 295 climb
   on course. All others cross Paradise VORTAC at or above R-
   141 CW R-214, 3900; R-296 CW R-314, 4400; R-316 CW R-
   104, 6700.

Oroville Muni, CA

Rwy 1: 900 and 1½ or standard with a minimum climb of 300'
   per NM to 1000'.

IFR Departure Procedure
Rwys 1 and 30: Turn left.
Rwys 12 and 19: Turn right.
Climb via Maxwell R-045 to 3000' or above. Then proceed on
   course.

Oxford, CT

Waterbury-Oxford

Rwy 13: 300-1
Rwy 36: 300-1

IFR Departure Procedure
Rwy 13: Climb runway heading to 1400' before turning
   eastbound.

Plainfield, IL
Clow Intl

IFR Departure Procedure
Rwy 36: Climb runway heading to 1100' before turning left.

Red Bluff Muni, CA
IFR Departure Procedure
Climb along Red Bluff R-346 to 5000'. Then proceed on
course.

Reno Cannon Intl, NV
Rwy 7: 1600-2
Rwy 16: 2500-2
Rwy 25 (Categories A and B): 1500-2
Rwy 25 (Categories C and D): 4000-3
Rwy 34: 1700-2

IFR Departure Procedure
Rwys 7 and 16: Turn left.
Rwy 25: Turn right.
Rwy 34: Climb to 8500' heading 344° before proceeding on
course.

Renton Muni, WA
Rwy 15: 700-1
Rwy 33: 700-1

IFR Departure Procedure
Rwy 33: Climb runway heading to 700'.
Rwy 15: Climb visually over the airport to 700'.
Then climb direct Seattle VORTAC. Aircraft departing on Se-
attle R-307 CW 011 or R-141 CW 227 climb on course. All
others climb on R-227 within 10 NM to cross Seattle
VORTAC at or above R-012 CW 101, 2000; R-102 CW 140,
9000; R-228 CW 306, 3000.

Riverside Muni, CA
Rwy 9: 1100-2 or standard with minimum climb of 235' per
NM to 2200'.
Rwy 16: NA
Rwy 27: standard

Rwy 34: 700-2 or 400-1 with minimum climb of 360' per NM to 1600'.

IFR Departure Procedure
Rwy 9: Climb runway heading to 1300'; then climbing right turn to 4000' direct Paradise VORTAC.
Rwy 34: Turn left.
Rwys 27 and 34: Climb heading 280° to 2000'; then climbing left turn to 4000' direct Paradise VORTAC.

Romeoville, IL
Lewis University

Rwy 6: 400-1
Rwy 9: 300-1

IFR Departure Procedure
Rwys 9, 24, and 27: When weather is below 400-1, climb on runway heading to 1100' before turning on course.

Sacramento, CA
Sacramento Executive

Rwy 2: ½ mile*
Rwy 12: 300-1

Federal Air Regulation 135

IFR Departure Procedure
Climb direct to Sacramento VORTAC.

Salinas Muni, CA
Rwys 3, 14, 21, and 32: NA
Rwy 31: RVR/24*
Rwy 8 (Categories C and D): 3600-2 or standard with minimum climb of 420' per NM to 4100'.
Rwy 13 (Categories C and D): 3600-2 or standard with minimum climb of 500' per NM to 4000'.

Federal Air Regulation 135

IFR Departure Procedure
Rwys 8, 13, and 26: Turn right.
Rwy 31: Turn left.
Climb on Salinas R-275 to 2000'; then climbing right turn to cross Salinas VORTAC at or above 3000'.

San Francisco Intl, CA

Rwys 28L and 28R: 1000-2 or standard with minimum climb
of 300' per NM to 1000'.
Rwy 19R (Categories A and B) and Rwy 19L: 1300-2 or standard with minimum climb of 480' per NM to 1400'.
Rwy 19R (Categories C and D): 2100-2 or standard with minimum climb of 530' per NM to 1800'.

IFR Departure Procedure

Rwys 1L/R and 28L/R: Climb runway heading to 2000'; then
climb on course.
Rwys 19L/R: Climbing left turn to 2000' to intercept San
Francisco R-090; then climb on course.
Rwys 10L/R: Climb to 2000' via San Francisco R-09 0; then
climb on course.

San Jose Intl, CA

Rwys 11, 12R, and 12L: 400-1 or standard with climb of 225'
per NM to 500'.

IFR Departure Procedure

Rwys 29, 30L, and 30R: Climb direct Oakland VORTAC.
Rwys 11, 12L, and 12R: Climbing right turn direct Oakland
VORTAC.

Santa Ana, CA

John Wayne Airport—Orange County

Rwy 19L: 400-1
Rwy 19R: RVR/24*

* *Federal Air Regulation 135*

IFR Departure Procedure

Rwys 1L and 1R: Climb runway heading to 700'; climbing left
turn to 2000', direct Seal Beach VORTAC.
Rwys 19L and 19R: Climb runway heading to 500'; climbing
left turn to 2000' on Santa Ana R-190; then climb on course.
When control zone not in effect, reduction NA.

Santa Monica Muni, CA

Rwy 3: 800-1

IFR Departure Procedure
Rwy 3: Climb runway heading to 1100'; turn right direct Santa Monica VOR.
All aircraft proceed via Santa Monica R-261 to Santa Monica 15 DME.

Santa Rosa, CA
Sonoma County
Rwy 1: 1100-3 or standard with minimum climb of 235' per NM to 1100'.

IFR Departure Procedure
Rwy 1: Turn left.
Rwy 14: Turn right.
Rwy 19: Climb straight ahead.
Rwy 32: Climb straight ahead to 1800'; climbing left turn direct Santa Rosa VOR.
Intercept and climb southbound on R-200 Santa Rosa VOR within 15 miles to recross Santa Rosa VOR at or above 5900'.

Seattle, WA
Seattle-Tacoma Intl

Rwy 16R: RVR/18*
Rwy 34R: RVR/24*

* *Federal Air Regulation 135*

IFR Departure Procedure
Aircraft departing on Seattle VORTAC R-307 CW 011 or R-141 CW 227 climb on course.
All others climb on R-227 within 10 NM to cross Seattle VORTAC at or above R-012 CW 101, 2000; R-102 CW 140, 9000; R-228 CW 306, 3000.

Boeing Field/King County Intl

Rwys 13L/R: 500-1
Rwys 31L/R: 600-1

IFR Departure Procedure
Climb visually over the airport to 300', then direct to Seattle VORTAC.

Aircraft departing on Seattle R-307 CW 011 or R-141 CW 227 climb on course.
All others climb on R-227 within 10 NM to cross Seattle VORTAC at or above R-012 CW 101, 2000; R-102 CW 140, 9000; R-228 CW 306, 3000.

Shelton, WA
Sanderson Field

Rwys 5 and 23: 500-1

IFR Departure Procedure
Climb visually over the airport to 700', then direct Mason County NDB before proceeding on course.

South Lake Tahoe, CA
Lake Tahoe

Rwy 18: 1200-3*
Rwy 36: Standard*
Night takeoff Rwy 18 not authorized.
* Minimum climb of 350' per NM to 9000' required.

IFR Departure Procedure
Rwy 18: Turn right; climb visually within 2 NM to cross airport heading 330°.
Rwy 36: Left turn heading 330°.
To intercept Lake Tahoe R-115 to Lake Tahoe VORTAC.

Southbridge Muni, MA
Rwys 2 and 20: 300-1

Tacoma Narrows, WA
Rwy 17: ½ mile*
Rwys 17 and 35: Maneuvering east of the airport not authorized.

* Federal Air Regulation 135

Torrance Muni, CA
Rwys 11L/R: 400-1 or standard with a minimum climb of 325' per NM to 500'.

IFR Departure Procedure
Rwys 29L/R: Climb runway heading.
Rwys 11L/R: Climbing left turn to heading 290°.
Both departures: Climb to 3000'; intercept Los Angeles R-170 to Los Angeles 10 DME.

Van Nuys, CA
Rwys 16L/R and 34L/R: 2500-2 or standard with minimum climb of 270' per NM to 3500'.

IFR Departure Procedure
Rwys 16L/R: climbing left turn
Rwys 34L/R: climbing right turn
To intercept Van Nuys R-096 to Van Nuys 10 DME

Visalia Muni, CA
IFR Departure Procedure
Rwy 30: Turn left.
Rwy 12: Turn right.
Climb heading 230° to 2000'.

Watsonville Muni, CA
Rwy 1: 1800-2 or standard with minimum climb of 370' per NM to 2000'.
Rwy 26: 400-1 or standard with minimum climb of 230' per NM to 600'.

IFR Departure Procedure
Rwys 1 and 8: Turn right.
Rwy 26: Turn left.
All aircraft proceed direct Pajar NDB and follow Pajar NDB bearing 196° while climbing to 4000'. Then proceed on course.

White Plains, NY
Westchester County

Rwys 11 and 29: 300-1
Rwy 16: 300-1

Willimantic, CT
Windham

Rwys 6, 18, 27, and 36: 300-1
Rwy 9: 700-1
Rwy 24: 500-1

Willows–Glenn County, CA
Climb direct to Maxwell VORTAC.

Windsor Locks, CT
Bradley Intl

Rwy 15: 300-1
Rwy 33: 700-1

IFR Departure Procedure
Rwy 1: Climb to 1000' via runway heading before turning
    westbound.

Appendix B
Selected IAP Charts for *Flight Simulator*

List of IAP Charts

Appendix B

Airport	City	State	Approach	Page #
Everett/Snohomish Co	Everett	WA	ILS RWY 16	156
Everett/Snohomish Co	Everett	WA	VOR RWY 16	157
Everett/Snohomish Co	Everett	WA	VOR RWY 34	158
Farmingdale/Republic	Farmingdale	NY	NDB RWY 1	159
Frankfort	Frankfort	IL	VOR RWY 27	160
Fresno Air Terminal	Fresno	CA	VOR RWY 11L	161
Fresno-Chandler Downtown	Fresno	CA	NDB-B	162
Fresno-Chandler Downtown	Fresno	CA	VOR/DME-C	163
Gibson City Muni	Gibson City	IL	VOR-A	164
Hartford-Brainard	Hartford	CT	VOR-A	165
Hawthorne Muni	Hawthorne	CA	VOR RWY 25	166
Joliet Park District	Joliet	IL	VOR RWY 12	167
Kankakee/Greater Kankakee	Kankakee	IL	VOR RWY 4	168
Kankakee/Greater Kankakee	Kankakee	IL	VOR RWY 22	169
Lodi	Lodi	CA	VOR-A	170
Los Angeles International	Los Angeles	CA	VOR RWY 7L/R	171
Los Angeles International	Los Angeles	CA	VOR RWY 25L/R	172
Martha's Vineyard	Martha's Vineyard	MA	ILS RWY 24	173
Martha's Vineyard	Martha's Vineyard	MA	VOR RWY 6	174
Martha's Vineyard	Martha's Vineyard	MA	VOR RWY 24	175
Marysville/Yuba Co	Marysville	CA	VOR RWY 14	176
Marysville/Yuba Co	Marysville	CA	VOR RWY 32	177
Merced Muni	Merced	CA	VOR RWY 30	178
Meriden Markham Muni	Meriden	CT	NDB RWY 36	179
Meriden Markham Muni	Meriden	CT	VOR RWY 36	180
Modesto City–County Airport–Harry Sham Field	Modesto	CA	VOR RWY 28R	181
Monee/Sanger	Monee	IL	VOR RWY 5	182
Morris Muni	Morris	IL	VOR-A	183
Napa County	Napa	CA	VOR RWY 6	184
New Haven/Tweed–New Haven	New Haven	CT	VOR RWY 2	185
New Haven/Tweed–New Haven	New Haven	CT	VOR RWY 20	186
NY/John F. Kennedy Intl	NY	NY	VOR-D	187
NY/John F. Kennedy Intl	NY	NY	VOR RWY 4L/R	188
NY/John F. Kennedy Intl	NY	NY	VOR RWY 31L	189
NY/John F. Kennedy Intl	NY	NY	VOR/DME RWY 22L	190
NY/La Guardia	NY	NY	VOR-A	191
NY/La Guardia	NY	NY	VOR-B	192
NY/La Guardia	NY	NY	VOR-C	193
NY/La Guardia	NY	NY	VOR RWY 4	194
Oakland/Metropolitan Oakland Intl	Oakland	CA	ILS RWY 11	195
Oakland/Metropolitan Oakland Intl	Oakland	CA	VOR RWY 9R	196
Oakland/Metropolitan Oakland Intl	Oakland	CA	VOR/DME RWY 27L	197
Oceanside Muni	Oceanside	CA	VOR-A	198
Olympia	Olympia	WA	VOR RWY 17	199
Olympia	Olympia	WA	VOR/DME RWY 35	200
Ontario International	Ontario	CA	VOR RWY 26R	201
Oroville Muni	Oroville	CA	VOR-A	202
Oxford/Waterbury-Oxford	Oxford	CT	NDB RWY 18	203
Plainfield/Clow Intl	Plainfield	IL	VOR-A	204
Red Bluff Muni	Red Bluff	CA	VOR RWY 33	205
Red Bluff Muni	Red Bluff	CA	VOR/DME RWY 15	206
Reno Cannon Intl	Reno	NV	NDB RWY 16R	207
Reno Cannon Intl	Reno	NV	VOR-D	208
Renton Muni	Renton	WA	NDB RWY 15	209
Romeoville/Lewis University	Romeoville	IL	VOR RWY 9	210

Appendix B

GENERAL INFORMATION & ABBREVIATIONS

★ Indicates control tower or ATIS operates non-continuously.
Distances in nautical miles (except visibility in statute miles and Runway Visual Range in hundreds of feet).
Runway Dimensions in feet.
Elevations in feet Mean Sea Level (MSL).
Ceilings in feet above airport elevation.
Radials/bearings/headings/courses are magnetic.
\# Indicates control tower temporarily closed UFN.

ADF	Automatic Direction Finder
ALS	Approach Light System
APP CON	Approach Control
ARR	Arrival
ASR/PAR	Published Radar Minimums at this Airport
ATIS	Automatic Terminal Information Service
AWOS	Automated Weather Observing System
AZ	Azimuth
BC	Back Course
C	Circling
CAT	Category
CCW	Counter Clockwise
Chan	Channel
CLNC DEL	clearance delivery
CTAF	Common Traffic Advisory Frequency
CW	Clockwise
DH	Decision Height
DME	Distance Measuring Equipment
DR	Dead Reckoning
ELEV	elevation
FAF	Final Approach Fix
FM	Fan Marker
GPI	Ground Point of Intercept(ion)
GS	Glide Slope
HAA	Height Above Airport
HAL	Height Above Landing
HAT	Height Above Touchdown
HIRL	High Intensity Runway Lights
IAF	Initial Approach Fix
ICAO	International Civil Aviation Organization
IM	Inner Marker
Intcp	Intercept
INT	Intersection
LDA	Localizer Type Directional Aid
Ldg	Landing
LDIN	Lead in Light System
LIRL	Low Intensity Runway Lights
LOC	Localizer
LR	Lead Radial. Provides at least 2 NM (Copter 1 NM) of lead to assist in turning onto the intermediate/final course
MALS	Medium Intensity Approach Light System
MALSR	Medium Intensity Approach Light Systems with RAIL
MAP	Missed Approach Point
MDA	Minimum Descent Altitude
MIRL	Medium Intensity Runways Lights
MLS	Microwave Landing System
MM	Middle Marker
NA	Not Authorized
NDB	Non-directional Radio Beacon
NM	Nautical Miles
NoPT	No Procedure Turn Required (Procedure Turn shall not be executed without ATC clearance)
ODALS	Omnidirectional Approach Light System
OM	Outer Marker
R	Radial
RA	Radio Altimeter setting height
Radar Required	Radar vectoring required for this approach
RAIL	Runway Alignment Indicator Lights
REIL	Runway End Identifier Lights
RNAV	Area Navigation
RPI	Runway Point of Intercept
RRL	Runway Remaining Lights
Runway Touchdown Zone	First 3000' of Runway
RVR	Runway Visual Range
S	Straight-in
SALS	Short Approach Light System
SSALR	Simplified Short Approach Light System with RAIL
SDF	Simplified Directional Facility
TA	Transition Altitude
TAC	TACAN
TCH	Threshold Crossing Height (height in feet Above Ground Level)
TDZ	Touchdown Zone
TDZE	Touchdown Zone Elevation
TDZ/CL	Touchdown Zone and Runway Centerline Lighting
TLv	Transition Level
VASI	Visual Approach Slope Indicator
VDP	Visual Descent Point
WPT	Waypoint (RNAV)
X	Radar Only Frequency

RADIO CONTROL
AIRPORT LIGHTING SYSTEM

KEY MIKE	FUNCTION
7 times within 5 seconds	Highest intensity available
5 times within 5 seconds	Medium or lower intensity (Lower REIL or REIL-off)
3 times within 5 seconds	Lowest intensity available (Lower REIL or REIL-off)

Available systems will be indicated on Instrument Approach Procedure (IAP) Charts, below the Minimums Data, as follows:
ACTIVATE MIRL Rwy 36-UNICOM.
ACTIVATE MIRL Rwy 36-122.8, ACTIVATE MALSR Rwy 7-122.8
ACTIVATE VASI and REIL Rwy 7-122.8, ACTIVATE HIRL Rwy 7-25 – 122.8

Appendix B

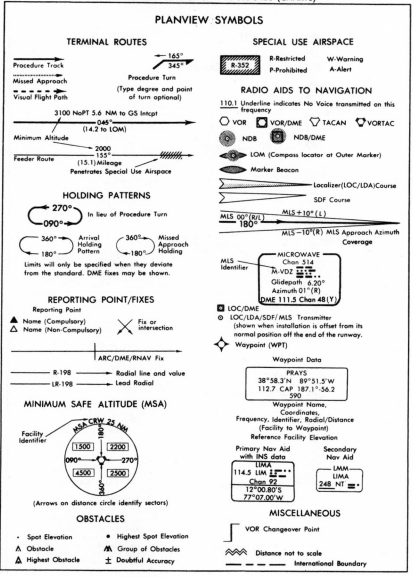

LEGEND
INSTRUMENT APPROACH PROCEDURES (CHARTS)

PLANVIEW SYMBOLS

TERMINAL ROUTES

Procedure Track

Missed Approach

Visual Flight Path

```
          ← 165°
            345° ←
```
Procedure Turn

(Type degree and point of turn optional)

3100 NoPT 5.6 NM to GS Intcpt

045°
(14.2 to LOM)

Minimum Altitude

2000
155°
(15.1) Mileage

Feeder Route

Penetrates Special Use Airspace

HOLDING PATTERNS

270°

090°

In lieu of Procedure Turn

360°

180°

Arrival Holding Pattern

360°

180°

Missed Approach Holding

Limits will only be specified when they deviate from the standard. DME fixes may be shown.

REPORTING POINT/FIXES

Reporting Point

▲ Name (Compulsory)

△ Name (Non-Compulsory)

✕ Fix or intersection

ARC/DME/RNAV Fix

R-198 → Radial line and value

LR-198 → Lead Radial

MINIMUM SAFE ALTITUDE (MSA)

MSA CRW 25 NM

180°

Facility Identifier

| 1500 | 2200 |
| 4500 | 2500 |

090° 270°

360°

(Arrows on distance circle identify sectors)

OBSTACLES

· Spot Elevation

⋀ Obstacle

Ａ Highest Obstacle

● Highest Spot Elevation

⋀⋀ Group of Obstacles

± Doubtful Accuracy

SPECIAL USE AIRSPACE

R-352

R-Restricted   W-Warning
P-Prohibited   A-Alert

RADIO AIDS TO NAVIGATION

110.1 Underline indicates No Voice transmitted on this frequency

○ VOR   ◻ VOR/DME   ▽ TACAN   ⬡ VORTAC

NDB   NDB/DME

LOM (Compass locator at Outer Marker)

Marker Beacon

Localizer(LOC/LDA)Course

SDF Course

MLS 00°(R/L)   MLS +10°(L)
180°
MLS −10°(R) MLS Approach Azimuth
Coverage

MLS Identifier

```
MICROWAVE
Chan 514
M-VDZ ▪▄▪▪··
Glidepath 6.20°
Azimuth 01°(R)
DME 111.5 Chan 48(Y)
```

◻ LOC/DME

⊙ LOC/LDA/SDF/MLS Transmitter
(shown when installation is offset from its normal position off the end of the runway.

✛ Waypoint (WPT)

Waypoint Data

```
PRAYS
38°58.3'N  89°51.5'W
112.7 CAP 187.1°-56.2
590
```
Waypoint Name,
Coordinates,
Frequency, Identifier, Radial/Distance
(Facility to Waypoint)
Reference Facility Elevation

Primary Nav Aid
with INS data

```
LIMA
114.5 LIM ▪▄▪·▪
Chan 92
12°00.80'S
77°07.00'W
```

Secondary
Nav Aid

```
LMM
LIMA
248 NT ▪▄▪
```

MISCELLANEOUS

⌐ VOR Changeover Point

〰〰 Distance not to scale

— — — — International Boundary

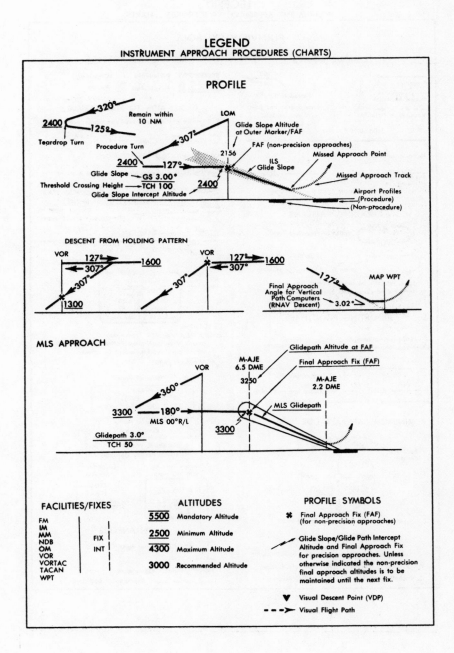

LEGEND
INSTRUMENT APPROACH PROCEDURES (CHARTS)

PROFILE

320°
2400
125°
Teardrop Turn
Remain within 10 NM
307°
Procedure Turn
2400 — 127°
Glide Slope — GS 3.00°
Threshold Crossing Height — TCH 100
Glide Slope Intercept Altitude
2400
LOM
Glide Slope Altitude at Outer Marker/FAF
2156
FAF (non-precision approaches)
ILS Glide Slope
Missed Approach Point
Missed Approach Track
Airport Profiles
(Procedure)
(Non-procedure)

DESCENT FROM HOLDING PATTERN

VOR 127° 1600
307°
307°
1300
VOR 127° 1600
307°
307°
Final Approach Angle for Vertical Path Computers (RNAV Descent)
127°
3.02°
MAP WPT

MLS APPROACH

VOR
3300 — 180°
MLS 00°R/L
Glidepath 3.0°
TCH 50
M-AJE 6.5 DME
3250
3300
Glidepath Altitude at FAF
Final Approach Fix (FAF)
M-AJE 2.2 DME
MLS Glidepath

FACILITIES/FIXES

FM
IM
MM
NDB
OM   FIX
VOR   INT
VORTAC
TACAN
WPT

ALTITUDES

5500 Mandatory Altitude

2500 Minimum Altitude

4300 Maximum Altitude

3000 Recommended Altitude

PROFILE SYMBOLS

✳ Final Approach Fix (FAF) (for non-precision approaches)

Glide Slope/Glide Path Intercept Altitude and Final Approach Fix for precision approaches. Unless otherwise indicated the non-precision final approach altitudes is to be maintained until the next fix.

▼ Visual Descent Point (VDP)

- - -► Visual Flight Path

LEGEND
INSTRUMENT APPROACH PROCEDURES (CHARTS)

AIRPORT SKETCH

Runways

Hard Surface Other Than Hard Surface Hardstands/Taxiways

Closed Runways Under Construction Metal Surface

Over-run Displaced Threshold Runway Centerline Lighting

Arresting Gear

uni-directional bi-directional Jet Barrier

- Control Tower
  When Control Tower and Rotating Beacon are co-located, Beacon symbol will be used and further identified as TWR.

★ Rotating Airport Beacon

Helicopter Alighting Areas

Negative Symbols used to identify Copter Procedure landing point.

Note: The prop type symbol is being phased out.

TDZE 123 Runway TDZ elevation

0.8% → up Total Runway Gradient
(shown when runway gradient exceeds 0.3%)

- U.S. Navy Optical Landing System (OLS) "OLS" location is shown because of its height of approximately 7 feet and proximity to edge of runway may create on obstruction for some types of aircraft.

Approach light symbols are shown on a separate legend.

MINIMA DATA

Alternate Minimums not standard. Civil users refer to tabulation. USA/USN/USAF pilots refer to appropriate regulations.

NA Alternate minimums are Not Authorized due to unmonitored facility or absence of weather reporting service.

Take-off Minimums not standard and/or Departure Procedures are published. Refer to tabulation.

LEGEND

AIRPORT DIAGRAMS

GENERAL INFORMATION (NOS)

SCOPE

Airport diagrams are specifically designed to assist in the movement of ground traffic at locations with complex runway/taxiway configurations and provide information for updating Inertial Navigation Systems (INS) aboard aircraft. Airport diagrams are not intended to be used for approach and landing or departure operations. Requisition for the creation of airport diagrams must meet the above criteria and will be approved by the FAA or DOD on a case-by-case basis.

NEW REQUIREMENTS/CORRECTIONS

National Ocean Service, NOAA, N/CG31
6010 Executive Boulevard
Rockville, Maryland 20852

Federal Aviation Administration, ATO-250
800 Independence Avenue, S.W.
Washington, D.C. 20591

LEGEND

Airport diagram scales are variable.

True/magnetic North orientation may vary from diagram to diagram.

Coordinate values are shown in one (1) minute increments. They are further broken down into six (6) second ticks, within each one (1) minute increment.

NOTE:

All new and revised airport diagrams are shown referenced to the World Geodetic System (WGS) (noted on appropriate diagram), and may not be compatible with local coordinates published in FLIP.

Arresting Gear

⌐ uni-directional   ⌐ bi-directional   ⫞ Jet Barrier

REFERENCE FEATURES

Buildings	■
Tanks	●
Obstruction	⚠
Airport Beacon	★
Runway Radar Reflectors	⚓
Control Tower	●
Helicopter Alighting Areas	Ⓗ ⊞ Ⓗ ⚠ ⊞
Negative Symbols used to identify Copter Procedures landing point	● ⊞ ⬛ ▲ ⊞

TAXIWAY/RUNWAY DATA

Hard Surface Runway

Other Than Hard Surface Runway

Closed Runway, Taxiways

Under Construction

Overruns, Taxiways, Parking Areas

Runway Gradient

FIELD ELEV 174

Runway Identification

0.7% UP

9000 X 200   ← 023.2° 1000 X 200

Runway End Elevation   ELEV 164   Runway Dimensions (In feet)   Runway Heading (Magnetic)   Overrun Dimensions (in feet)

Appendix B

INSTRUMENT APPROACH PROCEDURE CHARTS
RATE OF DESCENT TABLE
(ft. per min.)

A rate of descent table is provided for use in planning and executing precision descents under known or approximate ground speed conditions. It will be especially useful for approaches when the localizer only is used for course guidance. A best speed, power, attitude combination can be programmed which will result in a stable glide rate and attitude favorable for executing a landing if minimums exist upon breakout. Care should always be exercised so that the minimum descent altitude and missed approach point are not exceeded.

ANGLE OF DESCENT (degrees and tenths)	GROUND SPEED (knots)										
	30	45	60	75	90	105	120	135	150	165	180
2.0	105	160	210	265	320	370	425	475	530	585	635
2.5	130	200	265	330	395	465	530	595	665	730	795
3.0	160	240	320	395	480	555	635	715	795	875	955
3.5	185	280	370	465	555	650	740	835	925	1020	1110
4.0	210	315	425	530	635	740	845	955	1060	1165	1270
4.5	240	355	475	595	715	835	955	1075	1190	1310	1430
5.0	265	395	530	660	795	925	1060	1190	1325	1455	1590
5.5	290	435	580	730	875	1020	1165	1310	1455	1600	1745
6.0	315	475	635	795	955	1110	1270	1430	1590	1745	1905
6.5	345	515	690	860	1030	1205	1375	1550	1720	1890	2065
7.0	370	555	740	925	1110	1295	1480	1665	1850	2035	2220
7.5	395	595	795	990	1190	1390	1585	1785	1985	2180	2380
8.0	425	635	845	1055	1270	1480	1690	1905	2115	2325	2540
8.5	450	675	900	1120	1345	1570	1795	2020	2245	2470	2695
9.0	475	715	950	1190	1425	1665	1900	2140	2375	2615	2855
9.5	500	750	1005	1255	1505	1755	2005	2255	2510	2760	3010
10.0	530	790	1055	1320	1585	1845	2110	2375	2640	2900	3165
10.5	555	830	1105	1385	1660	1940	2215	2490	2770	3045	3320
11.0	580	870	1160	1450	1740	2030	2320	2610	2900	3190	3480
11.5	605	910	1210	1515	1820	2120	2425	2725	3030	3335	3635
12.0	630	945	1260	1575	1890	2205	2520	2835	3150	3465	3780

Not for use in Navigation

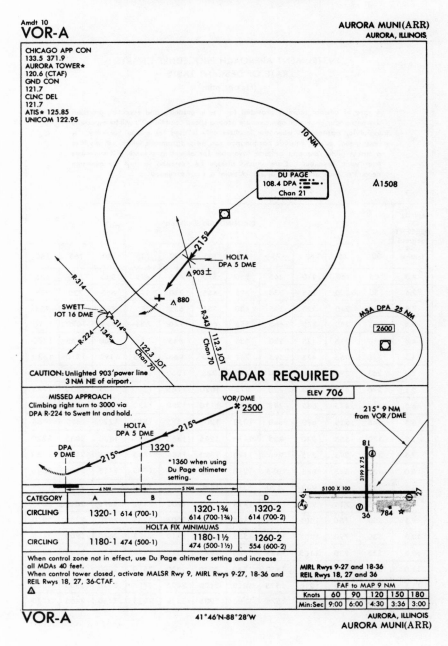

VOR-A

AURORA MUNI(ARR)
AURORA, ILLINOIS

CHICAGO APP CON
133.5 371.9
AURORA TOWER★
120.6 (CTAF)
GND CON
121.7
CLNC DEL
121.7
ATIS★ 125.85
UNICOM 122.95

DU PAGE
108.4 DPA ▬▬ ▪ ▪
Chan 21

△1508

215°

HOLTA
DPA 5 DME

△903±

△880

R-314

SWETT
IOT 16 DME

R-314°

134°

R-224

122.3 IOT
Chan 70

R-343

112.3 IOT
Chan 70

MSA DPA 25 NM

2600

CAUTION: Unlighted 903'power line
3 NM NE of airport.

RADAR REQUIRED

ELEV 706

MISSED APPROACH
Climbing right turn to 3000 via
DPA R-224 to Swett Int and hold.

VOR/DME
★2500

215° 9 NM
from VOR/DME

HOLTA
DPA 5 DME   215°

DPA
9 DME   215°   1320*

*1360 when using
Du Page altimeter
setting.

81

3199 X 75

5100 X 100

36   784 ★

27

CATEGORY	A	B	C	D
CIRCLING	1320-1 614 (700-1)		1320-1¾ 614 (700-1¾)	1320-2 614 (700-2)
HOLTA FIX MINIMUMS				
CIRCLING	1180-1 474 (500-1)		1180-1½ 474 (500-1½)	1260-2 554 (600-2)

When control zone not in effect, use Du Page altimeter setting and increase
all MDAs 40 feet.
When control tower closed, activate MALSR Rwy 9, MIRL Rwys 9-27, 18-36 and
REIL Rwys 18, 27, 36-CTAF.
△

MIRL Rwys 9-27 and 18-36
REIL Rwys 18, 27 and 36

FAF to MAP 9 NM					
Knots	60	90	120	150	180
Min:Sec	9:00	6:00	4:30	3:36	3:00

VOR-A

41°46'N-88°28'W

AURORA, ILLINOIS
AURORA MUNI(ARR)

Not for use in Navigation

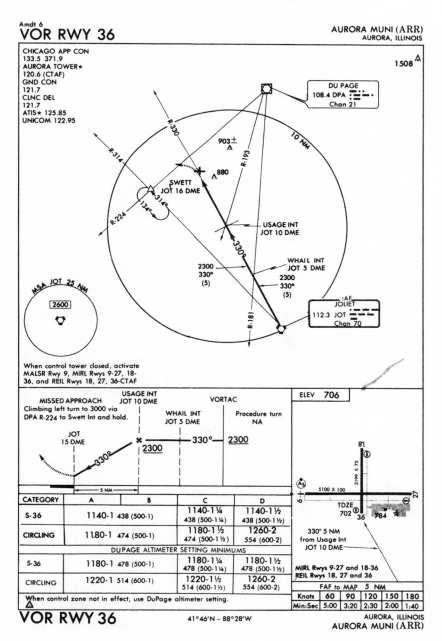

Amdt 6
VOR RWY 36

AURORA MUNI (ARR)
AURORA, ILLINOIS

CHICAGO APP CON
133.5 371.9
AURORA TOWER★
120.6 (CTAF)
GND CON
121.7
CLNC DEL
121.7
ATIS★ 125.85
UNICOM 122.95

DU PAGE
108.4 DPA
Chan 21

1508

903±

880

SWETT
JOT 16 DME

USAGE INT
JOT 10 DME

WHAIL INT
JOT 5 DME

2300
330°
(5)

2300
330°
(5)

IAF
JOLIET
112.3 JOT
Chan 70

MSA JOT 25 NM

2600

When control tower closed, activate
MALSR Rwy 9, MIRL Rwys 9-27, 18-
36, and REIL Rwys 18, 27, 36-CTAF

MISSED APPROACH	USAGE INT JOT 10 DME	VORTAC
Climbing left turn to 3000 via DPA R-224 to Swett Int and hold.	WHAIL INT JOT 5 DME	Procedure turn NA

JOT
15 DME

330°

2300

330° — 2300

ELEV 706

TDZE
702

330° 5 NM
from Usage Int
JOT 10 DME

MIRL Rwys 9-27 and 18-36
REIL Rwys 18, 27 and 36

FAF to MAP 5 NM

5 NM

CATEGORY	A	B	C	D
S-36	1140-1 438 (500-1)		1140-1¼ 438 (500-1¼)	1140-1½ 438 (500-1½)
CIRCLING	1180-1 474 (500-1)		1180-1½ 474 (500-1½)	1260-2 554 (600-2)
DUPAGE ALTIMETER SETTING MINIMUMS				
S-36	1180-1 478 (500-1)		1180-1¼ 478 (500-1¼)	1180-1½ 478 (500-1½)
CIRCLING	1220-1 514 (600-1)		1220-1½ 514 (600-1½)	1260-2 554 (600-2)

When control zone not in effect, use DuPage altimeter setting.

Knots	60	90	120	150	180
Min:Sec	5:00	3:20	2:30	2:00	1:40

VOR RWY 36

41°46'N – 88°28'W

AURORA, ILLINOIS
AURORA MUNI (ARR)

115

Not for use in Navigation

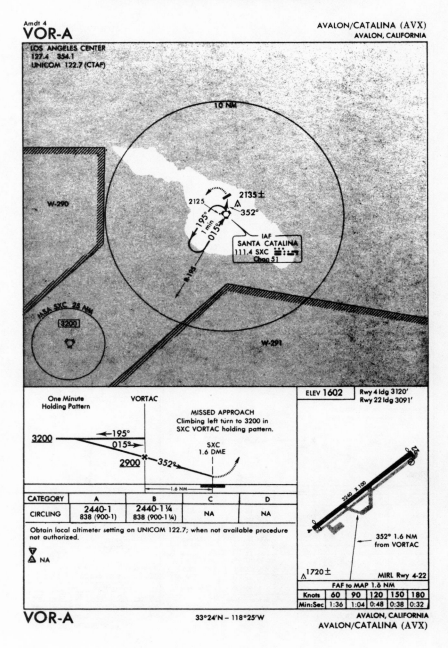

VOR-A

AVALON/CATALINA (AVX)
AVALON, CALIFORNIA

LOS ANGELES CENTER
127.4   354.1
UNICOM 122.7 (CTAF)

10 NM

W-290

2125   2135±
          352°
195°
1 min
015°

R-199

IAF
SANTA CATALINA
111.4 SXC
Chan 51

W-291

ARA SXC 25 NM
3200

One Minute
Holding Pattern   VORTAC

MISSED APPROACH
Climbing left turn to 3200 in
SXC VORTAC holding pattern.

3200   ←195°
            015°   SXC
2900   ―352°   1.6 DME

1.6 NM

ELEV 1602   Rwy 4 ldg 3120'
             Rwy 22 ldg 3091'

3240 X 100

352° 1.6 NM
from VORTAC

1720±   MIRL Rwy 4-22

CATEGORY	A	B	C	D
CIRCLING	2440-1 838 (900-1)	2440-1¼ 838 (900-1¼)	NA	NA

Obtain local altimeter setting on UNICOM 122.7; when not available procedure
not authorized.

NA

FAF to MAP 1.6 NM					
Knots	60	90	120	150	180
Min:Sec	1:36	1:04	0:48	0:38	0:32

VOR-A

33°24'N – 118°25'W

AVALON, CALIFORNIA
AVALON/CATALINA (AVX)

Not for use in Navigation

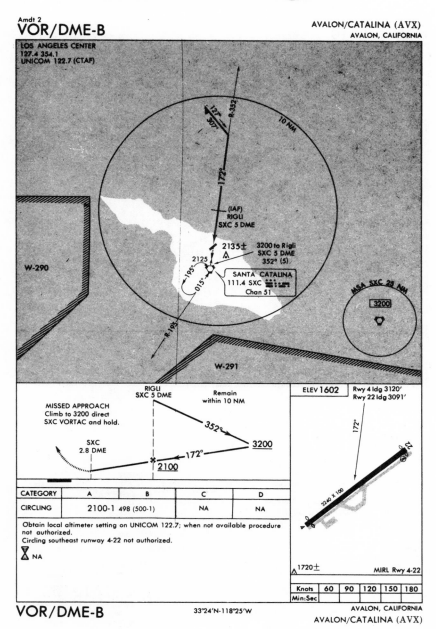

Amdt 2
VOR/DME-B

AVALON/CATALINA (AVX)
AVALON, CALIFORNIA

LOS ANGELES CENTER
127.4 354.1
UNICOM 122.7 (CTAF)

10 NM

127°
307°
R-352

172°

(IAF)
RIGLI
SXC 5 DME

2135±
3200 to Rigli
SXC 5 DME
352° (5)

2125

W-290

195°

015°

SANTA CATALINA
111.4 SXC
Chan 51

MSA SXC 25 NM

3200

R-195

W-291

RIGLI
SXC 5 DME

Remain
within 10 NM

MISSED APPROACH
Climb to 3200 direct
SXC VORTAC and hold.

352°

SXC
2.8 DME

172°

3200

2100

ELEV 1602

Rwy 4 ldg 3120'
Rwy 22 ldg 3091'

172°

3240 X 100

CATEGORY	A	B	C	D
CIRCLING	2100-1 498 (500-1)		NA	NA

Obtain local altimeter setting on UNICOM 122.7; when not available procedure
not authorized.
Circling southeast runway 4-22 not authorized.

NA

1720±

MIRL Rwy 4-22

Knots	60	90	120	150	180
Min:Sec					

VOR/DME-B

33°24'N-118°25'W

AVALON, CALIFORNIA
AVALON/CATALINA (AVX)

Not for use in Navigation

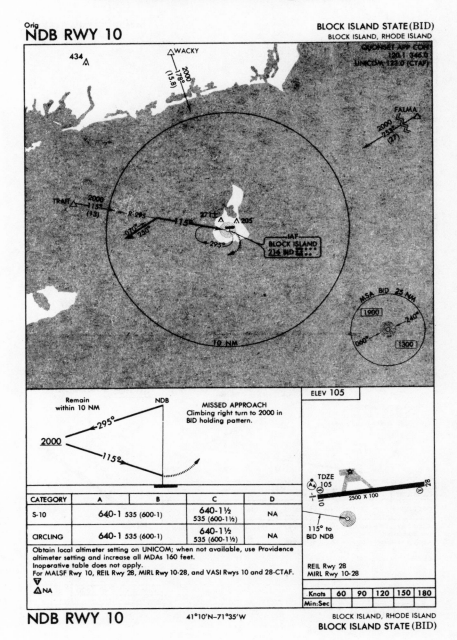

Orig
NDB RWY 10

BLOCK ISLAND STATE (BID)
BLOCK ISLAND, RHODE ISLAND

QUONSET APP CON
120.1 346.0
UNICOM 123.0 (CTAF)

434 △

△WACKY
2000
178°
(15.8)

FALMA △
2000
253°
(27)

TRAFF △
2000
115°
(13)

R-295
2000
250°

1150

271 △
△ 205

△ 295°

IAF
BLOCK ISLAND
216 BID

MSA BID 25 NM
1900
240°
060°
1300

10 NM

	Remain within 10 NM		NDB	MISSED APPROACH

Remain within 10 NM

NDB

295°

2000

115°

MISSED APPROACH
Climbing right turn to 2000 in BID holding pattern.

ELEV 105

TDZE 105

2500 X 100

28

10

115° to
BID NDB

CATEGORY	A	B	C	D
S-10	640-1	535 (600-1)	640-1½ 535 (600-1½)	NA
CIRCLING	640-1	535 (600-1)	640-1½ 535 (600-1½)	NA

Obtain local altimeter setting on UNICOM; when not available, use Providence altimeter setting and increase all MDAs 160 feet.
Inoperative table does not apply.
For MALSF Rwy 10, REIL Rwy 28, MIRL Rwy 10-28, and VASI Rwys 10 and 28-CTAF.
▽
△ NA

REIL Rwy 28
MIRL Rwy 10-28

Knots	60	90	120	150	180
Min:Sec					

NDB RWY 10

41°10'N–71°35'W

BLOCK ISLAND, RHODE ISLAND
BLOCK ISLAND STATE (BID)

Not for use in Navigation

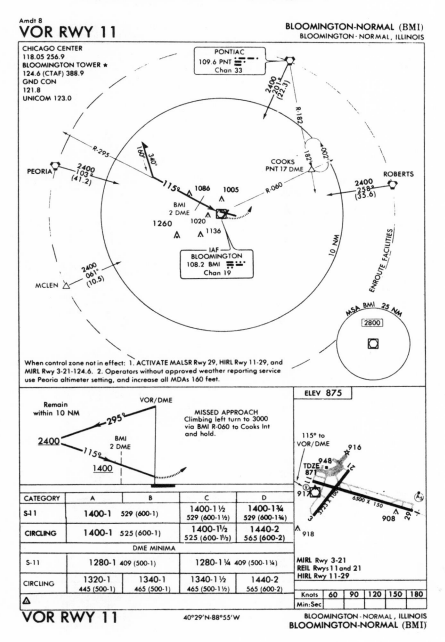

Amdt 8

VOR RWY 11

BLOOMINGTON-NORMAL (BMI)
BLOOMINGTON-NORMAL, ILLINOIS

CHICAGO CENTER
118.05 256.9
BLOOMINGTON TOWER ★
124.6 (CTAF) 388.9
GND CON
121.8
UNICOM 123.0

PONTIAC
109.6 PNT
Chan 33

PEORIA 2400 103° (41.2)

R-295

R-182

COOKS PNT 17 DME

ROBERTS 2400 258° (35.6)

R-060

1086   1005

BMI 2 DME

1260   1020   1136

IAF
BLOOMINGTON
108.2 BMI
Chan 19

MCLEN 2400 061° (10.5)

10 NM

ENROUTE FACILITIES

MSA BMI 25 NM
2800

When control zone not in effect: 1. ACTIVATE MALSR Rwy 29, HIRL Rwy 11-29, and MIRL Rwy 3-21-124.6. 2. Operators without approved weather reporting service use Peoria altimeter setting, and increase all MDAs 160 feet.

ELEV 875

Remain within 10 NM

VOR/DME

295°

2400

BMI 2 DME

115°

1400

MISSED APPROACH
Climbing left turn to 3000
via BMI R-060 to Cooks Int
and hold.

115° to
VOR/DME   916

TDZE   948
871

917

6500 X 150

908

918

CATEGORY	A	B	C	D
S-11	1400-1	529 (600-1)	1400-1½ 529 (600-1½)	1400-1¾ 529 (600-1¾)
CIRCLING	1400-1	525 (600-1)	1400-1½ 525 (600-1½)	1440-2 565 (600-2)
DME MINIMA				
S-11	1280-1 409 (500-1)		1280-1¼ 409 (500-1¼)	
CIRCLING	1320-1 445 (500-1)	1340-1 465 (500-1)	1340-1½ 465 (500-1½)	1440-2 565 (600-2)

MIRL Rwy 3-21
REIL Rwys 11 and 21
HIRL Rwy 11-29

Knots	60	90	120	150	180
Min:Sec					

VOR RWY 11

40°29'N-88°55'W

BLOOMINGTON-NORMAL, ILLINOIS
BLOOMINGTON-NORMAL (BMI)

Not for use in Navigation

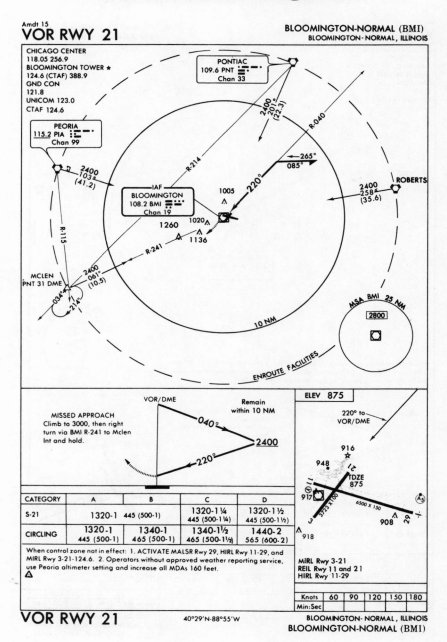

Amdt 15
VOR RWY 21

BLOOMINGTON-NORMAL (BMI)
BLOOMINGTON-NORMAL, ILLINOIS

CHICAGO CENTER
118.05 256.9
BLOOMINGTON TOWER ★
124.6 (CTAF) 388.9
GND CON
121.8
UNICOM 123.0
CTAF 124.6

PONTIAC
109.6 PNT
Chan 33

PEORIA
115.2 PIA
Chan 99

IAF
BLOOMINGTON
108.2 BMI
Chan 19

R-214

R-040

2400
201°
(22.3)

265°
085°

220°

ROBERTS

2400
258°
(35.6)

1005

1020

1260

1136

R-241

R-115

MCLEN
PNT 31 DME

2400
103°
(41.2)

034°
214°

2400
061°
(10.5)

10 NM

MSA BMI 25 NM

2800

ENROUTE FACILITIES

MISSED APPROACH
Climb to 3000, then right
turn via BMI R-241 to Mclen
Int and hold.

VOR/DME

Remain
within 10 NM

040°

2400

220°

ELEV 875

220° to
VOR/DME

916

948

918

917

TDZE
875

6500 X 150

3723 X 150

908

918

CATEGORY	A	B	C	D
S-21	1320-1 445 (500-1)		1320-1¼ 445 (500-1¼)	1320-1½ 445 (500-1½)
CIRCLING	1320-1 445 (500-1)	1340-1 465 (500-1)	1340-1½ 465 (500-1½)	1440-2 565 (600-2)

When control zone not in effect: 1. ACTIVATE MALSR Rwy 29, HIRL Rwy 11-29, and
MIRL Rwy 3-21-124.6. 2. Operators without approved weather reporting service,
use Peoria altimeter setting and increase all MDAs 160 feet.

MIRL Rwy 3-21
REIL Rwy 11 and 21
HIRL Rwy 11-29

Knots	60	90	120	150	180
Min:Sec					

VOR RWY 21

40°29'N-88°55'W

BLOOMINGTON-NORMAL, ILLINOIS
BLOOMINGTON-NORMAL (BMI)

Not for use in Navigation

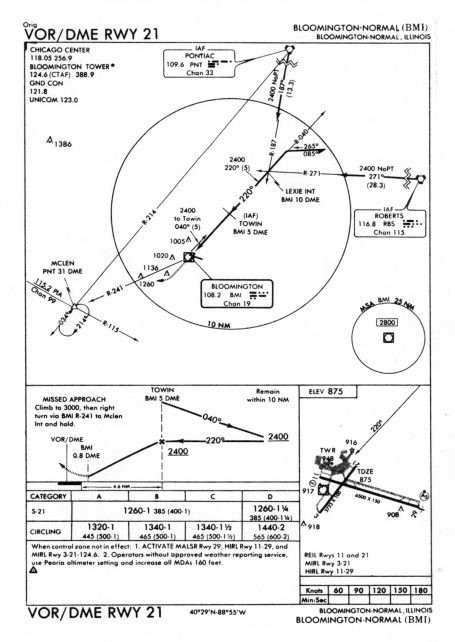

Orig
VOR/DME RWY 21

BLOOMINGTON-NORMAL (BMI)
BLOOMINGTON-NORMAL, ILLINOIS

CHICAGO CENTER
118.05 256.9
BLOOMINGTON TOWER ★
124.6 (CTAF) 388.9
GND CON
121.8
UNICOM 123.0

IAF
PONTIAC
109.6 PNT
Chan 33

2400 NoPT
187° (13.3)

265°
085°

R-040

R-187

R-271

2400 NoPT
271°
(28.3)

2400
220° (5)

LEXIE INT
BMI 10 DME

IAF
ROBERTS
116.8 RBS
Chan 115

A 1386

2400
to Towin
040° (5)

(IAF)
TOWIN
BMI 5 DME

R-214

220°

1005 A

1020 A

MCLEN
PNT 31 DME

1136

1260 A

BLOOMINGTON
108.2 BMI
Chan 19

115.2 PIA
Chan 99

R-241

R-115

034°

214°

10 NM

MSA BMI 25 NM

2800

ELEV 875

MISSED APPROACH
Climb to 3000, then right
turn via BMI R-241 to Mclen
Int and hold.

TOWIN
BMI 5 DME

Remain
within 10 NM

040°

VOR/DME
BMI
0.8 DME

220°

2400

2400

4.6 NM

220°

916

TWR
948

TDZE
875

917

6500 X 150

908

A 918

CATEGORY	A	B	C	D
S-21		1260-1 385 (400-1)		1260-1¼ 385 (400-1¼)
CIRCLING	1320-1 445 (500-1)	1340-1 465 (500-1)	1340-1½ 465 (500-1½)	1440-2 565 (600-2)

When control zone not in effect: 1. ACTIVATE MALSR Rwy 29, HIRL Rwy 11-29, and
MIRL Rwy 3-21-124.6. 2. Operators without approved weather reporting service,
⚠ use Peoria altimeter setting and increase all MDAs 160 feet.

REIL Rwys 11 and 21
MIRL Rwy 3-21
HIRL Rwy 11-29

Knots	60	90	120	150	180
Min:Sec					

VOR/DME RWY 21

40°29'N-88°55'W

BLOOMINGTON-NORMAL, ILLINOIS
BLOOMINGTON-NORMAL (BMI)

Not for use in Navigation

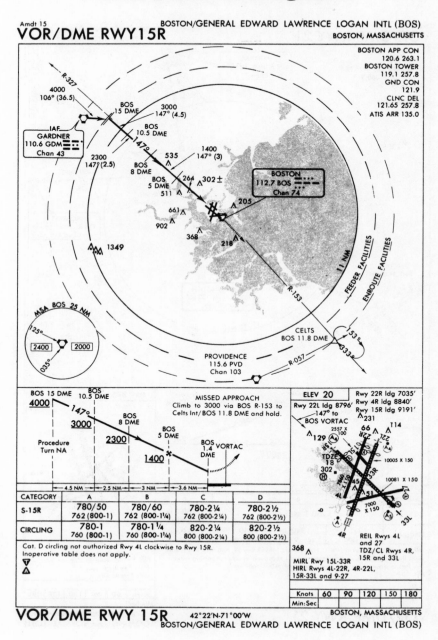

BOSTON/GENERAL EDWARD LAWRENCE LOGAN INTL (BOS)

VOR/DME RWY 15R

BOSTON, MASSACHUSETTS

BOSTON APP CON
120.6 263.1
BOSTON TOWER
119.1 257.8
GND CON
121.9
CLNC DEL
121.65 257.8
ATIS ARR 135.0

R-327

4000
106° (36.5)

IAF
GARDNER
110.6 GDM
Chan 43

BOS
15 DME
3000
147° (4.5)

147°

BOS
10.5 DME

2300
147° (2.5)

1400
147° (3)

535

BOS
8 DME

302±

264

BOS
5 DME

511

205

BOSTON
112.7 BOS
Chan 74

661

902

368

218

1349

R-153

MSA BOS 25 NM

125°
2400 2000
035°

CELTS
BOS 11.8 DME

-53°

333°

PROVIDENCE
115.6 PVD
Chan 103

R-057

FEEDER FACILITIES
ENROUTE FACILITIES

11 NM

MISSED APPROACH
Climb to 3000 via BOS R-153 to
Celts Int/BOS 11.8 DME and hold.

BOS 15 DME
4000

BOS
10.5 DME

147°

3000

BOS
8 DME

2300

BOS
5 DME

Procedure
Turn NA

1400

BOS
1.4
DME

VORTAC

| | | | 4.5 NM | 2.5 NM | 3 NM | 3.6 NM | |

CATEGORY	A	B	C	D
S-15R	780/50 762 (800-1)	780/60 762 (800-1¼)	780-2¼ 762 (800-2¼)	780-2½ 762 (800-2½)
CIRCLING	780-1 760 (800-1)	780-1¼ 760 (800-1¼)	820-2¼ 800 (800-2¼)	820-2½ 800 (800-2½)

Cat. D circling not authorized Rwy 4L clockwise to Rwy 15R.
Inoperative table does not apply.

ELEV 20

Rwy 22R ldg 7035'
Rwy 4R ldg 8840'
Rwy 15R ldg 9191'

Rwy 22L ldg 8796'
147° to
BOS VORTAC

231

129

66

114

2557 X
100

TDZE
18

302

10005 X 150

10081 X 150

45

51

7000
X 150

33L

4R

368

MIRL Rwy 15L-33R
HIRL Rwys 4L-22R, 4R-22L,
15R-33L and 9-27

REIL Rwys 4L
and 27
TDZ/CL Rwys 4R,
15R and 33L

Knots	60	90	120	150	180
Min:Sec					

VOR/DME RWY 15R

42°22'N-71°00'W

BOSTON, MASSACHUSETTS
BOSTON/GENERAL EDWARD LAWRENCE LOGAN INTL (BOS)

Not for use in Navigation

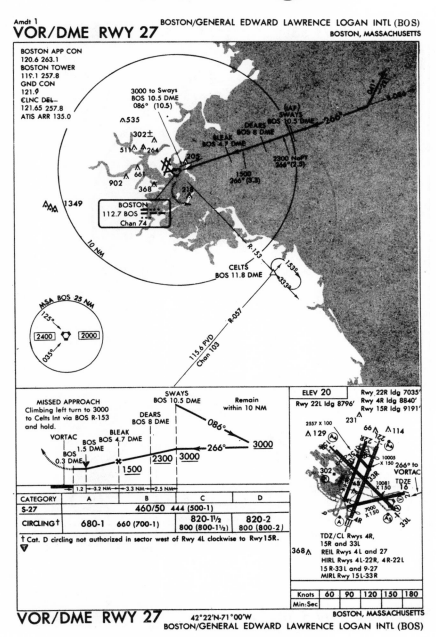

BOSTON APP CON
120.6 263.1
BOSTON TOWER
119.1 257.8
GND CON
121.9
CLNC DEL
121.65 257.8
ATIS ARR 135.0

3000 to Sways
BOS 10.5 DME
086° (10.5)

∧535

302±
∧
511∧ ∧264
∧ 661

902

368∧

BOSTON
112.7 BOS
Chan 74

(IAF)
SWAYS
BOS 10.5 DME — 266°

DEARS
BOS 8 DME
BLEAK
BOS 4.7 DME

2300 NoPT
266°(2.5)

1500
266° (3.3)

218

R-153

CELTS
BOS 11.8 DME

153°

333°

115.6 PVD
Chan 103

R-057

∧∧∧ 1349

10 NM

MSA BOS 25 NM
125°
2400 ⬠ 2000
035°

MISSED APPROACH
Climbing left turn to 3000
to Celts Int via BOS R-153
and hold.

SWAYS
BOS 10.5 DME

DEARS
BOS 8 DME

Remain
within 10 NM

086°

BLEAK
BOS 4.7 DME

VORTAC
BOS 1.5 DME

BOS
0.3 DME

266°

3000

3000

2300 3000

1500

1.2 ← 3.2 NM → ← 3.3 NM → ←2.5 NM→

CATEGORY	A	B	C	D
S-27		460/50 444 (500-1)		
CIRCLING†	680-1	660 (700-1)	820-1½ 800 (800-1½)	820-2 800 (800-2)

† Cat. D circling not authorized in sector west of Rwy 4L clockwise to Rwy 15R.
▽

ELEV 20

Rwy 22R ldg 7035'
Rwy 22L ldg 8796'
Rwy 4R ldg 8840'
Rwy 15R ldg 9191'

2557 X 100
231∧
∧129
66∧ ∧114
10005
X 150
266° to
VORTAC
302
10081
X 150
TDZE
16
7000
X 150
368∧
4R
33L

TDZ/CL Rwys 4R,
15R and 33L
REIL Rwys 4L and 27
HIRL Rwys 4L-22R, 4R-22L
15 R-33 L and 9-27
MIRL Rwy 15L-33R

Knots	60	90	120	150	180
Min:Sec					

Not for use in Navigation

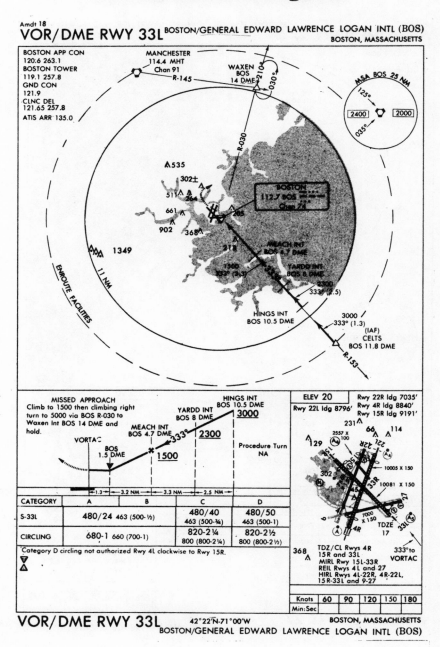

Amdt 18

VOR/DME RWY 33L BOSTON/GENERAL EDWARD LAWRENCE LOGAN INTL (BOS)
BOSTON, MASSACHUSETTS

BOSTON APP CON
120.6 263.1
BOSTON TOWER
119.1 257.8
GND CON
121.9
CLNC DEL
121.65 257.8
ATIS ARR 135.0

MANCHESTER
114.4 MHT
Chan 91
R-145

WAXEN
BOS
14 DME

MSA BOS 25 NM
125°
035°
2400 2000

MANCHESTER R-030

∆535

302±

511∆ 264

661∆

902∆ 368∆

∆785

BOSTON
112.7 BOS
Chan 74

∆218

MEACH INT
BOS 4.7 DME

1349

730D
333° (2.3)

YARDD INT
BOS 8 DME

2300
333° (2.5)

HINGS INT
BOS 10.5 DME

3000
333° (1.3)
(IAF)
CELTS
BOS 11.8 DME

R-153

11 NM

ENROUTE FACILITIES

MISSED APPROACH
Climb to 1500 then climbing right turn to 5000 via BOS R-030 to Waxen Int BOS 14 DME and hold.

HINGS INT
BOS 10.5 DME
3000

YARDD INT
BOS 8 DME

MEACH INT
BOS 4.7 DME
333° 2300

VORTAC
BOS
1.5 DME
1500

Procedure Turn
NA

1.3 → 3.2 NM → 3.3 NM → 2.5 NM

CATEGORY	A	B	C	D
S-33L	480/24 463 (500-½)		480/40 463 (500-¾)	480/50 463 (500-1)
CIRCLING	680-1 660 (700-1)		820-2¼ 800 (800-2¼)	820-2½ 800 (800-2½)

Category D circling not authorized Rwy 4L clockwise to Rwy 15R.

ELEV 20
Rwy 22L ldg 8796'

Rwy 22R ldg 7035'
Rwy 4R ldg 8840'
Rwy 15R ldg 9191'

231∆
66∆ 114∆
129∆ 2557 X 100

302∆

10005 X 150

10081 X 150

7000 X 150

TDZE 17

368∆

TDZ/CL Rwys 4R
15R and 33L
MIRL Rwy 15L-33R
REIL Rwys 4L and 27
HIRL Rwys 4L-22R, 4R-22L,
15R-33L and 9-27

333° to
VORTAC

	Knots	60	90	120	150	180
	Min:Sec					

VOR/DME RWY 33L   42°22'N-71°00'W   BOSTON, MASSACHUSETTS
BOSTON/GENERAL EDWARD LAWRENCE LOGAN INTL (BOS)

Not for use in Navigation

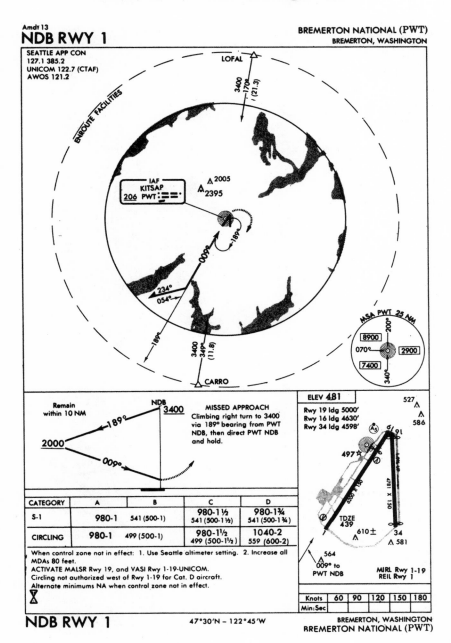

Amdt 13

NDB RWY 1

SEATTLE APP CON
127.1 385.2
UNICOM 122.7 (CTAF)
AWOS 121.2

BREMERTON NATIONAL (PWT)
BREMERTON, WASHINGTON

LOFAL

3400
1700
(21.3)

ENROUTE FACILITIES

IAF
KITSAP
206 PWT

∧ 2005
∧ 2395

189°

009°

234°
054°

189°

3400
349°
(11.8)

CARRO

MSA PWT 25 NM
200°
8900
070°   2900
7400
340°

Remain
within 10 NM

NDB
3400

189°

2000

009°

MISSED APPROACH
Climbing right turn to 3400
via 189° bearing from PWT
NDB, then direct PWT NDB
and hold.

ELEV 481

527 ∧
∧ 586

Rwy 19 ldg 5000'
Rwy 16 ldg 4630'
Rwy 34 ldg 4598'

497 ☆

TDZE
439

610± ∧

34
∧ 581

564
009° to
PWT NDB

MIRL Rwy 1-19
REIL Rwy 1

CATEGORY	A	B	C	D
S-1	980-1	541 (500-1)	980-1½ 541 (500-1½)	980-1¾ 541 (500-1¾)
CIRCLING	980-1	499 (500-1)	980-1½ 499 (500-1½)	1040-2 559 (600-2)

When control zone not in effect: 1. Use Seattle altimeter setting. 2. Increase all
MDAs 80 feet.
ACTIVATE MALSR Rwy 19, and VASI Rwy 1-19-UNICOM.
Circling not authorized west of Rwy 1-19 for Cat. D aircraft.
Alternate minimums NA when control zone not in effect.

Knots	60	90	120	150	180
Min:Sec					

NDB RWY 1

47°30'N – 122°45'W

BREMERTON, WASHINGTON
BREMERTON NATIONAL (PWT)

Not for use in Navigation

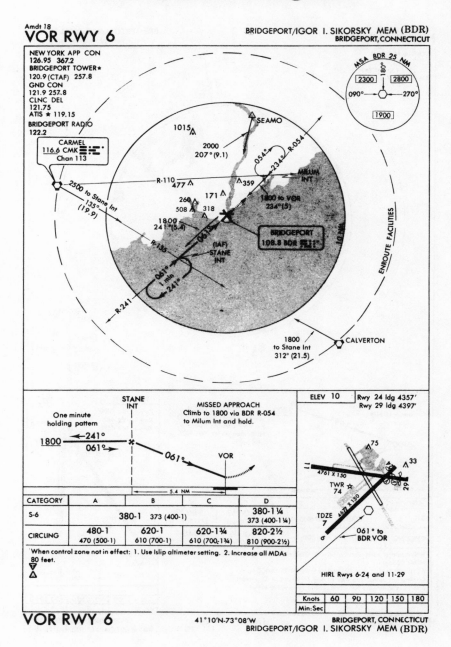

Amdt 18
VOR RWY 6

BRIDGEPORT/IGOR I. SIKORSKY MEM (BDR)
BRIDGEPORT, CONNECTICUT

NEW YORK APP CON
126.95 367.2
BRIDGEPORT TOWER ★
120.9 (CTAF) 257.8
GND CON
121.9 257.8
CLNC DEL
121.75
ATIS ★ 119.15
BRIDGEPORT RADIO
122.2

CARMEL
116.6 CMK
Chan 113

MSA BDR 25 NM
180°
2300 | 2800
090° ——————— 270°
1900

1015
SEAMO
2000
207° (9.1)
054°
234° R-054
R-110 477
359
MILUM INT
260
508
171
318
1800 to VOR
234° (5)
1800
241° (5.4)
061°
BRIDGEPORT
108.8 BDR
(IAF)
STANE INT
R-135
2500 to Stane Int
135°
(19.9)
R-241
061°
1 min
241°
ENROUTE FACILITIES

1800
to Stane Int
312° (21.5)
CALVERTON

| | STANE INT | MISSED APPROACH | ELEV 10 | Rwy 24 ldg 4357' |
| | | Climb to 1800 via BDR R-054 | | Rwy 29 ldg 4397' |

One minute
holding pattern

1800 ←—241°
061°→

061°

VOR

MISSED APPROACH
Climb to 1800 via BDR R-054
to Milum Int and hold.

5.4 NM

CATEGORY	A	B	C	D
S-6	380-1 373 (400-1)			380-1¼ 373 (400-1¼)
CIRCLING	480-1 470 (500-1)	620-1 610 (700-1)	620-1¾ 610 (700-1¾)	820-2½ 810 (900-2½)

When control zone not in effect: 1. Use Islip altimeter setting. 2. Increase all MDAs
80 feet.

ELEV 10

75
33
4761 X 150
TWR
74
TDZE
7
4677 X 150
29
061° to
BDR VOR

HIRL Rwys 6-24 and 11-29

Knots	60	90	120	150	180
Min:Sec					

VOR RWY 6

41°10'N-73°08'W

BRIDGEPORT, CONNECTICUT
BRIDGEPORT/IGOR I. SIKORSKY MEM (BDR)

Not for use in Navigation

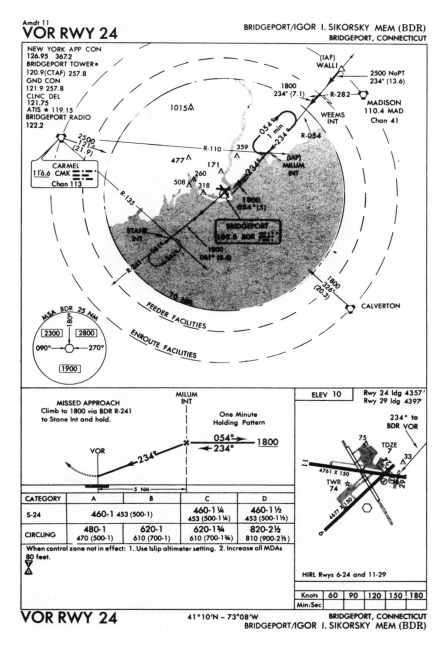

Not for use in Navigation

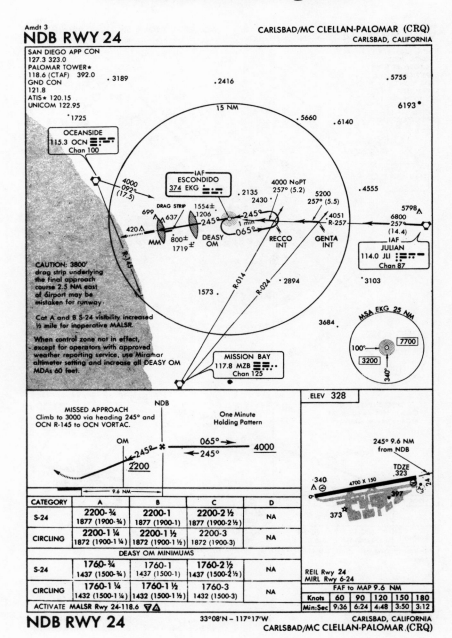

Amdt 3

NDB RWY 24

CARLSBAD/MC CLELLAN-PALOMAR (CRQ)
CARLSBAD, CALIFORNIA

SAN DIEGO APP CON
127.3 323.0
PALOMAR TOWER *
118.6 (CTAF) 392.0
GND CON
121.8
ATIS * 120.15
UNICOM 122.95

OCEANSIDE
115.3 OCN
Chan 100

IAF
ESCONDIDO
374 EKG

4000 NoPT
257° (5.2)

5200
257° (5.5)

. 4555

5798
6800
257°
(14.4)

4000
092°
(17.5)

DRAG STRIP
1554±
1206

699
4051
R-257

IAF
JULIAN
114.0 JLI
Chan 87

637
-245°
-245°
1 min
065°

RECCO
INT

GENTA
INT

420
MM
800±
1719±
DEASY
OM

. 3103

CAUTION: 3800'
drag strip underlying
the final approach
course 2.5 NM east
of airport may be
mistaken for runway.

1573 .

R-014
R-024

. 2894

MSA EKG 25 NM

100°
7700

Cat A and B S-24 visibility increased
½ mile for inoperative MALSR.

3684 .

3200
340°

When control zone not in effect,
except for operators with approved
weather reporting service, use Miramar
altimeter setting and increase all DEASY OM
MDAs 60 feet.

MISSION BAY
117.8 MZB
Chan 125

ELEV 328

MISSED APPROACH
Climb to 3000 via heading 245° and
OCN R-145 to OCN VORTAC.

NDB

One Minute
Holding Pattern

245° 9.6 NM
from NDB

TDZE
.323

OM
-245°
065°
-245°

4000

2200

.340

4700 X 150

.397

9.6 NM

373

CATEGORY	A	B	C	D
S-24	2200-¾ 1877 (1900-¾)	2200-1 1877 (1900-1)	2200-2½ 1877 (1900-2½)	NA
CIRCLING	2200-1¼ 1872 (1900-1¼)	2200-1½ 1872 (1900-1½)	2200-3 1872 (1900-3)	NA
DEASY OM MINIMUMS				
S-24	1760-¾ 1437 (1500-¾)	1760-1 1437 (1500-1)	1760-2½ 1437 (1500-2½)	NA
CIRCLING	1760-1¼ 1432 (1500-1¼)	1760-1½ 1432 (1500-1½)	1760-3 1432 (1500-3)	NA

ACTIVATE MALSR Rwy 24-118.6

REIL Rwy 24
MIRL Rwy 6-24

FAF to MAP 9.6 NM

Knots	60	90	120	150	180
Min:Sec	9:36	6:24	4:48	3:50	3:12

NDB RWY 24

33°08'N – 117°17'W

CARLSBAD, CALIFORNIA
CARLSBAD/MC CLELLAN-PALOMAR (CRQ)

Not for use in Navigation

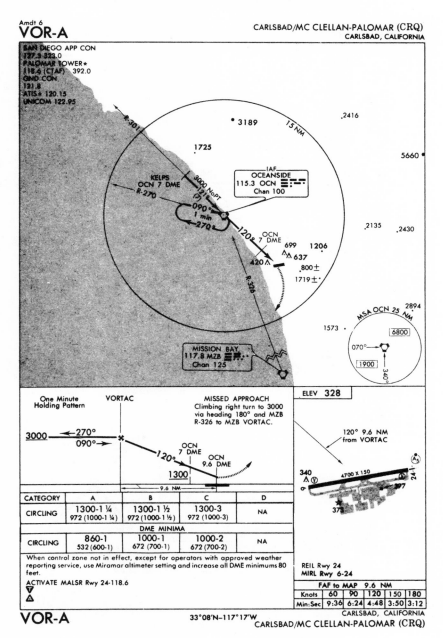

Amdt 6
VOR-A

CARLSBAD/MC CLELLAN-PALOMAR (CRQ)
CARLSBAD, CALIFORNIA

SAN DIEGO APP CON
127.3 323.0
PALOMAR TOWER★
118.6 (CTAF) 392.0
GND CON
121.8
ATIS★ 120.15
UNICOM 122.95

OCEANSIDE
115.3 OCN
Chan 100

KELPS
OCN 7 DME
R-270

MISSION BAY
117.8 MZB
Chan 125

MSA OCN 25 NM
6800
070°
1900
340°

ELEV 328

One Minute Holding Pattern	VORTAC	MISSED APPROACH Climbing right turn to 3000 via heading 180° and MZB R-326 to MZB VORTAC.

120° 9.6 NM
from VORTAC

340
4700 X 150

CATEGORY	A	B	C	D
CIRCLING	1300-1 ¼ 972 (1000-1 ¼)	1300-1 ½ 972 (1000-1 ½)	1300-3 972 (1000-3)	NA

DME MINIMA				
CIRCLING	860-1 532 (600-1)	1000-1 672 (700-1)	1000-2 672 (700-2)	NA

When control zone not in effect, except for operators with approved weather reporting service, use Miramar altimeter setting and increase all DME minimums 80 feet.

ACTIVATE MALSR Rwy 24-118.6

REIL Rwy 24
MIRL Rwy 6-24

FAF to MAP 9.6 NM					
Knots	60	90	120	150	180
Min:Sec	9:36	6:24	4:48	3:50	3:12

VOR-A

33°08'N–117°17'W

CARLSBAD, CALIFORNIA
CARLSBAD/MC CLELLAN-PALOMAR (CRQ)

Not for use in Navigation

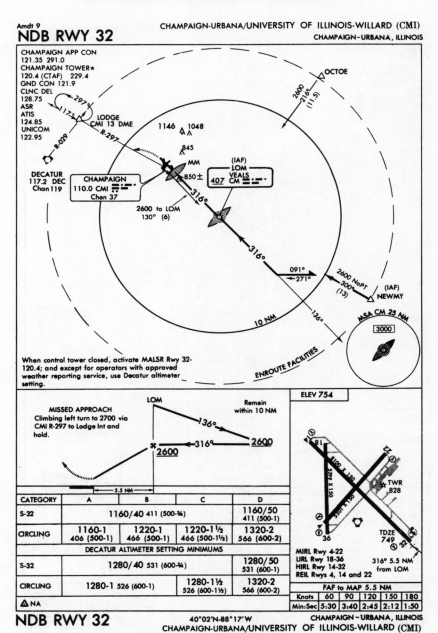

CHAMPAIGN-URBANA/UNIVERSITY OF ILLINOIS-WILLARD (CMI)
CHAMPAIGN-URBANA, ILLINOIS

CHAMPAIGN APP CON
121.35 291.0
CHAMPAIGN TOWER★
120.4 (CTAF) 229.4
GND CON 121.9
CLNC DEL
128.75
ASR
ATIS
124.85
UNICOM
122.95

OCTOE
2600
216° (11.5)

R-029
297°
173°
LODGE
CMI 13 DME
R-297

1146 1048
845

DECATUR
117.2 DEC
Chan 119

CHAMPAIGN
110.0 CMI
Chan 37

MM
850±

(IAF)
LOM
VEALS
CM
407

2600 to LOM
130° (6)

316°

316°

091°
271°

2600 NoPT
300°
(13)

(IAF)
NEWMY

136°

10 NM

MSA CM 25 NM
3000

When control tower closed, activate MALSR Rwy 32-120.4; and except for operators with approved weather reporting service, use Decatur altimeter setting.

ENROUTE FACILITIES

ELEV 754

MISSED APPROACH
Climbing left turn to 2700 via CMI R-297 to Lodge Int and hold.

LOM
Remain within 10 NM
136°
316° 2600
2600

5.5 NM

MIRL Rwy 4-22
LIRL Rwy 18-36
HIRL Rwy 14-32
REIL Rwys 4, 14 and 22

TWR 828
TDZE 749

316° 5.5 NM
from LOM

CATEGORY	A	B	C	D
S-32	1160/40 411 (500-¾)			1160/50 411 (500-1)
CIRCLING	1160-1 406 (500-1)	1220-1 466 (500-1)	1220-1½ 466 (500-1½)	1320-2 566 (600-2)
DECATUR ALTIMETER SETTING MINIMUMS				
S-32	1280/40 531 (600-¾)			1280/50 531 (600-1)
CIRCLING	1280-1 526 (600-1)		1280-1½ 526 (600-1½)	1320-2 566 (600-2)
⚠ NA				

FAF to MAP 5.5 NM					
Knots	60	90	120	150	180
Min:Sec	5:30	3:40	2:45	2:12	1:50

NDB RWY 32

40°02'N-88°17'W

CHAMPAIGN-URBANA, ILLINOIS
CHAMPAIGN-URBANA/UNIVERSITY OF ILLINOIS-WILLARD (CMI)

Not for use in Navigation

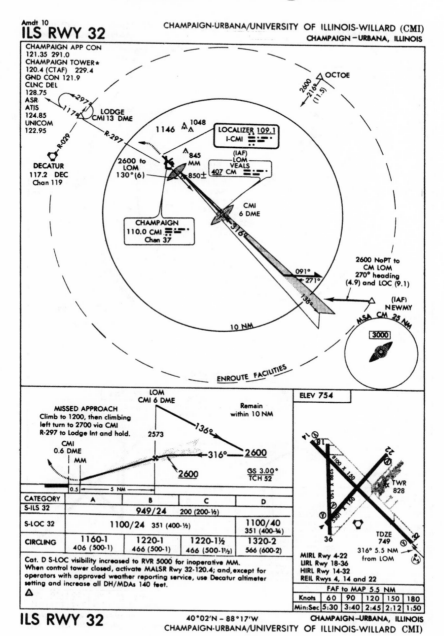

CHAMPAIGN APP CON
121.35 291.0
CHAMPAIGN TOWER★
120.4 (CTAF) 229.4
GND CON 121.9
CLNC DEL
128.75
ASR
ATIS
124.85
UNICOM
122.95

LODGE
CMI 13 DME

R-297

-297-
-117-
R-029

DECATUR
117.2 DEC
Chan 119

OCTOE
2600
-216°-
(11.5)

1146 ▲ 1048
▲ 845
MM

LOCALIZER 109.1
I-CMI

(IAF)
LOM
VEALS

407 CM
850±

2600 to
LOM
130°(6)

CMI
6 DME

CHAMPAIGN
110.0 CMI
Chan 37

316°

091°
271°

130°

2600 NoPT to
CM LOM
270° heading
(4.9) and LOC (9.1)

(IAF)
NEWMY

MSA CM 25 NM

3000

10 NM

ENROUTE FACILITIES

ELEV 754

LOM
CMI 6 DME

MISSED APPROACH
Climb to 1200, then climbing
left turn to 2700 via CMI
R-297 to Lodge Int and hold.

Remain
within 10 NM

136°

2573

CMI
0.6 DME
MM

316° 2600

2600

GS 3.00°
TCH 52

0.5 5 NM

TWR
828

TDZE
749

316° 5.5 NM
from LOM

CATEGORY	A	B	C	D
S-ILS 32		949/24 200 (200-½)		
S-LOC 32		1100/24 351 (400-½)		1100/40 351 (400-¾)
CIRCLING	1160-1 406 (500-1)	1220-1 466 (500-1)	1220-1½ 466 (500-1½)	1320-2 566 (600-2)

Cat. D S-LOC visibility increased to RVR 5000 for inoperative MM.
When control tower closed, activate MALSR Rwy 32-120.4; and, except for
operators with approved weather reporting service, use Decatur altimeter
setting and increase all DH/MDAs 140 feet.
△

MIRL Rwy 4-22
LIRL Rwy 18-36
HIRL Rwy 14-32
REIL Rwys 4, 14 and 22

FAF to MAP 5.5 NM					
Knots	60	90	120	150	180
Min:Sec	5:30	3:40	2:45	2:12	1:50

Not for use in Navigation

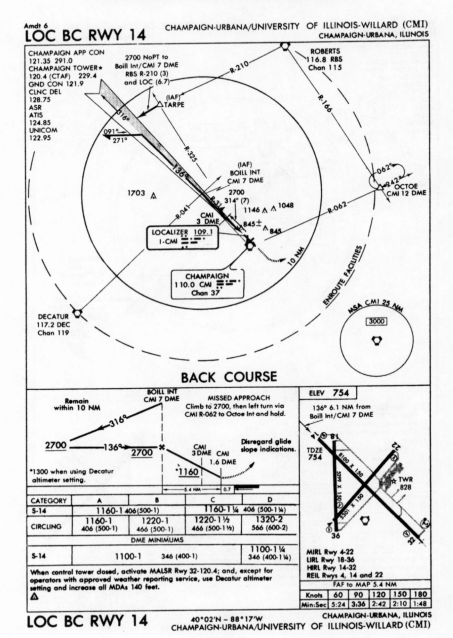

Amdt 6
LOC BC RWY 14

CHAMPAIGN-URBANA/UNIVERSITY OF ILLINOIS-WILLARD (CMI)
CHAMPAIGN-URBANA, ILLINOIS

CHAMPAIGN APP CON
121.35 291.0
CHAMPAIGN TOWER★
120.4 (CTAF) 229.4
GND CON 121.9
CLNC DEL
128.75
ASR
ATIS
124.85
UNICOM
122.95

2700 NoPT to
Boill Int/CMI 7 DME
RBS R-210 (3)
and LOC (6.7)

(IAF)
△ TARPE

ROBERTS
116.8 RBS
Chan 115

R-210

R-166

316°

091°
271°

R-325

136°

R-041

1703 ∆

(IAF)
BOILL INT
CMI 7 DME

R-231

2700
314° (7)

1146 ∆ ∆ 1048

CMI
3 DME

845±

∆ 845

R-062

-062°

⊙ 2424
OCTOE
CMI 12 DME

LOCALIZER 109.1
I-CMI

10 NM

CHAMPAIGN
110.0 CMI
Chan 37

ENROUTE FACILITIES

DECATUR
117.2 DEC
Chan 119

MSA CMI 25 NM

3000

BACK COURSE

Remain
within 10 NM

BOILL INT
CMI 7 DME

316°

2700 — 136° — 2700 ✕

*1300 when using Decatur
altimeter setting.

MISSED APPROACH
Climb to 2700, then left turn via
CMI R-062 to Octoe Int and hold.

CMI
3 DME
*1160

CMI
1.6 DME

Disregard glide
slope indications.

5.4 NM
0.7

CATEGORY	A	B	C	D
S-14	1160-1 406(500-1)		1160-1¼ 406 (500-1¼)	
CIRCLING	1160-1 406 (500-1)	1220-1 466 (500-1)	1220-1½ 466 (500-1½)	1320-2 566 (600-2)
DME MINIMUMS				
S-14	1100-1 346 (400-1)			1100-1¼ 346 (400-1¼)

When control tower closed, activate MALSR Rwy 32-120.4; and, except for
operators with approved weather reporting service, use Decatur altimeter
setting and increase all MDAs 140 feet.
⚠

ELEV 754

136° 6.1 NM from
Boill Int/CMI 7 DME

TDZE
754

TWR
828

4625 X 150

6100 X 100

5300 X 150

MIRL Rwy 4-22
LIRL Rwy 18-36
HIRL Rwy 14-32
REIL Rwys 4, 14 and 22

FAF to MAP 5.4 NM				
Knots	60	90	120	150	180
Min:Sec	5:24	3:36	2:42	2:10	1:48

LOC BC RWY 14

40°02'N – 88°17'W

CHAMPAIGN-URBANA, ILLINOIS
CHAMPAIGN-URBANA/UNIVERSITY OF ILLINOIS-WILLARD (CMI)

Not for use in Navigation

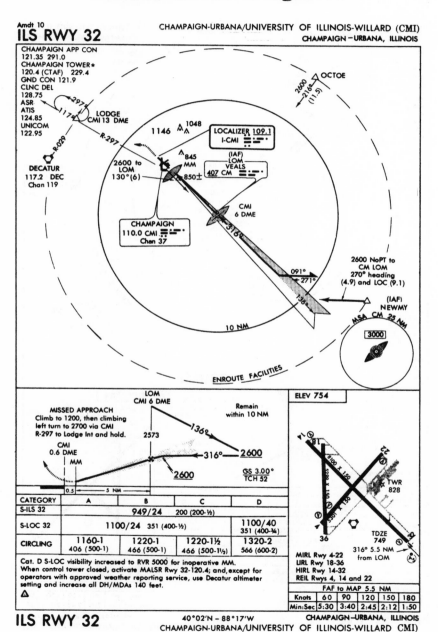

Not for use in Navigation

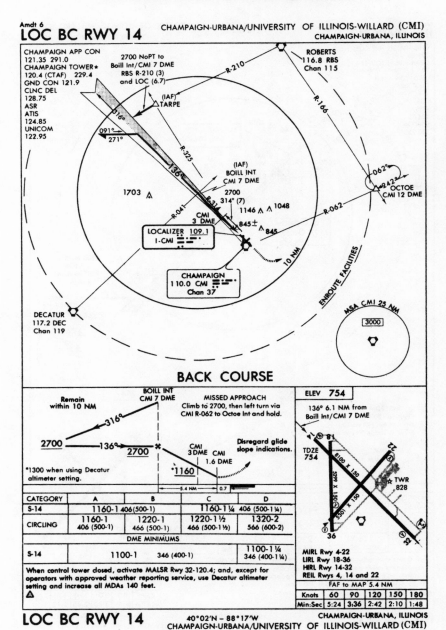

Amdt 6
LOC BC RWY 14

CHAMPAIGN-URBANA/UNIVERSITY OF ILLINOIS-WILLARD (CMI)
CHAMPAIGN-URBANA, ILLINOIS

CHAMPAIGN APP CON
121.35 291.0
CHAMPAIGN TOWER★
120.4 (CTAF) 229.4
GND CON 121.9
CLNC DEL
128.75
ASR
ATIS
124.85
UNICOM
122.95

2700 NoPT to
Boill Int/CMI 7 DME
RBS R-210 (3)
and LOC (6.7)

ROBERTS
116.8 RBS
Chan 115

(IAF)
△TARPE

(IAF)
BOILL INT
CMI 7 DME

OCTOE
CMI 12 DME

1703 △

2700
314° (7)

1146 △ △ 1048

CMI
3 DME

845± △ 845

LOCALIZER 109.1
I-CMI

CHAMPAIGN
110.0 CMI
Chan 37

DECATUR
117.2 DEC
Chan 119

MSA CMI 25 NM

3000

ENROUTE FACILITIES

10 NM

BACK COURSE

ELEV 754

Remain
within 10 NM

BOILL INT
CMI 7 DME

MISSED APPROACH
Climb to 2700, then left turn via
CMI R-062 to Octoe Int and hold.

136° 6.1 NM from
Boill Int/CMI 7 DME

2700 — 136°→ 2700 — ✕

CMI
3 DME   CMI
1.6 DME

Disregard glide
slope indications.

*1300 when using Decatur
altimeter setting.

*1160

5.4 NM   0.7

TDZE
754

TWR
828

CATEGORY	A	B	C	D
S-14	1160-1 406(500-1)		1160-1¼ 406 (500-1¼)	
CIRCLING	1160-1 406 (500-1)	1220-1 466 (500-1)	1220-1½ 466 (500-1½)	1320-2 566 (600-2)

DME MINIMUMS				
S-14	1100-1 346 (400-1)			1100-1¼ 346 (400-1¼)

When control tower closed, activate MALSR Rwy 32-120.4; and, except for
operators with approved weather reporting service, use Decatur altimeter
setting and increase all MDAs 140 feet.
⚠

MIRL Rwy 4-22
LIRL Rwy 18-36
HIRL Rwy 14-32
REIL Rwys 4, 14 and 22

FAF to MAP 5.4 NM

Knots	60	90	120	150	180
Min:Sec	5:24	3:36	2:42	2:10	1:48

LOC BC RWY 14

40°02'N – 88°17'W

CHAMPAIGN-URBANA, ILLINOIS
CHAMPAIGN-URBANA/UNIVERSITY OF ILLINOIS-WILLARD (CMI)

Not for use in Navigation

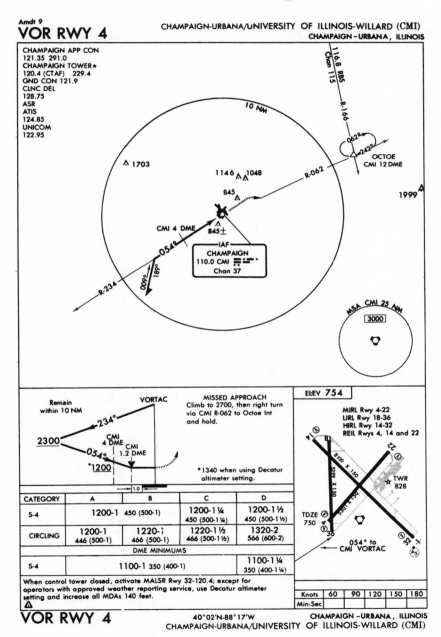

Amdt 9

VOR RWY 4

CHAMPAIGN-URBANA/UNIVERSITY OF ILLINOIS-WILLARD (CMI)
CHAMPAIGN – URBANA , ILLINOIS

CHAMPAIGN APP CON
121.35 291.0
CHAMPAIGN TOWER★
120.4 (CTAF)   229.4
GND CON ·121.9
CLNC DEL
128.75
ASR
ATIS
124.85
UNICOM
122.95

116.8 RBS
Chan 115
R-166
10 NM
062°
242°
OCTOE
CMI 12 DME
∧ 1703
1146 ∧∧1048
R-062
1999 ∧
845
∧
CMI 4 DME
845±
054°
IAF
CHAMPAIGN
110.0 CMI
Chan 37
009°
189°
R-234
MSA CMI 25 NM
3000

MISSED APPROACH
Climb to 2700, then right turn
via CMI R-062 to Octoe Int
and hold.

Remain
within 10 NM
234°
VORTAC
2300
CMI
4 DME
CMI
1.2 DME
054°
*1200
1.0

*1340 when using Decatur
altimeter setting.

ELEV 754

MIRL Rwy 4-22
LIRL Rwy 18-36
HIRL Rwy 14-32
REIL Rwys 4, 14 and 22

TWR
828
TDZE
750
054° to
CMI VORTAC

CATEGORY	A	B	C	D
S-4	1200-1 450 (500-1)		1200-1¼ 450 (500-1¼)	1200-1½ 450 (500-1½)
CIRCLING	1200-1 446 (500-1)	1220-1 466 (500-1)	1220-1½ 466 (500-1½)	1320-2 566 (600-2)
DME MINIMUMS				
S-4	1100-1 350 (400-1)			1100-1¼ 350 (400-1¼)

When control tower closed, activate MALSR Rwy 32-120.4; except for
operators with approved weather reporting service, use Decatur altimeter
setting and increase all MDAs 140 feet.

Knots	60	90	120	150	180
Min:Sec					

VOR RWY 4

40°02'N-88°17'W
CHAMPAIGN-URBANA/UNIVERSITY OF ILLINOIS-WILLARD (CMI)

CHAMPAIGN –URBANA , ILLINOIS

Not for use in Navigation

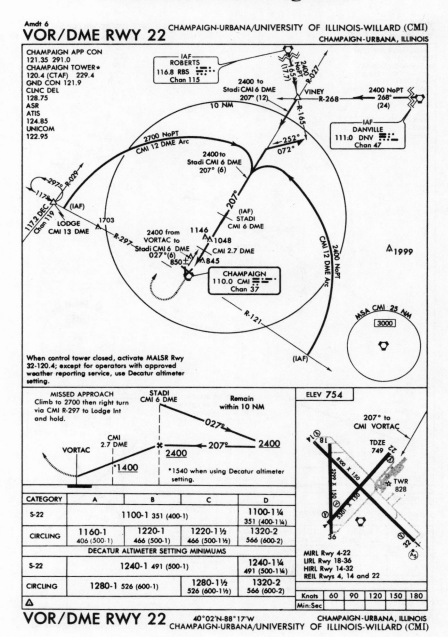

Amdt 6

VOR/DME RWY 22   CHAMPAIGN-URBANA/UNIVERSITY OF ILLINOIS-WILLARD (CMI)
CHAMPAIGN-URBANA, ILLINOIS

CHAMPAIGN APP CON
121.35 291.0
CHAMPAIGN TOWER*
120.4 (CTAF)   229.4
GND CON 121.9
CLNC DEL
128.75
ASR
ATIS
124.85
UNICOM
122.95

IAF
ROBERTS
116.8 RBS
Chan 115

2400 to
Stadi CMI 6 DME
207° (12)

VINEY
R-268

2400 NoPT
268°
(24)

10 NM

IAF
DANVILLE
111.0 DNV
Chan 47

2700 NoPT
CMI 12 DME Arc

2400 to
Stadi CMI 6 DME
207° (6)

252°
072°

207°

(IAF)
STADI
CMI 6 DME

117.2 DEC
Chan 119

(IAF)
LODGE
CMI 13 DME

1703
R-297

1146
1048
CMI 2.7 DME

2400 from
VORTAC to
Stadi CMI 6 DME
027° (6)
850±

845

CHAMPAIGN
110.0 CMI
Chan 37

CMI 12 DME Arc   2400 NoPT

1999

R-121

MSA CMI 25 NM
3000

When control tower closed, activate MALSR Rwy
32-120.4; except for operators with approved
weather reporting service, use Decatur altimeter
setting.

MISSED APPROACH		ELEV **754**

MISSED APPROACH
Climb to 2700 then right turn
via CMI R-297 to Lodge Int
and hold.

STADI
CMI 6 DME

Remain
within 10 NM

027°

CMI
2.7 DME

VORTAC

207°   2400

2400

*1400

*1540 when using Decatur altimeter
setting.

ELEV **754**

207° to
CMI VORTAC

TDZE
749

TWR
828

MIRL Rwy 4-22
LIRL Rwy 18-36
HIRL Rwy 14-32
REIL Rwys 4, 14 and 22

CATEGORY	A	B	C	D
S-22	1100-1 351 (400-1)			1100-1¼ 351 (400-1¼)
CIRCLING	1160-1 406 (500-1)	1220-1 466 (500-1)	1220-1½ 466 (500-1½)	1320-2 566 (600-2)
DECATUR ALTIMETER SETTING MINIMUMS				
S-22	1240-1 491 (500-1)			1240-1¼ 491 (500-1¼)
CIRCLING	1280-1 526 (600-1)		1280-1½ 526 (600-1½)	1320-2 566 (600-2)

Knots	60	90	120	150	180
Min:Sec					

VOR/DME RWY 22   40°02'N-88°17'W   CHAMPAIGN-URBANA, ILLINOIS
CHAMPAIGN-URBANA/UNIVERSITY OF ILLINOIS-WILLARD (CMI)

Not for use in Navigation

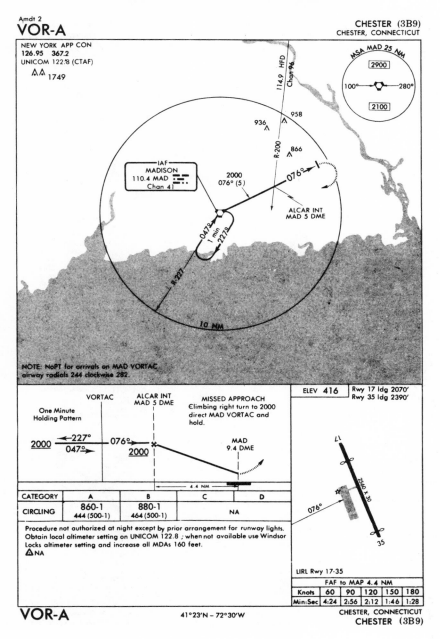

Not for use in Navigation

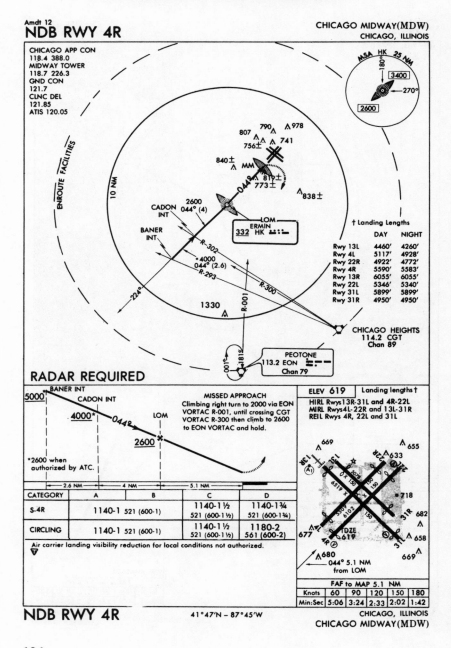

Amdt 12
NDB RWY 4R

CHICAGO MIDWAY(MDW)
CHICAGO, ILLINOIS

CHICAGO APP CON
118.4 388.0
MIDWAY TOWER
118.7 226.3
GND CON
121.7
CLNC DEL
121.85
ATIS 120.05

ENROUTE FACILITIES

10 NM

MSA HK 25 NM
180°
3400
270°
2600

790 △ △978
807 △ △741
756± △

840± △ MM

044°
819± △
773± △

△838±

CADON INT 2600 044° (4)

BANER INT

R-302
•4000
044° (2.6)
R-293

R-300

LOM
ERMIN
332 HK

-224°

R-001

1330 △

181°
001°

PEOTONE
113.2 EON
Chan 79

† Landing Lengths

	DAY	NIGHT
Rwy 13L	4460'	4260'
Rwy 4L	5117'	4928'
Rwy 22R	4922'	4772'
Rwy 4R	5590'	5583'
Rwy 13R	6055'	6055'
Rwy 22L	5346'	5340'
Rwy 31L	5899'	5899'
Rwy 31R	4950'	4950'

CHICAGO HEIGHTS
114.2 CGT
Chan 89

RADAR REQUIRED

BANER INT
5000
CADON INT
4000*
044°
LOM
2600
*2600 when authorized by ATC.

MISSED APPROACH
Climbing right turn to 2000 via EON VORTAC R-001, until crossing CGT VORTAC R-300 then climb to 2600 to EON VORTAC and hold.

ELEV 619 | Landing lengths †

HIRL Rwys13R-31L and 4R-22L
MIRL Rwys4L-22R and 13L-31R
REIL Rwys 4R, 22L and 31L

669 △ △ 655
△633
△718
TDZE 619
677 △619 △ 658
△680
669 △

044° 5.1 NM from LOM

	2.6 NM	4 NM	5.1 NM	
CATEGORY	A	B	C	D
S-4R	1140-1 521 (600-1)		1140-1½ 521 (600-1½)	1140-1¾ 521 (600-1¾)
CIRCLING	1140-1 521 (600-1)		1140-1½ 521 (600-1½)	1180-2 561 (600-2)

Air carrier landing visibility reduction for local conditions not authorized. ▽

FAF to MAP 5.1 NM					
Knots	60	90	120	150	180
Min:Sec	5:06	3:24	2:33	2:02	1:42

NDB RWY 4R

41°47'N – 87°45'W

CHICAGO, ILLINOIS
CHICAGO MIDWAY(MDW)

Not for use in Navigation

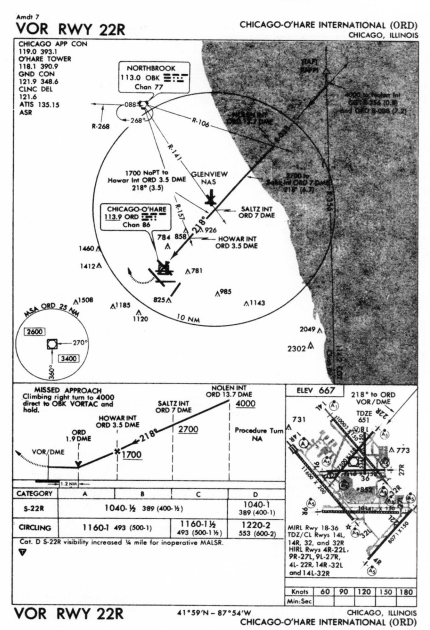

Amdt 7

VOR RWY 22R

CHICAGO-O'HARE INTERNATIONAL (ORD)
CHICAGO, ILLINOIS

CHICAGO APP CON
119.0 393.1
O'HARE TOWER
118.1 390.9
GND CON
121.9 348.6
CLNC DEL
121.6
ATIS 135.15
ASR

NORTHBROOK
113.0 OBK
Chan 77

CHICAGO-O'HARE
113.9 ORD
Chan 86

R-268

088°

268°

R-106

R-141

R-157

R-354

1700 NoPT to
Howar Int ORD 3.5 DME
218° (3.5)

GLENVIEW
NAS

218°

SALTZ INT
ORD 7 DME

784 858

926

HOWAR INT
ORD 3.5 DME

2700 to
Saltz Int ORD 7 DME
218° (4.7)

4000 to Nolen Int
Cont R-354 (0.9)
and ORD R-088 (7.2)

1460 ∆

∆781

1412 ∆

1508 ∆

∆1185

825 ∆

∆985

∆1143

1120 ∆

10 NM

2049 ∆

2302 ∆

MSA ORD 25 NM

2600

270°

3400

360°

MISSED APPROACH
Climbing right turn to 4000
direct to OBK VORTAC and
hold.

NOLEN INT
ORD 13.7 DME

4000

SALTZ INT
ORD 7 DME

HOWAR INT
ORD 3.5 DME

2700

Procedure Turn
NA

ORD
1.9 DME

218°

VOR/DME

1700

1.2 NM

CATEGORY	A	B	C	D
S-22R	1040- ½ 389 (400- ½)			1040-1 389 (400-1)
CIRCLING	1160-1 493 (500-1)		1160-1 ½ 493 (500-1 ½)	1220-2 553 (600-2)

Cat. D S-22R visibility increased ¼ mile for inoperative MALSR.

ELEV 667

218° to ORD
VOR/DME

731

TDZE
651

∆ 773

#852

27R

9R

32R

4R

MIRL Rwy 18-36
TDZ/CL Rwys 14L,
14R, 32, and 32R
HIRL Rwys 4R-22L,
9R-27L, 9L-27R,
4L-22R, 14R-32L
and 14L-32R

Knots	60	90	120	150	180
Min:Sec					

VOR RWY 22R

41°59'N – 87°54'W

CHICAGO, ILLINOIS
CHICAGO-O'HARE INTERNATIONAL (ORD)

Not for use in Navigation

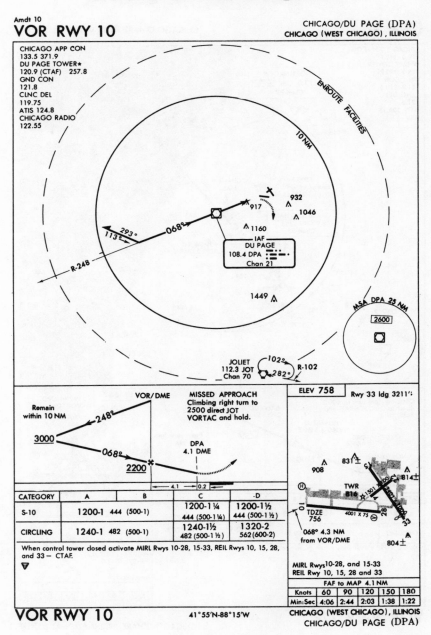

VOR RWY 10

CHICAGO/DU PAGE (DPA)
CHICAGO (WEST CHICAGO), ILLINOIS

CHICAGO APP CON
133.5 371.9
DU PAGE TOWER★
120.9 (CTAF)   257.8
GND CON
121.8
CLNC DEL
119.75
ATIS 124.8
CHICAGO RADIO
122.55

ENROUTE FACILITIES

10 NM

293°   068°
113±

R-248

IAF
DU PAGE
108.4 DPA
Chan 21

917   932
1046
1160

1449

MSA DPA 25 NM
2600

JOLIET
112.3 JOT
Chan 70
102°
282°   R-102

VOR/DME
Remain
within 10 NM
248°
3000
068°
2200

MISSED APPROACH
Climbing right turn to
2500 direct JOT
VORTAC and hold.

DPA
4.1 DME

4.1   0.2

ELEV 758   Rwy 33 ldg 3211'±

CATEGORY	A	B	C	-D
S-10	1200-1 444 (500-1)		1200-1¼ 444 (500-1¼)	1200-1½ 444 (500-1½)
CIRCLING	1240-1 482 (500-1)		1240-1½ 482 (500-1½)	1320-2 562 (600-2)

When control tower closed activate MIRL Rwys 10-28, 15-33, REIL Rwys 10, 15, 28, and 33 — CTAF.

831±   15
908   814±
TWR
816
TDZE
756
4001 X 75
28
068° 4.3 NM
from VOR/DME

804±

MIRL Rwys10-28, and 15-33
REIL Rwy 10, 15, 28 and 33

FAF to MAP 4.1 NM				
Knots	60	90	120	150	180
Min:Sec	4:06	2:44	2:03	1:38	1:22

VOR RWY 10

41°55'N-88°15'W

CHICAGO (WEST CHICAGO), ILLINOIS
CHICAGO/DU PAGE (DPA)

Not for use in Navigation

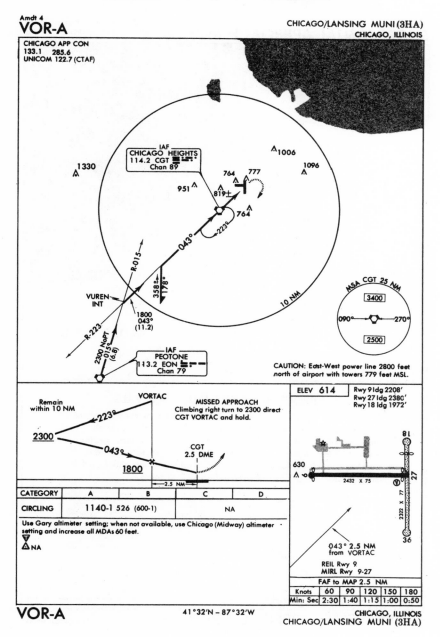

Amdt 4
VOR-A

CHICAGO/LANSING MUNI (3HA)
CHICAGO, ILLINOIS

CHICAGO APP CON
133.1   285.6
UNICOM 122.7 (CTAF)

IAF
CHICAGO HEIGHTS
114.2 CGT ⚋⚋ ⚌
Chan 89

∧1006

∧1330

764 ∧   777 ∧

951 ∧   819± ∧
764 ∧

043°
223°

R-015

VUREN
INT

358°
178°

1800
043°
(11.2)

R-223

2300 NoPT
015°
(6.8)

IAF
PEOTONE
113.2 EON ⚋⚋ ⚌
Chan 79

10 NM

MSA CGT 25 NM
3400
090° ◇ 270°
2500

CAUTION: East-West power line 2800 feet
north of airport with towers 779 feet MSL.

ELEV 614

Rwy 9 ldg 2208'
Rwy 27 ldg 2380'
Rwy 18 ldg 1972'

Remain
within 10 NM

VORTAC

MISSED APPROACH
Climbing right turn to 2300 direct
CGT VORTAC and hold.

223°

2300

043°

CGT
2.5 DME

1800

2.5 NM

630
∧

81

2432 X 75

27

2322 X 77

36

043° 2.5 NM
from VORTAC

REIL Rwy 9
MIRL Rwy 9-27

CATEGORY	A	B	C	D
CIRCLING	1140-1 526 (600-1)		NA	

Use Gary altimeter setting; when not available, use Chicago (Midway) altimeter
setting and increase all MDAs 60 feet.
▽
∧ NA

FAF to MAP 2.5 NM

Knots	60	90	120	150	180
Min: Sec	2:30	1:40	1:15	1:00	0:50

VOR-A

41°32'N – 87°32'W

CHICAGO, ILLINOIS
CHICAGO/LANSING MUNI (3HA)

Not for use in Navigation

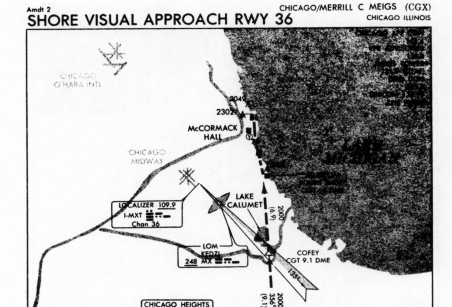

CHICAGO/MERRILL C MEIGS (CGX)
CHICAGO ILLINOIS

SHORE VISUAL APPROACH RWY 36

CHART NOT TO SCALE

RADAR REQUIRED

PROCEDURES FOR MEIGS ARRIVALS

ATC will not assign vectors to the traffic pattern or conduct Shore visual approaches, whenever Meigs is below visual approach minimums of ceiling 1900 feet, visibility 6 miles. If Meigs weather is below these minimums, pilots will be provided vectors to Midway's final approach for landing. If IFR is cancelled - Pilots should advise ATC - "Cancelling IFR and proceeding VFR to Meigs".

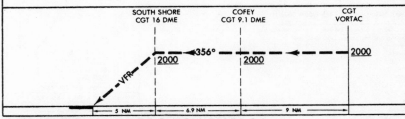

SHORE VISUAL APPROACH RWY 36

CHICAGO, ILLINOIS

41°52'N – 87°36'W

CHICAGO/MERRILL C MEIGS (CGX)

Not for use in Navigation

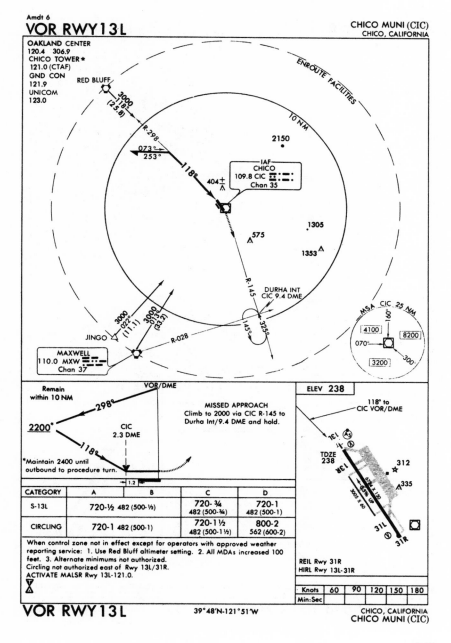

Amdt 6

VOR RWY13L

CHICO MUNI (CIC)
CHICO, CALIFORNIA

OAKLAND CENTER
120.4 306.9
CHICO TOWER *
121.0 (CTAF)
GND CON
121.9
UNICOM
123.0

RED BLUFF

ENROUTE FACILITIES

10 NM

3000
116°
(25.8)

2150

R-298

073°
253°

118°

IAF
CHICO
109.8 CIC
Chan 35

404 ±

.1305

575

1353

R-145

DURHA INT
CIC 9.4 DME

325°

145°

MSA CIC 25 NM

4100

8200

070°

3000
022°
(11.1)

3000
015°
(53.2)

JINGO

R-028

3200

300°

MAXWELL
110.0 MXW
Chan 37

Approach profile

Remain
within 10 NM

VOR/DME

298°

2200*

CIC
2.3 DME

118°

*Maintain 2400 until
outbound to procedure turn.

1.2

MISSED APPROACH
Climb to 2000 via CIC R-145 to
Durha Int/9.4 DME and hold.

ELEV 238

118° to
CIC VOR/DME

13L

TDZE
238

.312

335

31L

31R

REIL Rwy 31R
HIRL Rwy 13L-31R

CATEGORY	A	B	C	D
S-13L	720-½ 482 (500-½)		720-¾ 482 (500-¾)	720-1 482 (500-1)
CIRCLING	720-1 482 (500-1)		720-1½ 482 (500-1½)	800-2 562 (600-2)

When control zone not in effect except for operators with approved weather
reporting service: 1. Use Red Bluff altimeter setting. 2. All MDAs increased 100
feet. 3. Alternate minimums not authorized.
Circling not authorized east of Rwy 13L/31R.
ACTIVATE MALSR Rwy 13L-121.0.

Knots	60	90	120	150	180
Min:Sec					

VOR RWY13L

39°48'N-121°51'W

CHICO, CALIFORNIA
CHICO MUNI (CIC)

Not for use in Navigation

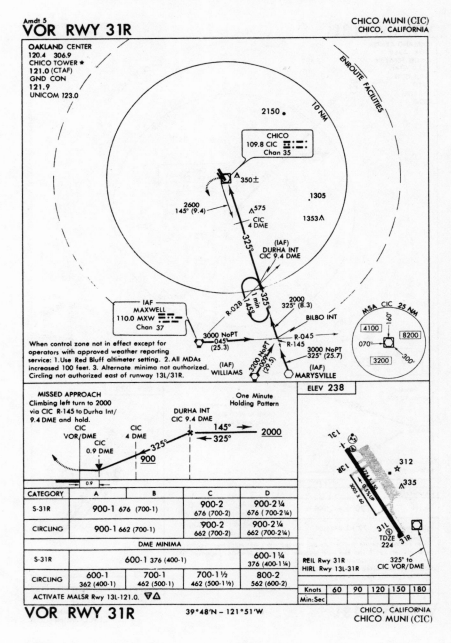

Not for use in Navigation

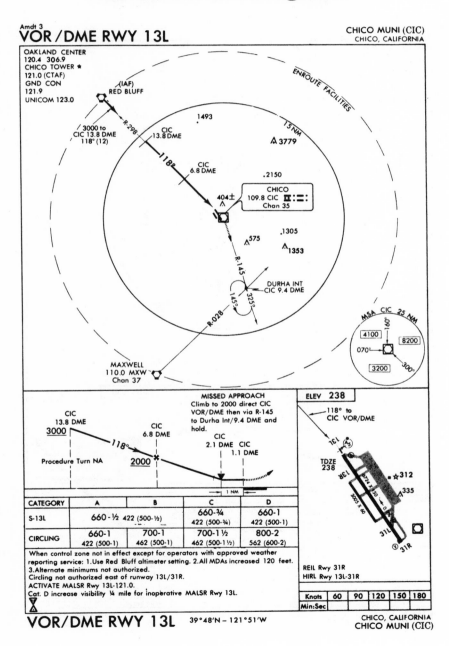

Not for use in Navigation

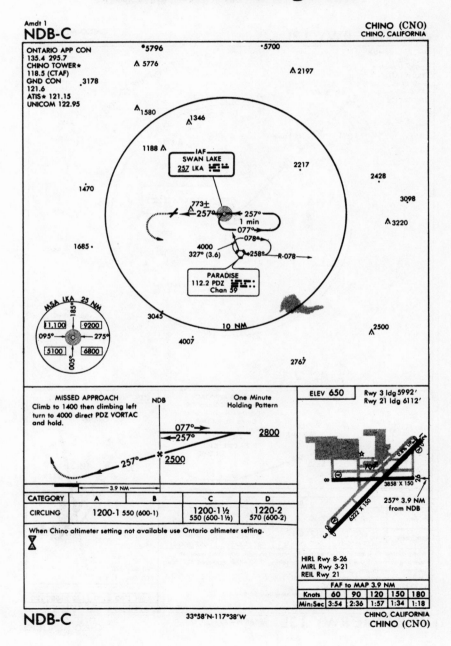

Amdt 1
NDB-C

CHINO (CNO)
CHINO, CALIFORNIA

ONTARIO APP CON
135.4 295.7
CHINO TOWER★
118.5 (CTAF)
GND CON
121.6
ATIS★ 121.15
UNICOM 122.95

•5796   •5700
Λ 5776   Λ 2197
.3178

Λ1580
Λ1346

1188 Λ   IAF
SWAN LAKE
257 LKA   2217

2428
1470   3098
773±
257°   257°   Λ 3220
1 min
077°
1685 •   078°
4000   077°
327° (3.6)   258°   R-078
PARADISE
112.2 PDZ
Chan 59

MSA LKA 25 NM

185°
11,100   9200
095°   275°
5100   6800
005°

3045
10 NM
4007   Λ2500

2767

MISSED APPROACH   NDB   One Minute
Climb to 1400 then climbing left   Holding Pattern
turn to 4000 direct PDZ VORTAC
and hold.
077°
257°   2800

257°   * 2500

3.9 NM

CATEGORY	A	B	C	D
CIRCLING	1200-1 550 (600-1)		1200-1½ 550 (600-1½)	1220-2 570 (600-2)

When Chino altimeter setting not available use Ontario altimeter setting.

ELEV 650   Rwy 3 ldg 5992'
Rwy 21 ldg 6112'

257° 3.9 NM
from NDB

3858' X 150

HIRL Rwy 8-26
MIRL Rwy 3-21
REIL Rwy 21

FAF to MAP 3.9 NM				
Knots	60	90	120	150	180
Min:Sec	3:54	2:36	1:57	1:34	1:18

NDB-C   33°58'N-117°38'W   CHINO, CALIFORNIA
CHINO (CNO)

Not for use in Navigation

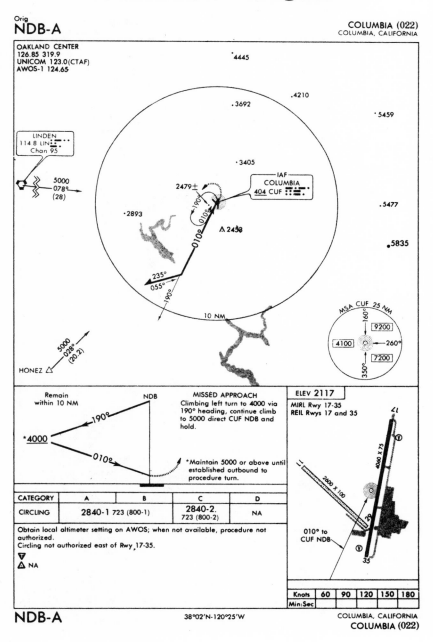

OAKLAND CENTER
126.85 319.9
UNICOM 123.0(CTAF)
AWOS-1 124.65

·4445

.4210

.3692

·5459

LINDEN
114.8 LIN
Chan 95

5000
078°
(28)

·3405

2479±

IAF
COLUMBIA
404 CUF

.5477

·2893

010°

Δ 2458

.5835

235°
055°

190°

MSA CUF 25 NM

10 NM

160°
9200
4100
260°
350°
7200

5000
028°
(20.2)

HONEZ Δ

Remain
within 10 NM

NDB

190°

*4000

010°

MISSED APPROACH
Climbing left turn to 4000 via
190° heading, continue climb
to 5000 direct CUF NDB and
hold.

*Maintain 5000 or above until
established outbound to
procedure turn.

ELEV 2117

MIRL Rwy 17-35
REIL Rwys 17 and 35

4000 X 75

2600 X 100

CATEGORY	A	B	C	D
CIRCLING	2840-1 723 (800-1)		2840-2 723 (800-2)	NA

Obtain local altimeter setting on AWOS; when not available, procedure not
authorized.
Circling not authorized east of Rwy 17-35.

▽
Δ NA

010° to
CUF NDB

Knots	60	90	120	150	180
Min:Sec					

NDB-A

38°02'N-120°25'W

Not for use in Navigation

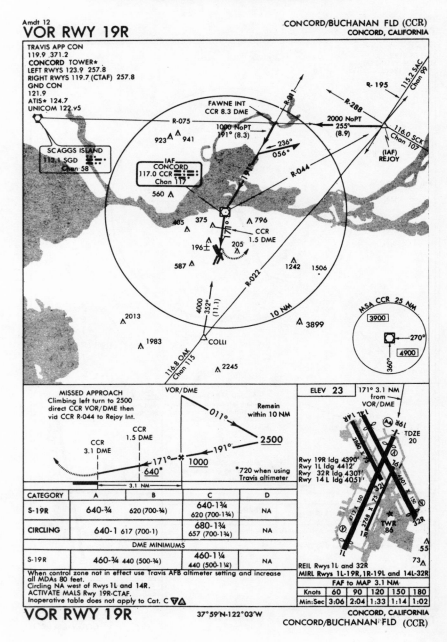

Not for use in Navigation

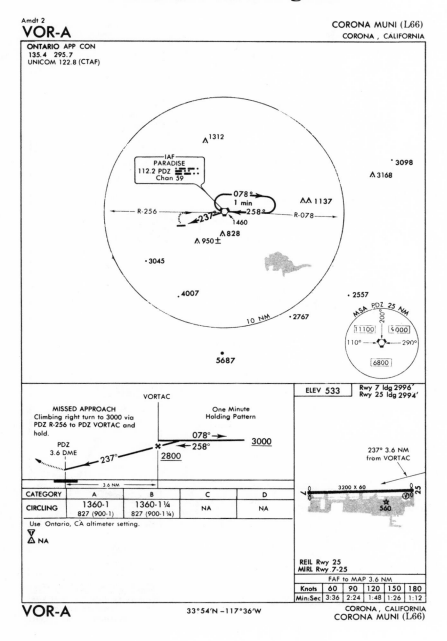

ONTARIO APP CON
135.4   295.7
UNICOM 122.8 (CTAF)

∧1312

IAF
PARADISE
112.2 PDZ
Chan 59

∧ 3098
∧ 3168

078°
1 min

R-256

237°   258°

∧∧ 1137

R-078

1460

∧828

∧ 950 ±

· 3045

· 2557

· 4007

10 NM   · 2767

MSA PDZ 25 NM
200°
11100   5000
110°   290°
6800

· 5687

VORTAC

ELEV 533

Rwy 7 ldg 2996'
Rwy 25 ldg 2994'

MISSED APPROACH
Climbing right turn to 3000 via
PDZ R-256 to PDZ VORTAC and
hold.

One Minute
Holding Pattern

078° →
← 258°   3000

PDZ
3.6 DME   237°
2800

237° 3.6 NM
from VORTAC

3.6 NM

3200 X 60

25

560

CATEGORY	A	B	C	D
CIRCLING	1360-1 827 (900-1)	1360-1¼ 827 (900-1¼)	NA	NA

Use Ontario, CA altimeter setting.

⊠ NA

REIL Rwy 25
MIRL Rwy 7-25

FAF to MAP 3.6 NM					
Knots	60	90	120	150	180
Min:Sec	3:36	2:24	1:48	1:26	1:12

Not for use in Navigation

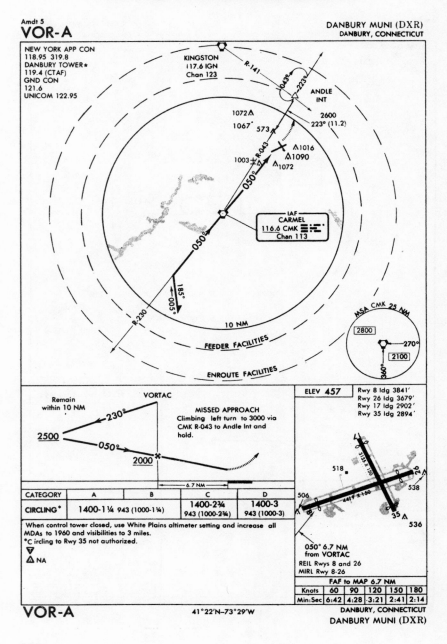

Not for use in Navigation

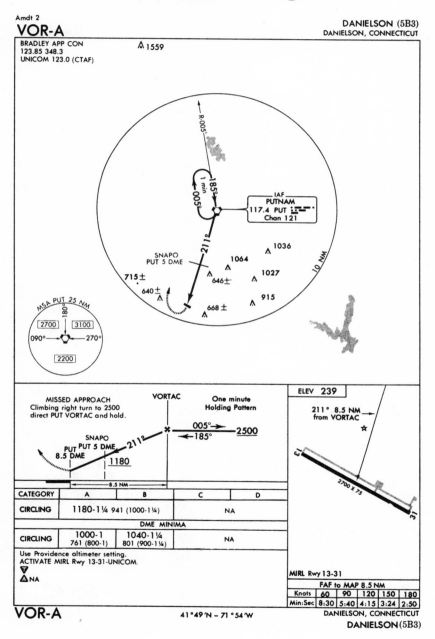

Amdt 2
VOR-A

DANIELSON (5B3)
DANIELSON, CONNECTICUT

BRADLEY APP CON
123.85 348.3
UNICOM 123.0 (CTAF)

△ 1559

R-005°

185°
1 min
005°

IAF
PUTNAM
117.4 PUT
Chan 121

211°

SNAPO
PUT 5 DME

△ 1036

1064
△

△ 1027

715±
.

646±
△

10 NM

640±
△

668 ±
△

△ 915

MSA PUT 25 NM

2700   3100

090°—   —270°

2200

MISSED APPROACH
Climbing right turn to 2500
direct PUT VORTAC and hold.

VORTAC

One minute
Holding Pattern

ELEV 239

211° 8.5 NM
from VORTAC

☆

SNAPO
PUT PUT 5 DME
8.5 DME

211°

005°
←185°

2500

1180

8.5 NM

2700 X 75

CATEGORY	A	B	C	D
CIRCLING	1180-1¼ 941 (1000-1¼)		NA	
	DME MINIMA			
CIRCLING	1000-1 761 (800-1)	1040-1¼ 801 (900-1¼)	NA	

Use Providence altimeter setting.
ACTIVATE MIRL Rwy 13-31-UNICOM.
▽
△NA

MIRL Rwy 13-31

FAF to MAP 8.5 NM					
Knots	60	90	120	150	180
Min:Sec	8:30	5:40	4:15	3:24	2:50

VOR-A

41°49'N – 71°54'W

DANIELSON, CONNECTICUT
DANIELSON(5B3)

Not for use in Navigation

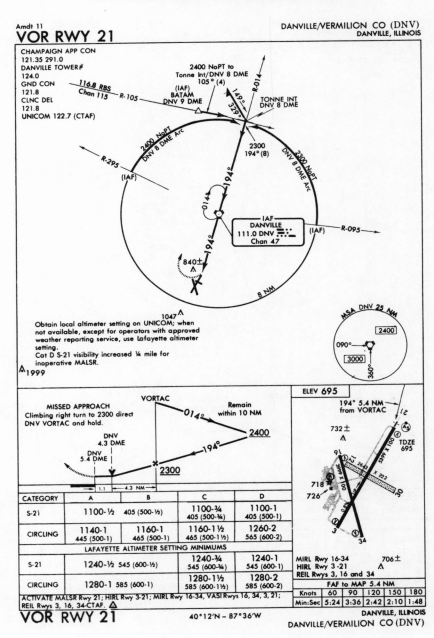

Not for use in Navigation

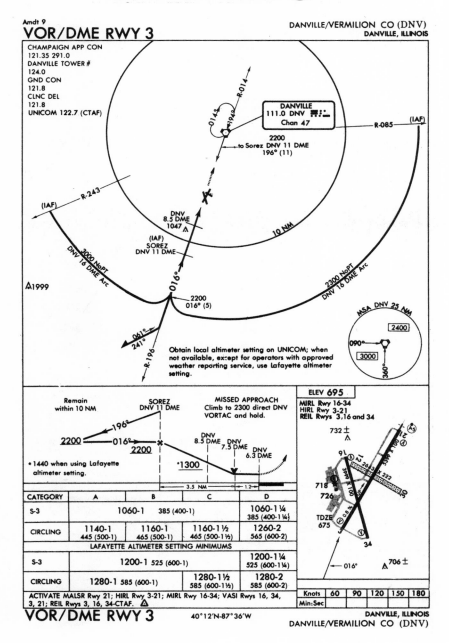

Amdt 9

VOR/DME RWY 3

DANVILLE/VERMILION CO (DNV)
DANVILLE, ILLINOIS

CHAMPAIGN APP CON
121.35 291.0
DANVILLE TOWER #
124.0
GND CON
121.8
CLNC DEL
121.8
UNICOM 122.7 (CTAF)

DANVILLE
111.0 DNV
Chan 47

R-085   (IAF)

2200
to Sorez DNV 11 DME
196° (11)

DNV
8.5 DME
1047

(IAF)
SOREZ
DNV 11 DME

016°

2200
016° (5)

Obtain local altimeter setting on UNICOM; when not available, except for operators with approved weather reporting service, use Lafayette altimeter setting.

MSA DNV 25 NM

2400

090°

3000

360°

ELEV 695

MIRL Rwy 16-34
HIRL Rwy 3-21
REIL Rwys 3,16 and 34

Remain
within 10 NM

SOREZ
DNV 11 DME

MISSED APPROACH
Climb to 2300 direct DNV
VORTAC and hold.

196°

2200   016°
2200

*1440 when using Lafayette altimeter setting.

DNV
8.5 DME DNV
7.5 DME DNV
6.3 DME

*1300

732

718
726

TDZE
675

3.5 NM   1.2

34

CATEGORY	A	B	C	D
S-3	1060-1 385 (400-1)			1060-1¼ 385 (400-1¼)
CIRCLING	1140-1 445 (500-1)	1160-1 465 (500-1)	1160-1½ 465 (500-1½)	1260-2 565 (600-2)
LAFAYETTE ALTIMETER SETTING MINIMUMS				
S-3	1200-1 525 (600-1)			1200-1¼ 525 (600-1¼)
CIRCLING	1280-1 585 (600-1)		1280-1½ 585 (600-1½)	1280-2 585 (600-2)

016°   706

ACTIVATE MALSR Rwy 21; HIRL Rwy 3-21; MIRL Rwy 16-34; VASI Rwys 16, 34, 3, 21; REIL Rwys 3, 16, 34-CTAF.

Knots	60	90	120	150	180
Min:Sec					

VOR/DME RWY 3

40°12'N-87°36'W

DANVILLE, ILLINOIS
DANVILLE/VERMILION CO (DNV)

Not for use in Navigation

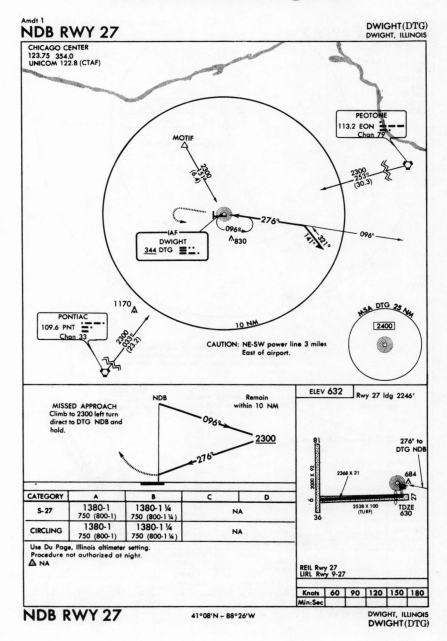

Amdt 1
NDB RWY 27

CHICAGO CENTER
123.75 354.0
UNICOM 122.8 (CTAF)

DWIGHT(DTG)
DWIGHT, ILLINOIS

MOTIF

PEOTONE
113.2 EON
Chan 79

2300
253°
(6.4)

2300
253°
(30.3)

IAF
DWIGHT
344 DTG

096°
276°
141°
321°
096°
830

1170

PONTIAC
109.6 PNT
Chan 33

2300
033°
(23.2)

10 NM

CAUTION: NE-SW power line 3 miles
East of airport.

MSA DTG 25 NM

2400

MISSED APPROACH
Climb to 2300 left turn
direct to DTG NDB and
hold.

NDB

Remain
within 10 NM

096°

2300

276°

ELEV 632   Rwy 27 ldg 2246'

276° to
DTG NDB

2368 X 21

684

2000 X 93

2538 X 100
(TURF)

TDZE
630

CATEGORY	A	B	C	D
S-27	1380-1 750 (800-1)	1380-1 ¼ 750 (800-1¼)	NA	
CIRCLING	1380-1 750 (800-1)	1380-1 ¼ 750 (800-1¼)	NA	

Use Du Page, Illinois altimeter setting.
Procedure not authorized at night.
⚠ NA

REIL Rwy 27
LIRL Rwy 9-27

Knots	60	90	120	150	180
Min:Sec					

NDB RWY 27

41°08'N – 88°26'W

DWIGHT, ILLINOIS
DWIGHT(DTG)

Not for use in Navigation

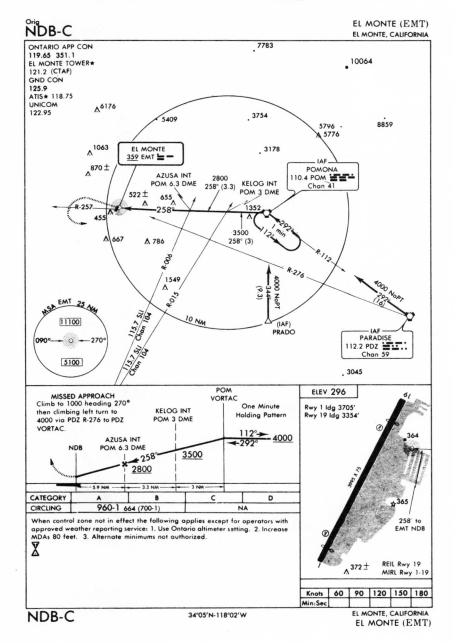

Not for use in Navigation

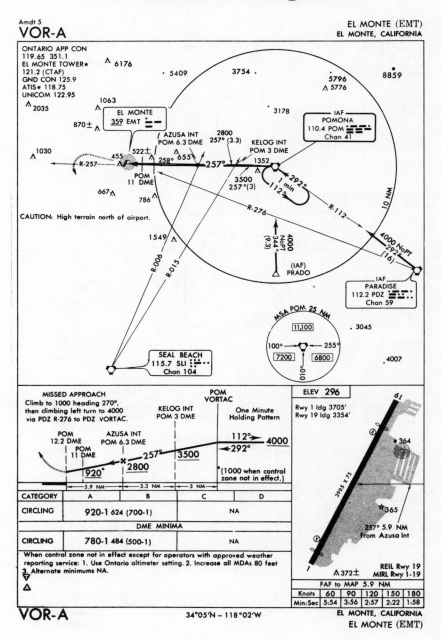

Not for use in Navigation

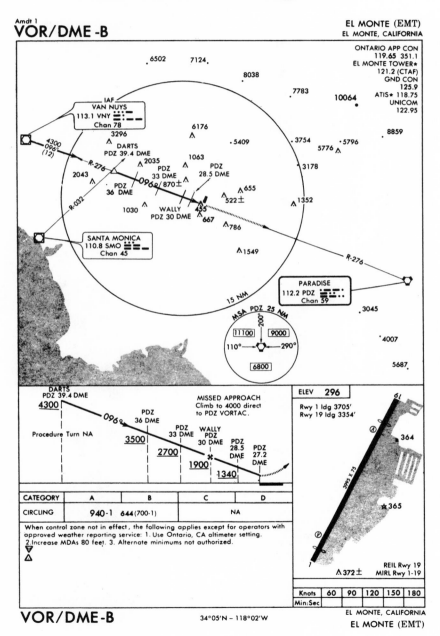

Amdt 1
VOR/DME -B

EL MONTE (EMT)
EL MONTE, CALIFORNIA

ONTARIO APP CON
119.65 351.1
EL MONTE TOWER*
121.2 (CTAF)
GND CON
125.9
ATIS* 118.75
UNICOM
122.95

.6502   7124.

8038

7783

10064

IAF
VAN NUYS
113.1 VNY
Chan 78

3296
∧
DARTS
PDZ 39.4 DME

6176
∧

.5409

.3754

5776 ∧ .5796

8859

4300
096°
(12)

R-276

∧2035
PDZ
33 DME

1063
∧

PDZ
28.5 DME

3178

2043
∧

PDZ
36 DME

096°/870±

∧

∧655
522±

∧1352

R-032

1030

WALLY
PDZ 30 DME

455
667 ∧

∧786

SANTA MONICA
110.8 SMO
Chan 45

∧1549

R-276

PARADISE
112.2 PDZ
Chan 59

15 NM

.3045

.4007

MSA PDZ 25 NM

5687.

200°
11100   9000
110° ◇ 290°
6800

DARTS PDZ 39.4 DME		MISSED APPROACH	ELEV	296	

4300

096°

PDZ
36 DME

PDZ
33 DME

WALLY
PDZ
30 DME

MISSED APPROACH
Climb to 4000 direct
to PDZ VORTAC.

ELEV   **296**

Rwy 1 ldg 3705'
Rwy 19 ldg 3354'

Procedure Turn NA

3500

2700

1900

PDZ
28.5
DME

PDZ
27.2
DME

1340

364

3925 X 75

★365

CATEGORY	A	B	C	D
CIRCLING	940-1	644(700-1)		NA

When control zone not in effect, the following applies except for operators with
approved weather reporting service: 1. Use Ontario, CA altimeter setting.
2.Increase MDAs 80 feet. 3. Alternate minimums not authorized.
▽
△

∧372±

REIL Rwy 19
MIRL Rwy 1-19

Knots	60	90	120	150	180
Min:Sec					

VOR/DME-B

34°05'N – 118°02'W

EL MONTE, CALIFORNIA
EL MONTE (EMT)

Not for use in Navigation

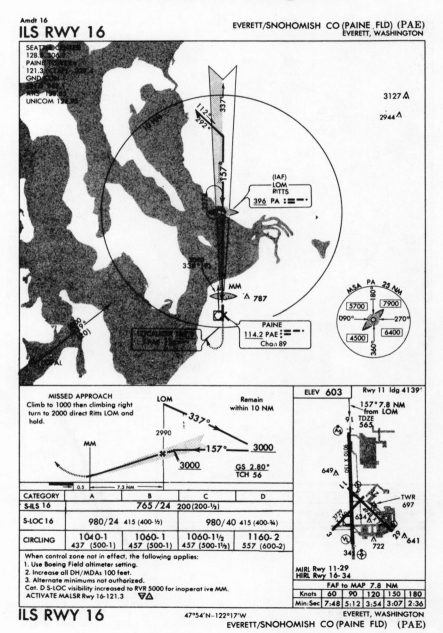

Amdt 16

ILS RWY 16

EVERETT/SNOHOMISH CO (PAINE FLD) (PAE)
EVERETT, WASHINGTON

SEATTLE CENTER
128.5 306
PAINE TOWER
121.3 (CTAF) 257.8
GND CON
AWRS 128.65
UNICOM 123.95

3127 ▲

2944 ▲

(IAF)
LOM
RITTS
396 PA ·=——·

337°
112°
292°
157°

335°

MM ▲ 787

PAINE
114.2 PAE ·=——·
Chan 89

MSA PA 25 NM
5700 | 7900
090° — 270°
4500 | 6400
360°

MISSED APPROACH
Climb to 1000 then climbing right turn to 2000 direct Ritts LOM and hold.

LOM

Remain within 10 NM

337°

2990

MM

157° ___3000

___3000

GS 2.80°
TCH 56

0.5 — 7.3 NM

ELEV 603 | Rwy 11 ldg 4139'

157° 7.8 NM from LOM
TDZE 565

TWR 697

722 ▲ 641

34

CATEGORY	A	B	C	D
S-ILS 16		765/24 200(200-½)		
S-LOC 16	980/24 415 (400-½)		980/40 415 (400-¾)	
CIRCLING	1040-1 437 (500-1)	1060-1 457 (500-1)	1060-1½ 457 (500-1½)	1160-2 557 (600-2)

When control zone not in effect, the following applies:
1. Use Boeing Field altimeter setting.
2. Increase all DH/MDAs 100 feet.
3. Alternate minimums not authorized.
Cat. D S-LOC visibility increased to RVR 5000 for inoperative MM.
ACTIVATE MALSR Rwy 16-121.3 ▼▲

MIRL Rwy 11-29
HIRL Rwy 16-34

FAF to MAP 7.8 NM				
Knots	60	90	120	150	180
Min:Sec	7:48	5:12	3:54	3:07	2:36

ILS RWY 16

47°54'N–122°17'W

EVERETT, WASHINGTON
EVERETT/SNOHOMISH CO (PAINE FLD) (PAE)

Not for use in Navigation

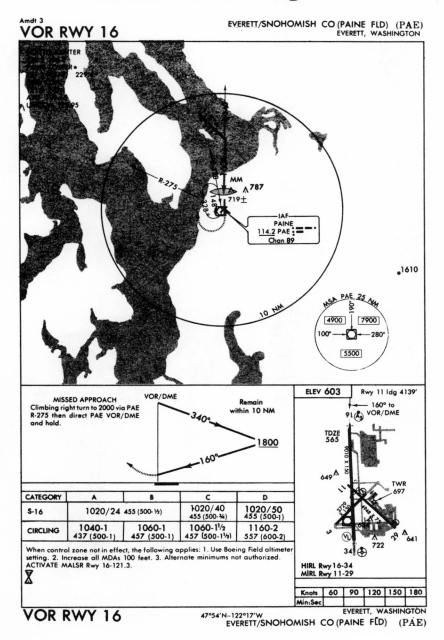

Amdt 3

VOR RWY 16

EVERETT/SNOHOMISH CO (PAINE FLD) (PAE)
EVERETT, WASHINGTON

R-275

MM ∧ 787
719±

148°
228°

IAF
PAINE
114.2 PAE
Chan 89

•1610

MSA PAE 25 NM

	190°	
4900		7900
100°		280°
	5500	

10 NM

MISSED APPROACH
Climbing right turn to 2000 via PAE
R-275 then direct PAE VOR/DME
and hold.

VOR/DME

Remain
within 10 NM

340°

1800

160°

ELEV 603   Rwy 11 ldg 4139'

160° to
VOR/DME

91

TDZE
565

649 ∧

TWR
697

37°

VL

34

722

∧
641

29 ∧

HIRL Rwy 16-34
MIRL Rwy 11-29

CATEGORY	A	B	C	D
S-16	1020/24 455 (500-½)		1020/40 455 (500-¾)	1020/50 455 (500-1)
CIRCLING	1040-1 437 (500-1)	1060-1 457 (500-1)	1060-1½ 457 (500-1½)	1160-2 557 (600-2)

When control zone not in effect, the following applies: 1. Use Boeing Field altimeter
setting. 2. Increase all MDAs 100 feet. 3. Alternate minimums not authorized.
ACTIVATE MALSR Rwy 16-121.3.

Knots	60	90	120	150	180
Min:Sec					

VOR RWY 16

47°54'N–122°17'W

EVERETT, WASHINGTON
EVERETT/SNOHOMISH CO (PAINE FLD)   (PAE)

157

Not for use in Navigation

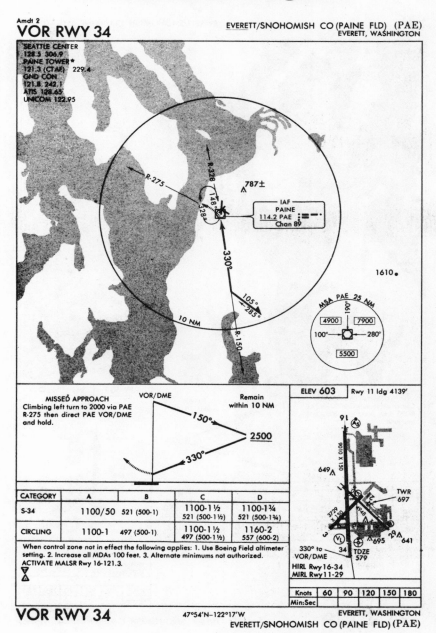

Amdt 2

VOR RWY 34

EVERETT/SNOHOMISH CO (PAINE FLD) (PAE)
EVERETT, WASHINGTON

SEATTLE CENTER
128.5 306.9
PAINE TOWER *
121.3 (CTAF) 229.4
GND CON
121.8 242.1
ATIS 128.65
UNICOM 122.95

787±

IAF
PAINE
114.2 PAE
Chan 89

R-328

R-275

148°
328°

330°

105°
285°

10 NM

R-150

1610.

MSA PAE 25 NM

4900	7900
100° ← □ → 280°	
5500	

190°
100°

MISSED APPROACH
Climbing left turn to 2000 via PAE
R-275 then direct PAE VOR/DME
and hold.

VOR/DME

Remain
within 10 NM

150°

2500

330°

ELEV 603   Rwy 11 ldg 4139'

91
A9

9010 X 150

649
A

3779
X 150

A948

TWR
697

3

A695
29
A641

VI

330° to
VOR/DME

34
TDZE
579

HIRL Rwy 16-34
MIRL Rwy 11-29

CATEGORY	A	B	C	D
S-34	1100/50	521 (500-1)	1100-1½ 521 (500-1½)	1100-1¾ 521 (500-1¾)
CIRCLING	1100-1	497 (500-1)	1100-1½ 497 (500-1½)	1160-2 557 (600-2)

When control zone not in effect the following applies: 1. Use Boeing Field altimeter
setting. 2. Increase all MDAs 100 feet. 3. Alternate minimums not authorized.
ACTIVATE MALSR Rwy 16-121.3.

Knots	60	90	120	150	180
Min:Sec					

VOR RWY 34

47°54'N-122°17'W

EVERETT, WASHINGTON
EVERETT/SNOHOMISH CO (PAINE FLD) (PAE)

Not for use in Navigation

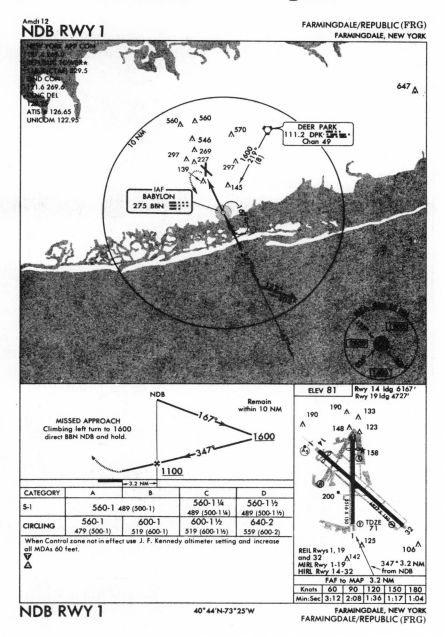

NDB RWY 1

FARMINGDALE/REPUBLIC (FRG)
FARMINGDALE, NEW YORK

NEW YORK APP CON
118.8 344.0
REPUBLIC TOWER★
118.8 (CTAF) 229.5
GND CON
121.6 269.6
CLNC DEL
121.
ATIS 126.65
UNICOM 122.95

DEER PARK
111.2 DPK
Chan 49

IAF
BABYLON
275 BBN

647

560   560
546
269
297   227
139
297
145
570
1600
219°
(8)

10 NM

NDB

MISSED APPROACH
Climbing left turn to 1600
direct BBN NDB and hold.

Remain
within 10 NM

167°
347°
1600
1100

3.2 NM

CATEGORY	A	B	C	D
S-1	560-1 489 (500-1)		560-1¼ 489 (500-1¼)	560-1½ 489 (500-1½)
CIRCLING	560-1 479 (500-1)	600-1 519 (600-1)	600-1½ 519 (600-1½)	640-2 559 (600-2)

When Control zone not in effect use J. F. Kennedy altimeter setting and increase
all MDAs 60 feet.

ELEV 81   Rwy 14 ldg 6167'
            Rwy 19 ldg 4727'

190   190   133
190   148   123
200   158
TDZE 71
125
142
106
516 X 150
4823 X 160

REIL Rwys 1, 19
and 32
MIRL Rwy 1-19
HIRL Rwy 14-32

347° 3.2 NM
from NDB

FAF to MAP 3.2 NM					
Knots	60	90	120	150	180
Min:Sec	3:12	2:08	1:36	1:17	1:04

NDB RWY 1

40°44'N-73°25'W

FARMINGDALE, NEW YORK
FARMINGDALE/REPUBLIC (FRG)

Not for use in Navigation

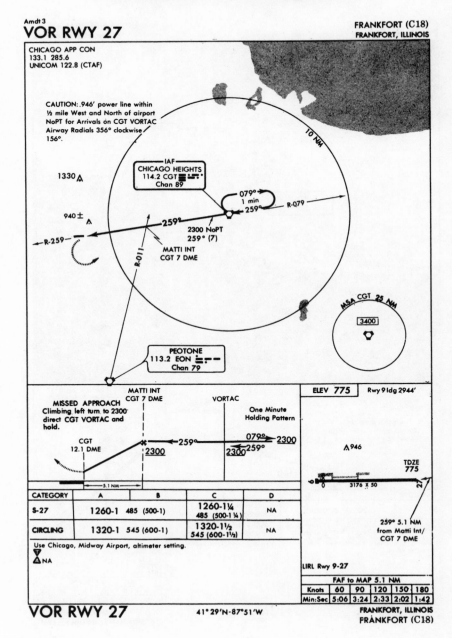

Amdt 3

VOR RWY 27

FRANKFORT (C18)
FRANKFORT, ILLINOIS

CHICAGO APP CON
133.1 285.6
UNICOM 122.8 (CTAF)

CAUTION: .946' power line within
½ mile West and North of airport
NoPT for Arrivals on CGT VORTAC
Airway Radials 356° clockwise
156°.

IAF
CHICAGO HEIGHTS
114.2 CGT
Chan 89

079°
1 min
259°   R-079

1330

940±

259°   R-079

R-259

259°
2300 NoPT
259° (7)
MATTI INT
CGT 7 DME

R-011

MSA CGT 25 NM
3400

PEOTONE
113.2 EON
Chan 79

MATTI INT
CGT 7 DME

VORTAC

ELEV 775   Rwy 9 ldg 2944'

MISSED APPROACH
Climbing left turn to 2300
direct CGT VORTAC and
hold.

One Minute
Holding Pattern

079°   2300
259°
2300 259°

946

CGT
12.1 DME

259°
2300

TDZE
775

5.1 NM

0   3176 X 50   27

CATEGORY	A	B	C	D
S-27	1260-1	485 (500-1)	1260-1¼ 485 (500-1¼)	NA
CIRCLING	1320-1	545 (600-1)	1320-1½ 545 (600-1½)	NA

Use Chicago, Midway Airport, altimeter setting.

NA

259° 5.1 NM
from Matti Int/
CGT 7 DME

LIRL Rwy 9-27

FAF to MAP 5.1 NM					
Knots	60	90	120	150	180
Min:Sec	5:06	3:24	2:33	2:02	1:42

VOR RWY 27

41°29'N-87°51'W

FRANKFORT, ILLINOIS
FRANKFORT (C18)

Not for use in Navigation

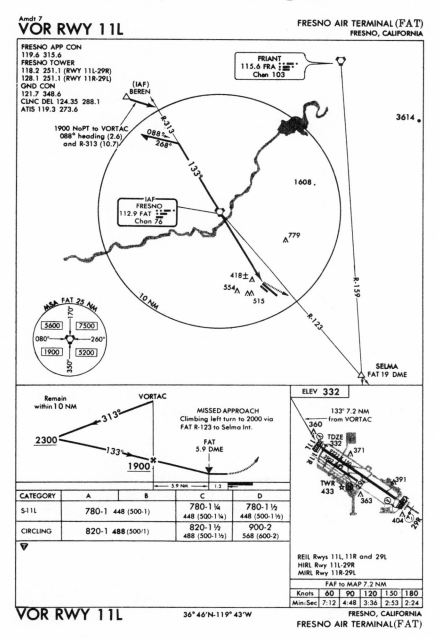

Not for use in Navigation

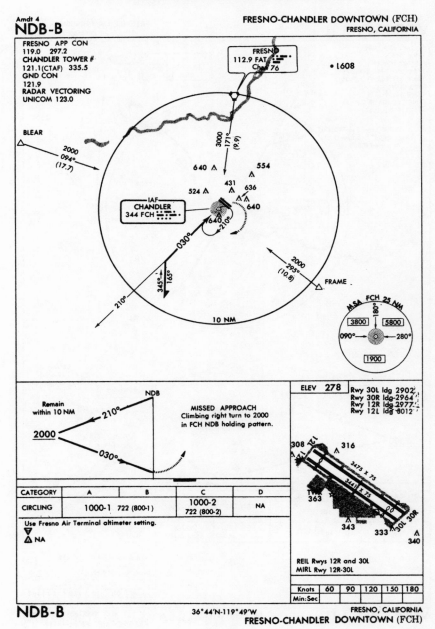

Amdt 4
NDB-B

FRESNO-CHANDLER DOWNTOWN (FCH)
FRESNO, CALIFORNIA

FRESNO APP CON
119.0 297.2
CHANDLER TOWER #
121.1(CTAF) 335.5
GND CON
121.9
RADAR VECTORING
UNICOM 123.0

FRESNO
112.9 FAT
Chan 76

• L608

BLEAR
2000
094°
(17.7)

3000
171°
(9.9)

640 ∧   554

524 ∧   431   636
         ∧   ∧
                640

IAF
CHANDLER
344 FCH

640   210°

030°

345° 165°

210°

2000
295°
(10.8)

FRAME

10 NM

MSA FCH 25 NM
180°
3800 | 5800
090°   280°
1900

ELEV 278
Rwy 30L ldg 2902
Rwy 30R ldg 2964
Rwy 12R ldg 2977
Rwy 12L ldg 3012

NDB

Remain
within 10 NM
210°

2000

030°

MISSED APPROACH
Climbing right turn to 2000
in FCH NDB holding pattern.

308   316
∧ 72   ∧

3475 X 75

344 X 75

TWR
363

343

333   340
∧   ∧ 30L 30R

REIL Rwys 12R and 30L
MIRL Rwy 12R-30L

CATEGORY	A	B	C	D
CIRCLING	1000-1 722 (800-1)		1000-2 722 (800-2)	NA

Use Fresno Air Terminal altimeter setting.
▽
⚠ NA

Knots	60	90	120	150	180
Min:Sec					

NDB-B

36°44'N-119°49'W

FRESNO, CALIFORNIA
FRESNO-CHANDLER DOWNTOWN (FCH)

Not for use in Navigation

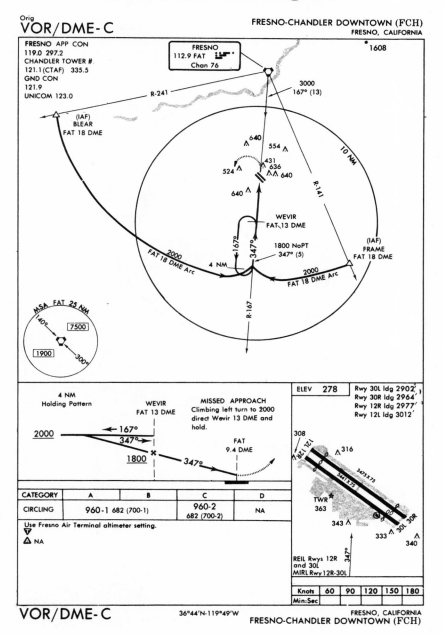

Not for use in Navigation

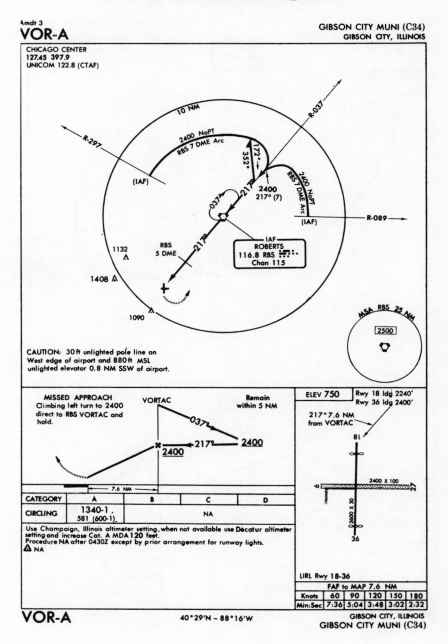

Amdt 3
VOR-A

GIBSON CITY MUNI (C34)
GIBSON CITY, ILLINOIS

CHICAGO CENTER
127.45 397.9
UNICOM 122.8 (CTAF)

10 NM

R-037

R-297

2400 NoPT
RBS 7 DME Arc

172°
352°

217°

2400
217° (7)

2400 NoPT
RBS 7 DME Arc

037°

(IAF)

R-089

(IAF)

217°

RBS
5 DME

IAF
ROBERTS
116.8 RBS
Chan 115

1132

1408

1090

MSA RBS 25 NM

2500

CAUTION: 30 ft unlighted pole line on
West edge of airport and 880 ft MSL
unlighted elevator 0.8 NM SSW of airport.

MISSED APPROACH
Climbing left turn to 2400
direct to RBS VORTAC and
hold.

VORTAC

Remain
within 5 NM

037°

217°   2400

2400

7.6 NM

ELEV 750 | Rwy 18 ldg 2240'
Rwy 36 ldg 2400'

217° 7.6 NM
from VORTAC

81

2400 X 100

27

36

CATEGORY	A	B	C	D
CIRCLING	1340-1, 581 (600-1)		NA	

Use Champaign, Illinois altimeter setting, when not available use Decatur altimeter
setting and increase Cat. A MDA 120 feet.
Procedure NA after 0430Z except by prior arrangement for runway lights.
△ NA

LIRL Rwy 18-36

FAF to MAP 7.6 NM					
Knots	60	90	120	150	180
Min:Sec	7:36	5:04	3:48	3:02	2:32

VOR-A

40°29'N – 88°16'W

GIBSON CITY, ILLINOIS
GIBSON CITY MUNI (C34)

Not for use in Navigation

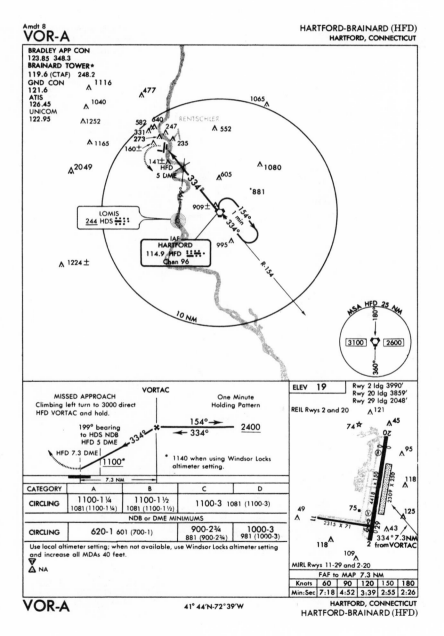

BRADLEY APP CON
123.85 348.3
BRAINARD TOWER*
119.6 (CTAF) 248.2
GND CON
121.6
ATIS
126.45
UNICOM
122.95

LOMIS
244 HDS

IAF
HARTFORD
114.9 HFD
Chan 96

MSA HFD 25 NM

MISSED APPROACH	VORTAC	One Minute Holding Pattern		ELEV 19	Rwy 2 ldg 3990'

MISSED APPROACH
Climbing left turn to 3000 direct
HFD VORTAC and hold.

199° bearing
to HDS NDB
HFD 5 DME

HFD 7.3 DME

1100*

7.3 NM

154° →
← 334°

2400

* 1140 when using Windsor Locks
altimeter setting.

ELEV 19
Rwy 2 ldg 3990'
Rwy 20 ldg 3859'
Rwy 29 ldg 2048'
REIL Rwys 2 and 20

334° 7.3NM
2 from VORTAC

CATEGORY	A	B	C	D
CIRCLING	1100-1¼ 1081(1100-1¼)	1100-1½ 1081 (1100-1½)	1100-3 1081 (1100-3)	
NDB or DME MINIMUMS				
CIRCLING	620-1 601 (700-1)		900-2¾ 881 (900-2¾)	1000-3 981 (1000-3)

Use local altimeter setting; when not available, use Windsor Locks altimeter setting
and increase all MDAs 40 feet.

NA

MIRL Rwys 11-29 and 2-20

FAF to MAP 7.3 NM

Knots	60	90	120	150	180
Min:Sec	7:18	4:52	3:39	2:55	2:26

Not for use in Navigation

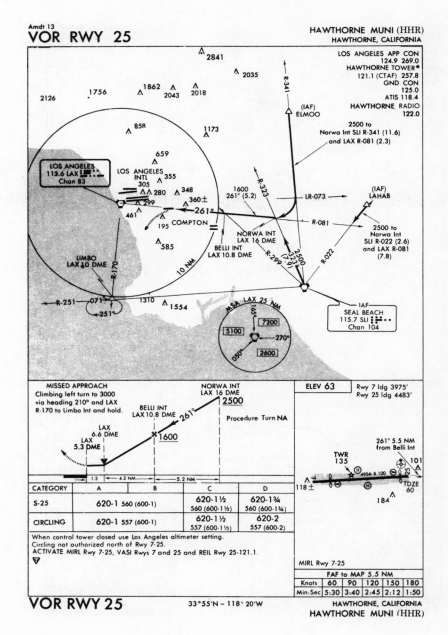

Amdt 13

VOR RWY 25

HAWTHORNE MUNI (HHR)
HAWTHORNE, CALIFORNIA

LOS ANGELES APP CON
124.9 269.0
HAWTHORNE TOWER*
121.1 (CTAF) 257.8
GND CON
125.0
ATIS 118.4
HAWTHORNE RADIO
122.0

2841

2035

R-341

(IAF)
ELMOO

2500 to
Norwa Int SLI R-341 (11.6)
and LAX R-081 (2.3)

1862   2018
2043

1756

2126

858

1173

659

LOS ANGELES
113.6 LAX
Chan 83

LOS ANGELES
INTL   355
305

R-323

1600
261° (5.2)

LR-073

(IAF)
LAHAB

280   348
299   360±
461   261°
195 COMPTON

R-081

2500 to
Norwa Int
SLI R-022 (2.6)
and LAX R-081
(7.8)

585

NORWA INT
LAX 16 DME

BELLI INT
LAX 10.8 DME

R-299   R-022

2500
(3.3)

10 NM

LIMBO
LAX 10 DME

R-170

R-251   071°
251°

1310   1554

MSA LAX 25 NM

IAF
SEAL BEACH
115.7 SLI
Chan 104

7200

5100   270°

090   2600

MISSED APPROACH
Climbing left turn to 3000
via heading 210° and LAX
R-170 to Limbo Int and hold.

NORWA INT
LAX 16 DME
2500

Procedure Turn NA

ELEV 63

Rwy 7 ldg 3975'
Rwy 25 ldg 4483'

BELLI INT
LAX 10.8 DME
261°
1600

LAX
6.6 DME
LAX
5.3 DME

261° 5.5 NM
from Belli Int

TWR
135

101

118±

4956 X 100

TDZE
60

184

1.3   4.2 NM   5.2 NM

CATEGORY	A	B	C	D
S-25	620-1 560 (600-1)		620-1½ 560 (600-1½)	620-1¾ 560 (600-1¾)
CIRCLING	620-1 557 (600-1)		620-1½ 557 (600-1½)	620-2 557 (600-2)

When control tower closed use Los Angeles altimeter setting.
Circling not authorized north of Rwy 7-25.
ACTIVATE MIRL Rwy 7-25, VASI Rwys 7 and 25 and REIL Rwy 25-121.1.

MIRL Rwy 7-25

FAF to MAP 5.5 NM					
Knots	60	90	120	150	180
Min:Sec	5:30	3:40	2:45	2:12	1:50

VOR RWY 25

33°55'N – 118°20'W

HAWTHORNE, CALIFORNIA
HAWTHORNE MUNI (HHR)

Not for use in Navigation

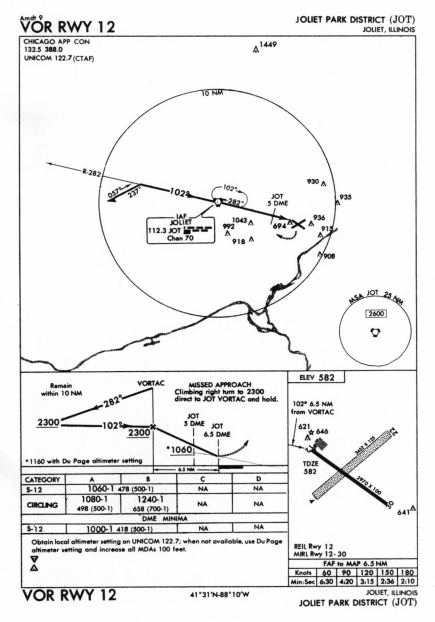

Amdt 9
VOR RWY 12

JOLIET PARK DISTRICT (JOT)
JOLIET, ILLINOIS

CHICAGO APP CON
133.5 388.0
UNICOM 122.7 (CTAF)

1449

10 NM

R-282

057° 237° 102°
282°
JOT 5 DME

930

935

936

694

915

908

IAF
JOLIET
112.3 JOT
Chan 70

1043
992
918

1029

MSA JOT 25 NM
2600

Remain within 10 NM

VORTAC

MISSED APPROACH
Climbing right turn to 2300
direct to JOT VORTAC and hold.

282°
2300
102°
2300
JOT 5 DME
JOT 6.5 DME
*1060

*1160 with Du Page altimeter setting

6.5 NM

ELEV 582

102° 6.5 NM
from VORTAC

621
646

TDZE 582

3452 X 125

2970 X 100

641

CATEGORY	A	B	C	D
S-12	1060-1 478 (500-1)		NA	NA
CIRCLING	1080-1 498 (500-1)	1240-1 658 (700-1)	NA	NA
DME MINIMA				
S-12	1000-1 418 (500-1)		NA	NA

Obtain local altimeter setting on UNICOM 122.7; when not available, use Du Page altimeter setting and increase all MDAs 100 feet.

REIL Rwy 12
MIRL Rwy 12-30

FAF to MAP 6.5 NM					
Knots	60	90	120	150	180
Min:Sec	6:30	4:20	3:15	2:36	2:10

VOR RWY 12

41°31'N-88°10'W

JOLIET, ILLINOIS
JOLIET PARK DISTRICT (JOT)

Not for use in Navigation

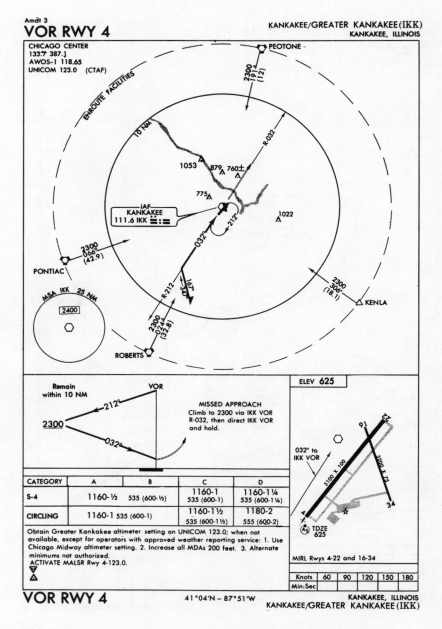

Amdt 3

VOR RWY 4

KANKAKEE/GREATER KANKAKEE (IKK)
KANKAKEE, ILLINOIS

CHICAGO CENTER
133.7 387.]
AWOS-1 118.65
UNICOM 123.0 (CTAF)

PEOTONE

ENROUTE FACILITIES

2300
191°
(12)

R-032

10 NM

1053
879
760±

775

IAF
KANKAKEE
111.6 IKK

-212°

1022

032°

2300
066°
(42.9)

PONTIAC

MSA IKK   25 NM

2400

R-212

167°
347°

2300
306°
(18.1)

KENLA

2300
024°
(32.8)

ROBERTS

Remain
within 10 NM

VOR

-212°

2300

032°

MISSED APPROACH
Climb to 2300 via IKK VOR
R-032, then direct IKK VOR
and hold.

ELEV 625

032° to
IKK VOR

5100 x 100

3200 x 75

91

22

34

TDZE
625

MIRL Rwys 4-22 and 16-34

CATEGORY	A	B	C	D
S-4	1160-½	535 (600-½)	1160-1 535 (600-1)	1160-1¼ 535 (600-1¼)
CIRCLING	1160-1	535 (600-1)	1160-1½ 535 (600-1½)	1180-2 555 (600-2)

Obtain Greater Kankakee altimeter setting on UNICOM 123.0; when not
available, except for operators with approved weather reporting service: 1. Use
Chicago Midway altimeter setting. 2. Increase all MDAs 200 feet. 3. Alternate
minimums not authorized.
ACTIVATE MALSR Rwy 4-123.0.

Knots	60	90	120	150	180
Min:Sec					

VOR RWY 4

41°04'N – 87°51'W

KANKAKEE, ILLINOIS
KANKAKEE/GREATER KANKAKEE (IKK)

Not for use in Navigation

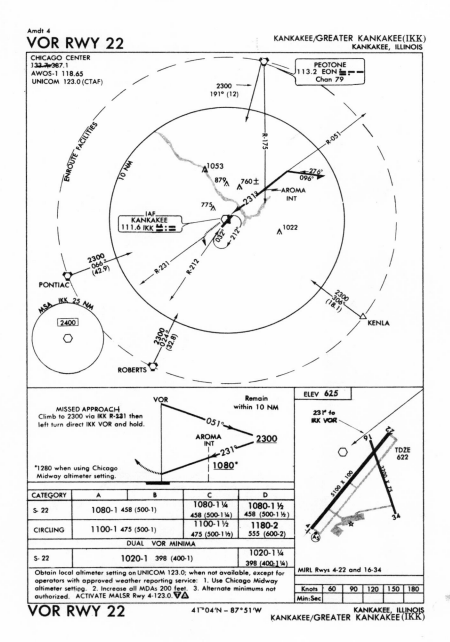

Amdt 4

VOR RWY 22

KANKAKEE/GREATER KANKAKEE(IKK)
KANKAKEE, ILLINOIS

CHICAGO CENTER
132.7–387.1
AWOS-1 118.65
UNICOM 123.0 (CTAF)

PEOTONE
113.2 EON
Chan 79

2300
191° (12)

R-175

R-051

276°
096°

AROMA
INT

1053
879
760±
2313
775
1022

IAF
KANKAKEE
111.6 IKK

032° 212°

2300
066°
(42.9)

R-231   R-212

PONTIAC

2300
306°
(18.1)

MSA IKK 25 NM

2400

KENLA

2300
024°
(32.8)

ROBERTS

ENROUTE FACILITIES

10 NM

Remain
within 10 NM

ELEV 625

VOR

MISSED APPROACH
Climb to 2300 via IKK R-231 then
left turn direct IKK VOR and hold.

051°

AROMA
INT

231°

2300

1080*

*1280 when using Chicago
Midway altimeter setting.

231° to
IKK VOR

91

TDZE
622

5100 x 100

3200 x 75

34

A3

MIRL Rwys 4-22 and 16-34

CATEGORY	A	B	C	D
S-22	1080-1 458 (500-1)		1080-1¼ 458 (500-1¼)	1080-1½ 458 (500-1½)
CIRCLING	1100-1 475 (500-1)		1100-1½ 475 (500-1½)	1180-2 555 (600-2)
DUAL VOR MINIMA				
S-22	1020-1 398 (400-1)			1020-1¼ 398 (400-1¼)

Obtain local altimeter setting on UNICOM 123.0; when not available, except for
operators with approved weather reporting service: 1. Use Chicago Midway
altimeter setting. 2. Increase all MDAs 200 feet. 3. Alternate minimums not
authorized. ACTIVATE MALSR Rwy 4-123.0.

Knots	60	90	120	150	180
Min:Sec					

VOR RWY 22

41°04'N – 87°51'W

KANKAKEE, ILLINOIS
KANKAKEE/GREATER KANKAKEE(IKK)

Not for use in Navigation

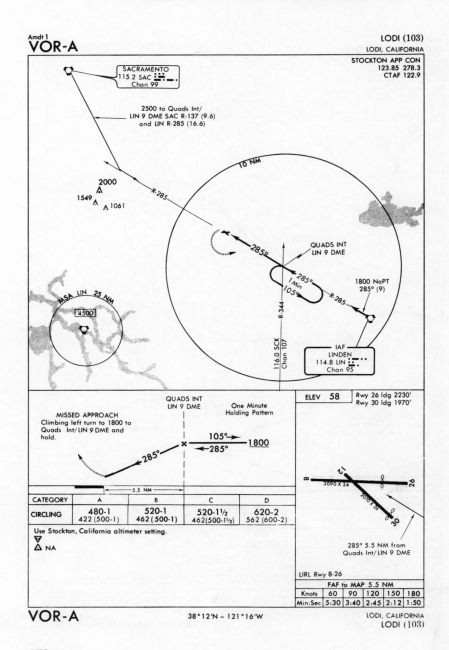

Not for use in Navigation

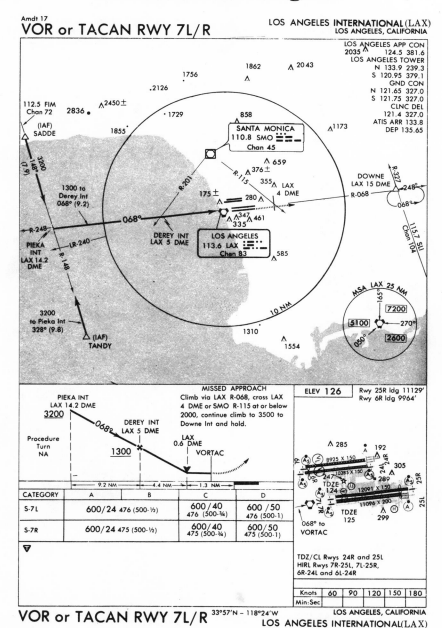

Amdt 17
VOR or TACAN RWY 7L/R

LOS ANGELES INTERNATIONAL (LAX)
LOS ANGELES, CALIFORNIA

LOS ANGELES APP CON
2035 ∧ 124.5 381.6
LOS ANGELES TOWER
N 133.9 239.3
S 120.95 379.1
GND CON
N 121.65 327.0
S 121.75 327.0
CLNC DEL
121.4 327.0
ATIS ARR 133.8
DEP 135.65

112.5 FIM
Chan 72
(IAF)
SADDE

SANTA MONICA
110.8 SMO
Chan 45

LOS ANGELES
113.6 LAX
Chan 83

PIEKA INT
LAX 14.2 DME

DEREY INT
LAX 5 DME

DOWNE
LAX 15 DME

MSA LAX 25 NM
7200
5100 270°
2600

MISSED APPROACH
Climb via LAX R-068, cross LAX 4 DME or SMO R-115 at or below 2000, continue climb to 3500 to Downe Int and hold.

ELEV 126 | Rwy 25R ldg 11129'
Rwy 6R ldg 9964'

PIEKA INT
LAX 14.2 DME
3200

DEREY INT
LAX 5 DME
068°

LAX 0.6 DME
VORTAC

1300

Procedure
Turn
NA

	9.2 NM	4.4 NM	1.3 NM	

TDZE 124
TDZE 125

068° to
VORTAC

CATEGORY	A	B	C	D
S-7L	600/24 476 (500-½)		600/40 476 (500-¾)	600/50 476 (500-1)
S-7R	600/24 475 (500-½)		600/40 475 (500-¾)	600/50 475 (500-1)

TDZ/CL Rwys 24R and 25L
HIRL Rwys 7R-25L, 7L-25R,
6R-24L and 6L-24R

Knots	60	90	120	150	180
Min:Sec					

VOR or TACAN RWY 7L/R
33°57'N – 118°24'W

LOS ANGELES, CALIFORNIA
LOS ANGELES INTERNATIONAL (LAX)

Not for use in Navigation

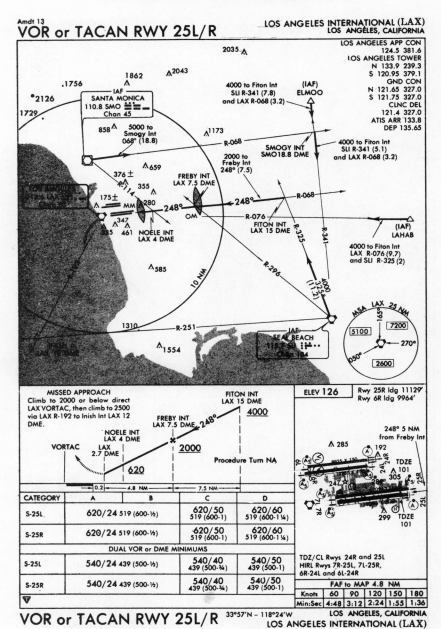

Amdt 13
VOR or TACAN RWY 25L/R

LOS ANGELES INTERNATIONAL (LAX)
LOS ANGELES, CALIFORNIA

LOS ANGELES APP CON
124.5 381.6
LOS ANGELES TOWER
N 133.9 239.3
S 120.95 379.1
GND CON
N 121.65 327.0
S 121.75 327.0
CLNC DEL
121.4 327.0
ATIS ARR 133.8
DEP 135.65

2035 ∧

.1756   1862 ∧   ∧2043
∧
.2126   IAF
1729   SANTA MONICA
110.8 SMO
Chan 45

4000 to Fiton Int
SLI R-341 (7.8)
and LAX R-068 (3.2)

(IAF)
ELMOO ∧

858 ∧   5000 to
Smogy Int
068° (18.8)

∧1173

R-068

SMOGY INT
SMO18.8 DME

4000 to Fiton Int
SLI R-341 (5.1)
and LAX R-068 (3.2)

376 ±   ∧659   FREBY INT
∧   LAX 7.5 DME
R-114   355
∧   ∧   2000 to
175 ±   280   Freby Int
∧   248°   248° (7.5)

248°   248°   R-068

MM
OM   R-076

347   FITON INT
∧   LAX 15 DME
235   461   NOELE INT
LAX 4 DME

R-325

R-341

(IAF)
LAHAB ∧

4000 to Fiton Int
LAX R-076 (9.7)
and SLI R-325 (2)

∧585

10 NM

R-296

4000
325
(11.2)

MSA LAX 25 NM
165°
5100   7200
050°   270°
2600

1310   R-251
∧1554   IAF
SEAL BEACH
115.7 SLI
Chan 104

MSA LAX 25 NM

MISSED APPROACH			FITON INT
Climb to 2000 or below direct			LAX 15 DME
LAX VORTAC, then climb to 2500			4000
via LAX R-192 to Inish Int LAX 12 DME.	FREBY INT LAX 7.5 DME 248°		

ELEV 126 | Rwy 25R ldg 11129'
Rwy 6R ldg 9964'

NOELE INT
LAX 4 DME
VORTAC   LAX
2.7 DME   2000   Procedure Turn NA

620

0.2   4.8 NM   7.5 NM

248° 5 NM
from Freby Int

∧ 285   192
TDZE
101
305
299   TDZE
101

CATEGORY	A	B	C	D
S-25L	620/24 519 (600-½)		620/50 519 (600-1)	620/60 519 (600-1¼)
S-25R	620/24 519 (600-½)		620/50 519 (600-1)	620/60 519 (600-1¼)
DUAL VOR or DME MINIMUMS				
S-25L	540/24 439 (500-½)		540/40 439 (500-¾)	540/50 439 (500-1)
S-25R	540/24 439 (500-½)		540/40 439 (500-¾)	540/50 439 (500-1)

TDZ/CL Rwys 24R and 25L
HIRL Rwys 7R-25L, 7L-25R,
6R-24L and 6L-24R

FAF to MAP 4.8 NM

Knots	60	90	120	150	180
Min:Sec	4:48	3:12	2:24	1:55	1:36

VOR or TACAN RWY 25L/R
33°57'N – 118°24'W

LOS ANGELES, CALIFORNIA
LOS ANGELES INTERNATIONAL (LAX)

Not for use in Navigation

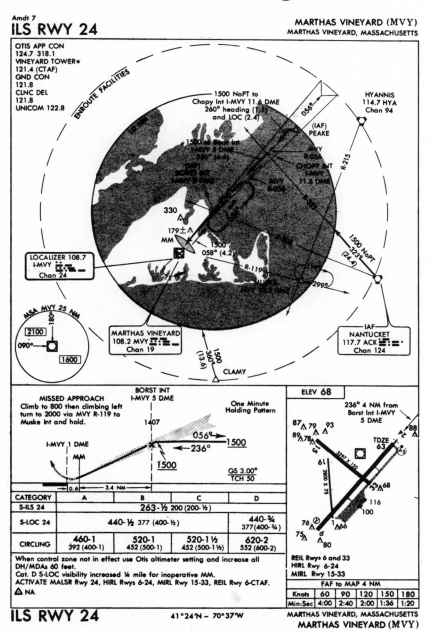

Amdt 7

ILS RWY 24

MARTHAS VINEYARD (MVY)
MARTHAS VINEYARD, MASSACHUSETTS

OTIS APP CON
124.7 318.1
VINEYARD TOWER★
121.4 (CTAF)
GND CON
121.8
CLNC DEL
121.8
UNICOM 122.8

LOCALIZER 108.7
I-MVY
Chan 24

MARTHAS VINEYARD
108.2 MVY
Chan 19

MSA MVY 25 NM
2100
1600
180°
090°

HYANNIS
114.7 HYA
Chan 94

(IAF)
PEAKE

IAF
NANTUCKET
117.7 ACK
Chan 124

CLAMY

ELEV 68

MISSED APPROACH
Climb to 800 then climbing left
turn to 2000 via MVY R-119 to
Muske Int and hold.

BORST INT
I-MVY 5 DME

One Minute
Holding Pattern

I-MVY 1 DME

1407

056°
236°
1500
1500

GS 3.00°
TCH 50

0.6   3.4 NM

TDZE 63
236° 4 NM from
Borst Int I-MVY
5 DME

REIL Rwys 6 and 33
HIRL Rwy 6-24
MIRL Rwy 15-33

CATEGORY	A	B	C	D
S-ILS 24		263-½ 200 (200-½)		
S-LOC 24		440-½ 377 (400-½)		440-¾ 377 (400-¾)
CIRCLING	460-1 392 (400-1)	520-1 452 (500-1)	520-1½ 452 (500-1½)	620-2 552 (600-2)

When control zone not in effect use Otis altimeter setting and increase all
DH/MDAs 60 feet.
Cat. D S-LOC visibility increased ¼ mile for inoperative MM.
ACTIVATE MALSR Rwy 24, HIRL Rwys 6-24, MIRL Rwy 15-33, REIL Rwy 6-CTAF.
⚠ NA

FAF to MAP 4 NM					
Knots	60	90	120	150	180
Min:Sec	4:00	2:40	2:00	1:36	1:20

ILS RWY 24

41°24'N – 70°37'W

MARTHAS VINEYARD, MASSACHUSETTS
MARTHAS VINEYARD (MVY)

Not for use in Navigation

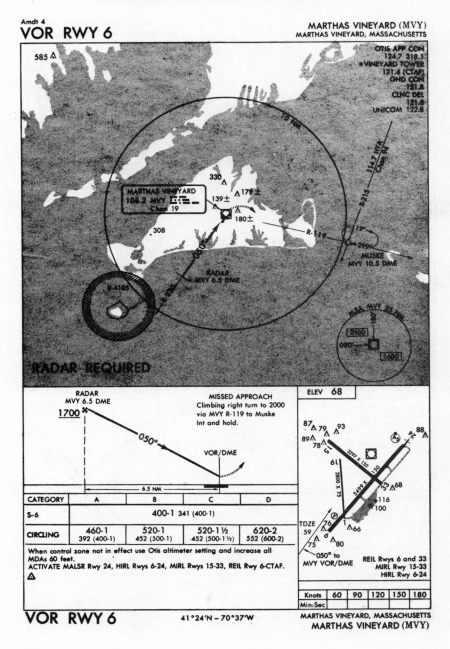

Amdt 4
VOR RWY 6

MARTHAS VINEYARD (MVY)
MARTHAS VINEYARD, MASSACHUSETTS

OTIS APP CON
124.7 318.1
★VINEYARD TOWER
121.4 (CTAF)
GND CON
121.8
CLNC DEL
121.8
UNICOM 122.8

585 ∧

10 NM

330 ∧

MARTHAS VINEYARD
108.2 MVY ⋯⋯
Chan 19

∧ 179±

139±

180±

R-119

308

114.7 HYA
Chan 94

R-213

19°

299°

MUSKE
MVY 10.5 DME

RADAR
MVY 6.5 DME

R-4102

MSA MVY 25 DME

180°
2100

070°
1600

RADAR REQUIRED

RADAR MVY 6.5 DME	MISSED APPROACH Climbing right turn to 2000 via MVY R-119 to Muske Int and hold.

1700

050°

VOR/DME

6.5 NM

CATEGORY	A	B	C	D
S-6	400-1 341 (400-1)			
CIRCLING	460-1 392 (400-1)	520-1 452 (500-1)	520-1½ 452 (500-1½)	620-2 552 (600-2)

When control zone not in effect use Otis altimeter setting and increase all
MDAs 60 feet.
ACTIVATE MALSR Rwy 24, HIRL Rwys 6-24, MIRL Rwys 15-33, REIL Rwy 6-CTAF.
⚠

ELEV 68

87 ∧ 79 ∧ ∧ 93
89 ∧ ∧ 78 3597 X 150
150
61
2800 X 75 5492 X 75
33 ∧ 68
∧ 116
∧ 100
TDZE
59 ∧ 76 ∧ 66
∧ 75
∧ 80
∧ 88

050° to
MVY VOR/DME

REIL Rwys 6 and 33
MIRL Rwy 15-33
HIRL Rwy 6-24

Knots	60	90	120	150	180
Min:Sec					

VOR RWY 6

41°24'N – 70°37'W

MARTHAS VINEYARD, MASSACHUSETTS
MARTHAS VINEYARD (MVY)

Not for use in Navigation

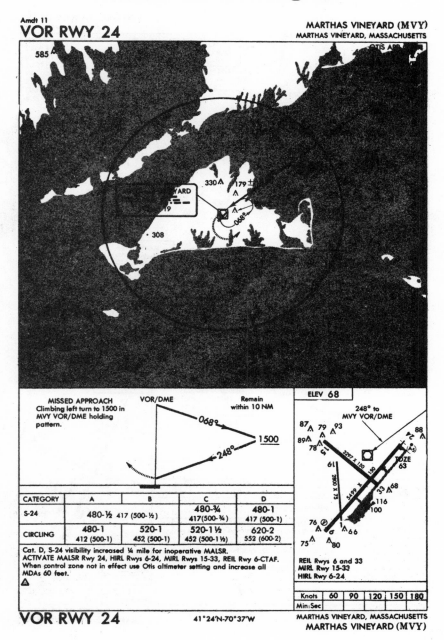

Amdt 11

VOR RWY 24

MARTHAS VINEYARD (MVY)
MARTHAS VINEYARD, MASSACHUSETTS

OTIS APP

585 ∆

330 ∆   179 ±

∆

YARD

068°

• 308

MISSED APPROACH
Climbing left turn to 1500 in
MVY VOR/DME holding
pattern.

VOR/DME

068°

Remain
within 10 NM

1500

248°

CATEGORY	A	B	C	D
S-24	480-½ 417 (500-½)		480-¾ 417(500-¾)	480-1 417 (500-1)
CIRCLING	480-1 412 (500-1)	520-1 452 (500-1)	520-1½ 452 (500-1½)	620-2 552 (600-2)

Cat. D, S-24 visibility increased ¼ mile for inoperative MALSR.
ACTIVATE MALSR Rwy 24, HIRL Rwys 6-24, MIRL Rwys 15-33, REIL Rwy 6-CTAF.
When control zone not in effect use Otis altimeter setting and increase all
MDAs 60 feet.
⚠

ELEV 68

248° to
MVY VOR/DME

87 ∆ 79 93
        ∆ ∆
89∆
   78
         3297 X 150

61
                        TOZE
                        63
       7800 X 75
                    33 ∆68
       5449 X 150

116
100

76 Ⓦ
 ∆   1 ∆ 66
75∆
   ᴼ ∆ 80

REIL Rwys 6 and 33
MIRL Rwy 15-33
HIRL Rwy 6-24

88
∆

Knots	60	90	120	150	180
Min:Sec					

VOR RWY 24

41°24'N-70°37'W

MARTHAS VINEYARD, MASSACHUSETTS
MARTHAS VINEYARD (MVY)

175

Not for use in Navigation

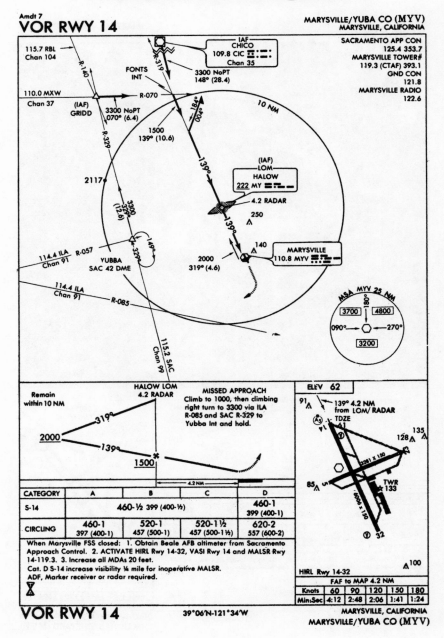

Not for use in Navigation

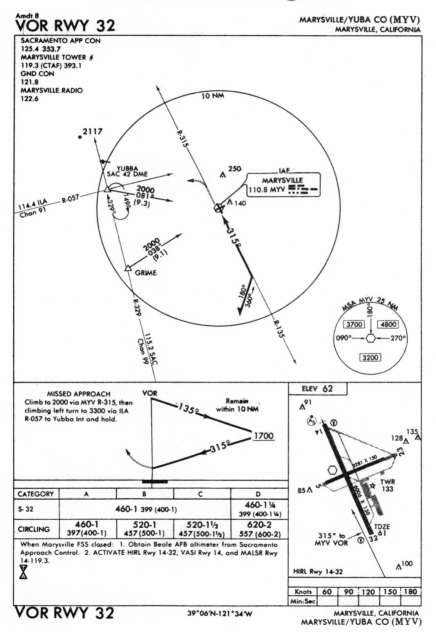

Amdt 8
VOR RWY 32

MARYSVILLE/YUBA CO (MYV)
MARYSVILLE, CALIFORNIA

SACRAMENTO APP CON
125.4 353.7
MARYSVILLE TOWER #
119.3 (CTAF) 393.1
GND CON
121.8
MARYSVILLE RADIO
122.6

MISSED APPROACH
Climb to 2000 via MYV R-315, then climbing left turn to 3300 via ILA R-057 to Yubba Int and hold.

Remain within 10 NM

ELEV 62

CATEGORY	A	B	C	D
S-32	460-1 399 (400-1)			460-1¼ 399 (400-1¼)
CIRCLING	460-1 397(400-1)	520-1 457(500-1)	520-1½ 457(500-1½)	620-2 557 (600-2)

When Marysville FSS closed: 1. Obtain Beale AFB altimeter from Sacramento Approach Control. 2. ACTIVATE HIRL Rwy 14-32, VASI Rwy 14, and MALSR Rwy 14-119.3.

315° to MYV VOR

TDZE 61

HIRL Rwy 14-32

Knots	60	90	120	150	180
Min:Sec					

VOR RWY 32

39°06'N-121°34'W

MARYSVILLE, CALIFORNIA
MARYSVILLE/YUBA CO (MYV)

Not for use in Navigation

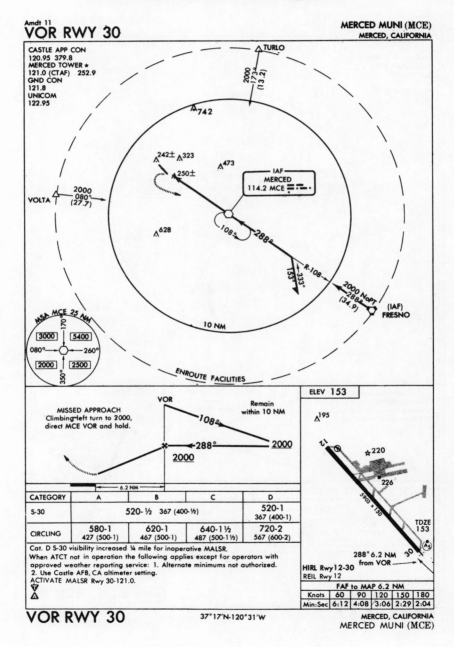

Not for use in Navigation

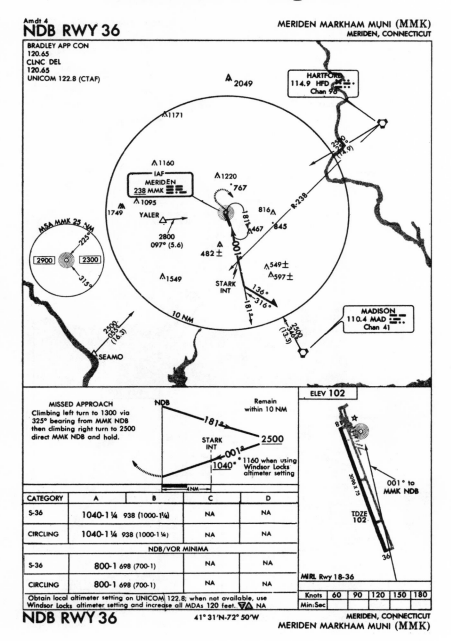

Amdt 4
NDB RWY 36

MERIDEN MARKHAM MUNI (MMK)
MERIDEN, CONNECTICUT

BRADLEY APP CON
120.65
CLNC DEL
120.65
UNICOM 122.8 (CTAF)

MISSED APPROACH
Climbing left turn to 1300 via 325° bearing from MMK NDB then climbing right turn to 2500 direct MMK NDB and hold.

Remain within 10 NM

* 1160 when using Windsor Locks altimeter setting

ELEV 102

001° to MMK NDB

TDZE 102

MIRL Rwy 18-36

CATEGORY	A	B	C	D
S-36	1040-1¼ 938 (1000-1¼)		NA	NA
CIRCLING	1040-1¼ 938 (1000-1¼)		NA	NA
NDB/VOR MINIMA				
S-36	800-1 698 (700-1)		NA	NA
CIRCLING	800-1 698 (700-1)		NA	NA

Obtain local altimeter setting on UNICOM 122.8; when not available, use Windsor Locks altimeter setting and increase all MDAs 120 feet. ▽△ NA

Knots	60	90	120	150	180
Min:Sec					

NDB RWY 36

41°31'N-72°50'W

MERIDEN, CONNECTICUT
MERIDEN MARKHAM MUNI (MMK)

179

Not for use in Navigation

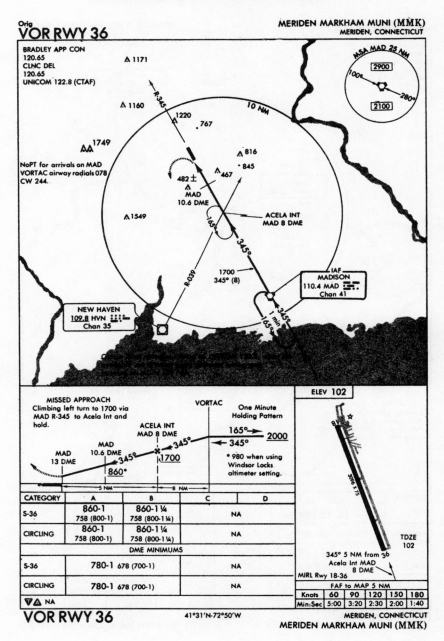

Orig
VOR RWY 36

MERIDEN MARKHAM MUNI (MMK)
MERIDEN, CONNECTICUT

BRADLEY APP CON
120.65
CLNC DEL
120.65
UNICOM 122.8 (CTAF)

MSA MAD 25 NM
2900
100°   280°
2100

NoPT for arrivals on MAD
VORTAC airway radials 078
CW 244.

▲ 1171
▲ 1160
▲▲ 1749
1220
.767
▲ 816
.845
▲ 467
482 ± MAD 10.6 DME
▲ 1549
ACELA INT MAD 8 DME
345°
R-039
10 NM
R-345
165°
1700 345° (8)
IAF MADISON 110.4 MAD Chan 41
NEW HAVEN 109.8 HVN Chan 35
165°   345°   1 min

MISSED APPROACH
Climbing left turn to 1700 via
MAD R-345 to Acela Int and
hold.

ELEV 102

VORTAC
One Minute Holding Pattern

ACELA INT MAD 8 DME
165°   2000
345°
* 980 when using Windsor Locks altimeter setting.

MAD 10.6 DME
345°   345°
1700

MAD 13 DME
345°
860*

5 NM   8 NM

TDZE 102

345° 5 NM from 36
Acela Int MAD 8 DME
MIRL Rwy 18-36

CATEGORY	A	B	C	D
S-36	860-1 758 (800-1)	860-1¼ 758 (800-1¼)	NA	
CIRCLING	860-1 758 (800-1)	860-1¼ 758 (800-1¼)	NA	
DME MINIMUMS				
S-36	780-1 678 (700-1)		NA	
CIRCLING	780-1 678 (700-1)		NA	
▽△ NA				

FAF to MAP 5 NM

Knots	60	90	120	150	180
Min:Sec	5:00	3:20	2:30	2:00	1:40

VOR RWY 36

41°31'N-72°50'W

MERIDEN, CONNECTICUT
MERIDEN MARKHAM MUNI (MMK)

Not for use in Navigation

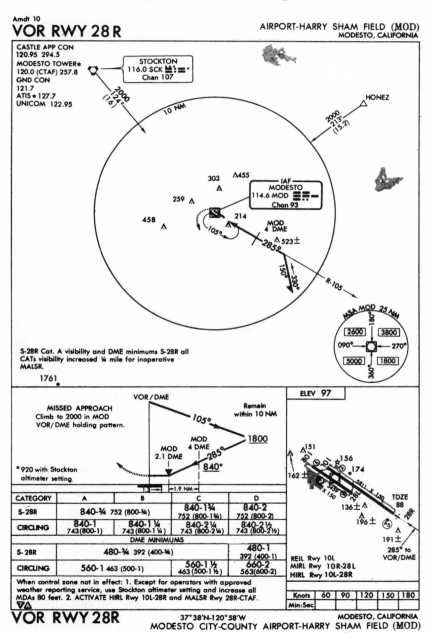

Amdt 10

VOR RWY 28R

AIRPORT-HARRY SHAM FIELD (MOD)
MODESTO, CALIFORNIA

CASTLE APP CON
120.95 294.5
MODESTO TOWER★
120.0 (CTAF) 257.8
GND CON
121.7
ATIS ★ 127.7
UNICOM 122.95

STOCKTON
116.0 SCK
Chan 107

10 NM

HONEZ

2000
213°
(15.2)

303
∧455

259

IAF
MODESTO
114.6 MOD
Chan 93

458

214

MOD
4 DME

∧ 523±

105°

285°

150°

330°

R-105

MSA MOD 25 NM

2600 | 3800
090°   270°
5000 | 1800
360°

S-28R Cat. A visibility and DME minimums S-28R all
CATs visibility increased ¼ mile for inoperative
MALSR.

1761

ELEV 97

MISSED APPROACH
Climb to 2000 in MOD
VOR/DME holding pattern.

VOR/DME

105°

Remain
within 10 NM

1800

MOD
4 DME

MOD
2.1 DME

285°

*920 with Stockton
altimeter setting.

840*

1.3 | 1.9 NM

151
∧

156

101

174

162±

136±∧

TDZE
88

CATEGORY	A	B	C	D
S-28R	840-¾ 752 (800-¾)		840-1¾ 752 (800-1¾)	840-2 752 (800-2)
CIRCLING	840-1 743(800-1)	840-1¼ 743(800-1¼)	840-2¼ 743(800-2¼)	840-2½ 743(800-2½)
DME MINIMUMS				
S-28R	480-¾ 392 (400-¾)			480-1 392 (400-1)
CIRCLING	560-1 463 (500-1)		560-1½ 463(500-1½)	660-2 563(600-2)

196±

191±

285° to
VOR/DME

REIL Rwy 10L
MIRL Rwy 10R-28L
HIRL Rwy 10L-28R

When control zone not in effect: 1. Except for operators with approved
weather reporting service, use Stockton altimeter setting and increase all
MDAs 80 feet. 2. ACTIVATE HIRL Rwy 10L-28R and MALSR Rwy 28R-CTAF.

Knots	60	90	120	150	180
Min:Sec					

VOR RWY 28R

37°38'N-120°58'W
MODESTO CITY-COUNTY AIRPORT-HARRY SHAM FIELD (MOD)

MODESTO, CALIFORNIA

181

Not for use in Navigation

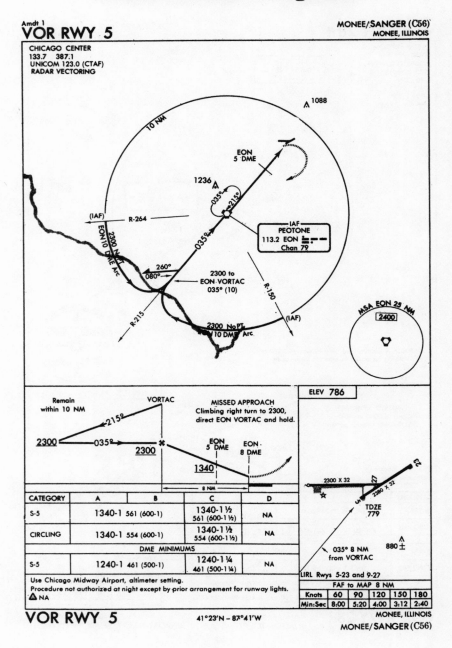

Amdt 1
VOR RWY 5

CHICAGO CENTER
133.7   387.1
UNICOM 123.0 (CTAF)
RADAR VECTORING

ELEV 786

Remain within 10 NM

MISSED APPROACH
Climbing right turn to 2300, direct EON VORTAC and hold.

2300 to EON VORTAC 035° (10)

2300 NoPT 10 DME Arc

MSA EON 25 NM   2400

IAF
PEOTONE
113.2 EON
Chan 79

CATEGORY	A	B	C	D
S-5	1340-1 561 (600-1)		1340-1½ 561 (600-1½)	NA
CIRCLING	1340-1 554 (600-1)		1340-1½ 554 (600-1½)	NA
DME MINIMUMS				
S-5	1240-1 461 (500-1)		1240-1¼ 461 (500-1¼)	NA

Use Chicago Midway Airport, altimeter setting.
Procedure not authorized at night except by prior arrangement for runway lights.
⚠ NA

TDZE 779

035° 8 NM from VORTAC

880 ±

LIRL Rwys 5-23 and 9-27

FAF to MAP 8 NM					
Knots	60	90	120	150	180
Min:Sec	8:00	5:20	4:00	3:12	2:40

VOR RWY 5

41°23'N – 87°41'W

Not for use in Navigation

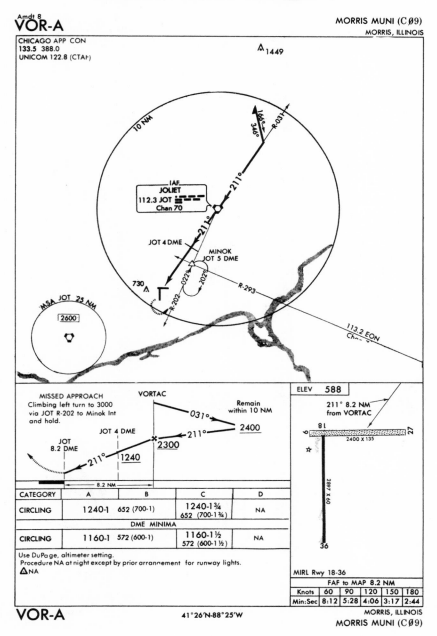

Amdt 8
VOR-A

MORRIS MUNI (C Ø9)
MORRIS, ILLINOIS

CHICAGO APP CON
133.5 388.0
UNICOM 122.8 (CTAF)

A 1449

IAF
JOLIET
112.3 JOT
Chan 70

211°

346°
R-031°

JOT 4 DME

MINOK
JOT 5 DME

730 A

R-202
022°

202°

R-293

113.2 EON

MSA JOT 25 NM

2600

MISSED APPROACH
Climbing left turn to 3000
via JOT R-202 to Minok Int
and hold.

VORTAC

031°

Remain
within 10 NM

2400

JOT 4 DME

211°

2300

JOT
8.2 DME

211°

1240

8.2 NM

ELEV 588

211° 8.2 NM
from VORTAC

81

6

27

2400 x 135

2897 X 60

36

CATEGORY	A	B	C	D
CIRCLING	1240-1	652 (700-1)	1240-1¾ 652 (700-1¾)	NA
DME MINIMA				
CIRCLING	1160-1	572 (600-1)	1160-1½ 572 (600-1½)	NA

Use DuPage, altimeter setting.
Procedure NA at night except by prior arrangement for runway lights.
△NA

MIRL Rwy 18-36

FAF to MAP 8.2 NM					
Knots	60	90	120	150	180
Min:Sec	8:12	5:28	4:06	3:17	2:44

VOR-A

41°26'N-88°25'W

MORRIS, ILLINOIS
MORRIS MUNI (C Ø9)

Not for use in Navigation

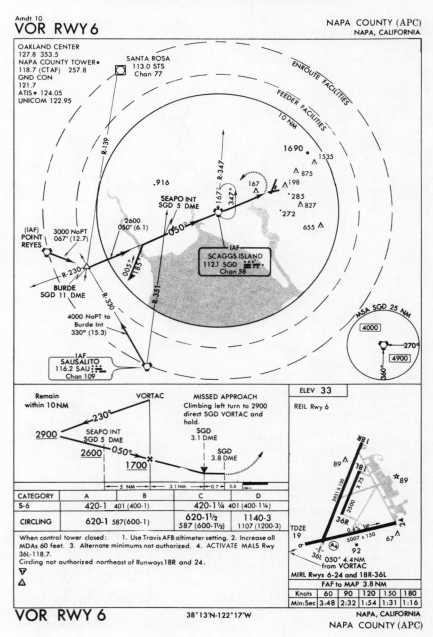

Amdt 10

VOR RWY 6

NAPA COUNTY (APC)
NAPA, CALIFORNIA

OAKLAND CENTER
127.8 353.5
NAPA COUNTY TOWER★
118.7 (CTAF) 257.8
GND CON
121.7
ATIS★ 124.05
UNICOM 122.95

SANTA ROSA
113.0 STS
Chan 77

ENROUTE FACILITIES
FEEDER FACILITIES
10 NM

R-139

1690 •
1535
875
167
198
285
827
272
655

.916

SEAPO INT
SGD 5 DME

167° R-347
347°

(IAF)
POINT
REYES

3000 NoPT
067° (12.7)

2600
050° (6.1)

050°

005°

185°

IAF
SCAGGS ISLAND
112.1 SGD
Chan 58

R-230

BURDE
SGD 11 DME

R-330

R-351

MSA SGD 25 NM

4000 NoPT to
Burde Int
330° (15.3)

4000
270°
360°
4900

IAF
SAUSALITO
116.2 SAU
Chan 109

ELEV 33

Remain
within 10 NM

VORTAC

MISSED APPROACH
Climbing left turn to 2900
direct SGD VORTAC and
hold.

REIL Rwy 6

230°
2900

SEAPO INT
SGD 5 DME

050°
2600

1700

SGD
3.1 DME

SGD
3.8 DME

5 NM   3.1 NM   0.7   0.6

89
18L
181
89

TDZE
19

36R

24

67

92

5007 x 150

3500

5921 x 150

36L 050° 4.4NM
from VORTAC

CATEGORY	A	B	C	D
S-6	420-1 401 (400-1)		420-1¼ 401 (400-1¼)	
CIRCLING	620-1 587(600-1)		620-1½ 587 (600-1½)	1140-3 1107 (1200-3)

When control tower closed: 1. Use Travis AFB altimeter setting. 2. Increase all
MDAs 60 feet. 3. Alternate minimums not authorized. 4. ACTIVATE MALS Rwy
36L-118.7.
Circling not authorized northeast of Runways 18R and 24.

MIRL Rwys 6-24 and 18R-36L

FAF to MAP 3.8 NM

Knots	60	90	120	150	180
Min:Sec	3:48	2:32	1:54	1:31	1:16

VOR RWY 6

38°13'N-122°17'W

NAPA, CALIFORNIA
NAPA COUNTY (APC)

Not for use in Navigation

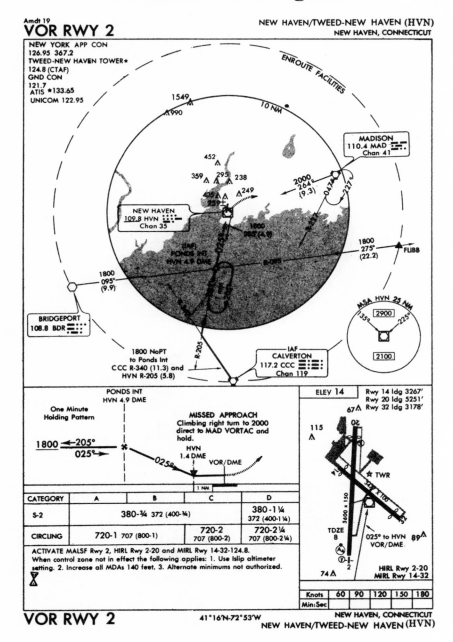

NEW YORK APP CON
126.95 367.2
TWEED-NEW HAVEN TOWER*
124.8 (CTAF)
GND CON
121.7
ATIS *133.65
UNICOM 122.95

ENROUTE FACILITIES

1549
990
10 NM

MADISON
110.4 MAD
Chan 41

452
359 295 238
249
405 259

2000
264°
(9.3)
047°
227°

NEW HAVEN
109.8 HVN
Chan 35

1800
265° (4.9)

1800
275°
(22.2)   FLIBB

(IAF)
PONDS INT
HVN 4.9 DME

1800
095°
(9.9)

MSA HVN 25 NM
135° 2900 225°

BRIDGEPORT
108.8 BDR

R-205

2100

1800 NoPT
to Ponds Int
CCC R-340 (11.3) and
HVN R-205 (5.8)

IAF
CALVERTON
117.2 CCC
Chan 119

		ELEY 14	Rwy 14 ldg 3267'
		67	Rwy 20 ldg 5251'
			Rwy 32 ldg 3178'

PONDS INT
HVN 4.9 DME

One Minute
Holding Pattern

MISSED APPROACH
Climbing right turn to 2000
direct to MAD VORTAC and
hold.

1800 ←205°
025°

HVN
1.4 DME
VOR/DME

025°

1 NM

115

TWR

5600 x 150

TDZE
8

025° to HVN
VOR/DME.   89

CATEGORY	A	B	C	D
S-2	380-¾ 372 (400-¾)			380-1¼ 372 (400-1¼)
CIRCLING	720-1 707 (800-1)		720-2 707 (800-2)	720-2¼ 707 (800-2¼)

ACTIVATE MALSF Rwy 2, HIRL Rwy 2-20 and MIRL Rwy 14-32-124.8.
When control zone not in effect the following applies: 1. Use Islip altimeter
setting. 2. Increase all MDAs 140 feet. 3. Alternate minimums not authorized.

74

HIRL Rwy 2-20
MIRL Rwy 14-32

Knots	60	90	120	150	180
Min:Sec					

Not for use in Navigation

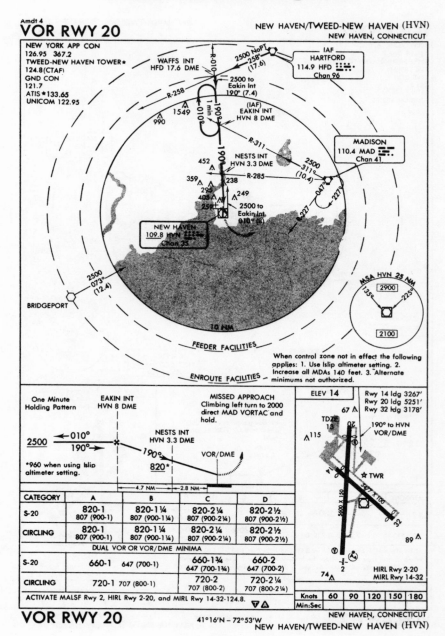

Amdt 4

VOR RWY 20

NEW HAVEN/TWEED-NEW HAVEN (HVN)
NEW HAVEN, CONNECTICUT

NEW YORK APP CON
126.95 367.2
TWEED-NEW HAVEN TOWER*
124.8(CTAF)
GND CON
121.7
ATIS *133.65
UNICOM 122.95

When control zone not in effect the following applies: 1. Use Islip altimeter setting. 2. Increase all MDAs 140 feet. 3. Alternate minimums not authorized.

One Minute
Holding Pattern

EAKIN INT
HVN 8 DME

MISSED APPROACH
Climbing left turn to 2000
direct MAD VORTAC and
hold.

2500 ←010°
190°→

*960 when using Islip
altimeter setting.

NESTS INT
HVN 3.3 DME

190°

820*

VOR/DME

←— 4.7 NM —→|←— 2.8 NM —→

ELEV 14

Rwy 14 ldg 3267'
Rwy 20 ldg 5251'
Rwy 32 ldg 3178'

190° to HVN
VOR/DME

CATEGORY	A	B	C	D
S-20	820-1 807 (900-1)	820-1¼ 807 (900-1¼)	820-2¼ 807 (900-2¼)	820-2½ 807 (900-2½)
CIRCLING	820-1 807 (900-1)	820-1¼ 807 (900-1¼)	820-2¼ 807 (900-2¼)	820-2½ 807 (900-2½)
DUAL VOR OR VOR/DME MINIMA				
S-20	660-1 647 (700-1)		660-1¾ 647 (700-1¾)	660-2 647 (700-2)
CIRCLING	720-1 707 (800-1)		720-2 707 (800-2)	720-2¼ 707 (800-2¼)

ACTIVATE MALSF Rwy 2, HIRL Rwy 2-20, and MIRL Rwy 14-32-124.8.

HIRL Rwy 2-20
MIRL Rwy 14-32

Knots	60	90	120	150	180
Min:Sec					

VOR RWY 20

41°16'N – 72°53'W

NEW HAVEN, CONNECTICUT
NEW HAVEN/TWEED-NEW HAVEN (HVN)

Not for use in Navigation

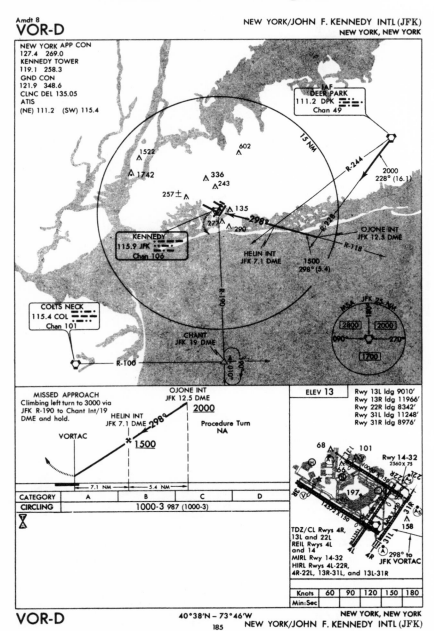

Amdt 8
VOR-D

NEW YORK/JOHN F. KENNEDY INTL (JFK)
NEW YORK, NEW YORK

NEW YORK APP CON
127.4 269.0
KENNEDY TOWER
119.1 258.3
GND CON
121.9 348.6
CLNC DEL 135.05
ATIS
(NE) 111.2 (SW) 115.4

IAF
DEER PARK
111.2 DPK
Chan 49

1522

602

1742

336
243

257±

135

KENNEDY
115.9 JFK
Chan 106

273

290

298°

OJONE INT
JFK 12.5 DME

R-244

2000
228° (16.1)

R-228

R-118

HELIN INT
JFK 7.1 DME

1500
298° (5.4)

COLTS NECK
115.4 COL
Chan 101

R-100

CHANT
JFK 19 DME

JFK 25 NM

2800   2000

090°   270°

1700

MISSED APPROACH
Climbing left turn to 3000 via
JFK R-190 to Chant Int/19
DME and hold.

OJONE INT
JFK 12.5 DME

2000

HELIN INT
JFK 7.1 DME   298°

Procedure Turn
NA

VORTAC

1500

7.1 NM   5.4 NM

ELEV 13

Rwy 13L ldg 9010'
Rwy 13R ldg 11966'
Rwy 22R ldg 8342'
Rwy 31L ldg 11248'
Rwy 31R ldg 8976'

68   101

Rwy 14-32
2560 x 75

197

158

298° to
JFK VORTAC

CATEGORY	A	B	C	D
CIRCLING		1000-3 987 (1000-3)		

TDZ/CL Rwys 4R,
13L and 22L
REIL Rwys 4L
and 14
MIRL Rwy 14-32
HIRL Rwys 4L-22R,
4R-22L, 13R-31L, and 13L-31R

Knots	60	90	120	150	180
Min:Sec					

VOR-D

40°38'N – 73°46'W
185

NEW YORK, NEW YORK
NEW YORK/JOHN F. KENNEDY INTL (JFK)

Not for use in Navigation

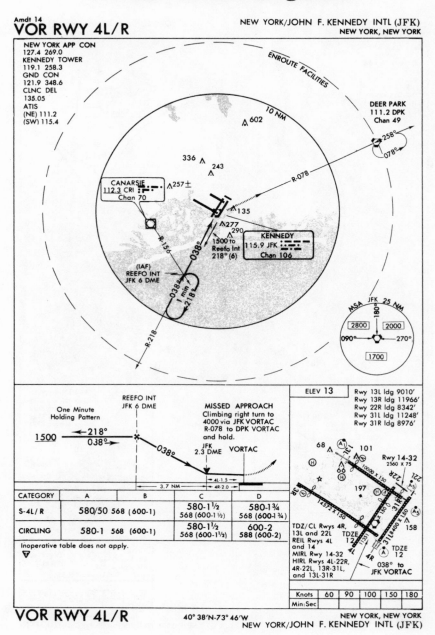

Not for use in Navigation

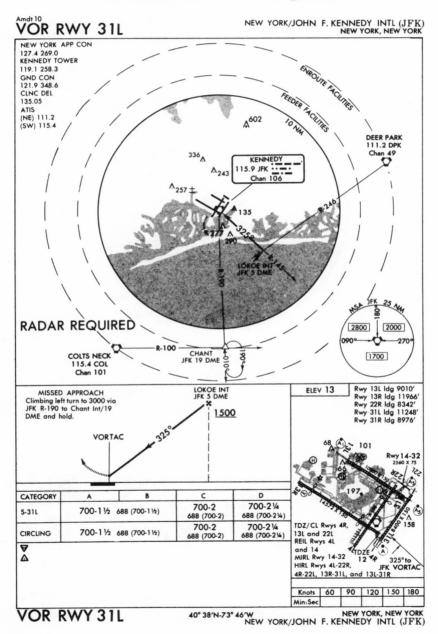

Amdt 10

VOR RWY 31L

NEW YORK/JOHN F. KENNEDY INTL (JFK)
NEW YORK, NEW YORK

NEW YORK APP CON
127.4 269.0
KENNEDY TOWER
119.1 258.3
GND CON
121.9 348.6
CLNC DEL
135.05
ATIS
(NE) 111.2
(SW) 115.4

ENROUTE FACILITIES

FEEDER FACILITIES

10 NM

∧602

DEER PARK
111.2 DPK
Chan 49

336 ∧
∧243

KENNEDY
115.9 JFK ---··-
Chan 106

∧257 ‡

R-246

∧ 135

R-277

325°

∧
290

LOKOE INT
JFK 5 DME

R-145

R-190

MSA JFK 25 NM

2800   2000

090°   270°

1700

RADAR REQUIRED

COLTS NECK
115.4 COL
Chan 101

R-100

CHANT
JFK 19 DME

010°

190°

| MISSED APPROACH | LOKOE INT
JFK 5 DME | ELEV 13 | Rwy 13L ldg 9010'
Rwy 13R ldg 11966'
Rwy 22R ldg 8342'
Rwy 31L ldg 11248'
Rwy 31R ldg 8976' |

MISSED APPROACH
Climbing left turn to 3000 via
JFK R-190 to Chant Int/19
DME and hold.

LOKOE INT
JFK 5 DME

1500

VORTAC

325°

CATEGORY	A	B	C	D
S-31L	700-1½	688 (700-1½)	700-2 688 (700-2)	700-2¼ 688 (700-2¼)
CIRCLING	700-1½	688 (700-1½)	700-2 688 (700-2)	700-2¼ 688 (700-2¼)

TDZ/CL Rwys 4R,
13L and 22L
REIL Rwys 4L
and 14
MIRL Rwy 14-32
HIRL Rwys 4L-22R,
4R-22L, 13R-31L, and 13L-31R

Rwy 14-32
2560 X 75

197

TDZE
12

325° to
JFK VORTAC

Knots	60	90	120	150	180
Min:Sec					

VOR RWY 31L

40°38'N-73°46'W

NEW YORK, NEW YORK
NEW YORK/JOHN F. KENNEDY INTL (JFK)

189

Not for use in Navigation

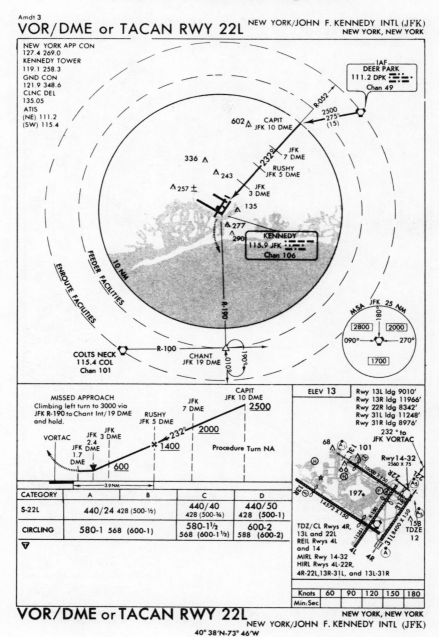

Amdt 3

VOR/DME or TACAN RWY 22L
NEW YORK/JOHN F. KENNEDY INTL (JFK)
NEW YORK, NEW YORK

NEW YORK APP CON
127.4 269.0
KENNEDY TOWER
119.1 258.3
GND CON
121.9 348.6
CLNC DEL
135.05
ATIS
(NE) 111.2
(SW) 115.4

IAF
DEER PARK
111.2 DPK
Chan 49

R-052

2500
275°
(15)

602 CAPIT
JFK 10 DME

336

243

257 ±

JFK
7 DME

RUSHY
JFK 5 DME

JFK
3 DME

135

277
290

KENNEDY
115.9 JFK
Chan 106

232°

FEEDER FACILITIES

ENROUTE FACILITIES

10 NM

R-190

MSA JFK 25 NM
180°
2800   2000
090°   270°
1700

COLTS NECK
115.4 COL
Chan 101

R-100

CHANT
JFK 19 DME

R-010

280°

ELEV 13

Rwy 13L ldg 9010'
Rwy 13R ldg 11966'
Rwy 22R ldg 8342'
Rwy 31L ldg 11248'
Rwy 31R ldg 8976'

232° to
JFK VORTAC

MISSED APPROACH
Climbing left turn to 3000 via
JFK R-190 to Chant Int/19 DME
and hold.

CAPIT
JFK 10 DME
2500

JFK
7 DME

RUSHY
JFK 5 DME

232°   2000

VORTAC

JFK 3 DME

JFK
2.4
DME

JFK
1.7
DME

1400

600

Procedure Turn NA

3.9NM

CATEGORY	A	B	C	D
S-22L	440/24 428 (500-½)		440/40 428 (500-¾)	440/50 428 (500-1)
CIRCLING	580-1 568 (600-1)		580-1½ 568 (600-1½)	600-2 588 (600-2)

68
101
66
197

14572 X 150

11800 X 150

10000 X 200

Rwy 14-32
2560 x 75

TDZ/CL Rwys 4R,
13L and 22L
REIL Rwys 4L
and 14
MIRL Rwy 14-32
HIRL Rwys 4L-22R,
4R-22L, 13R-31L, and 13L-31R

TDZE
12

4L
4R

Knots	60	90	120	150	180
Min:Sec					

VOR/DME or TACAN RWY 22L
NEW YORK, NEW YORK
NEW YORK/JOHN F. KENNEDY INTL (JFK)
40° 38'N-73° 46'W

Not for use in Navigation

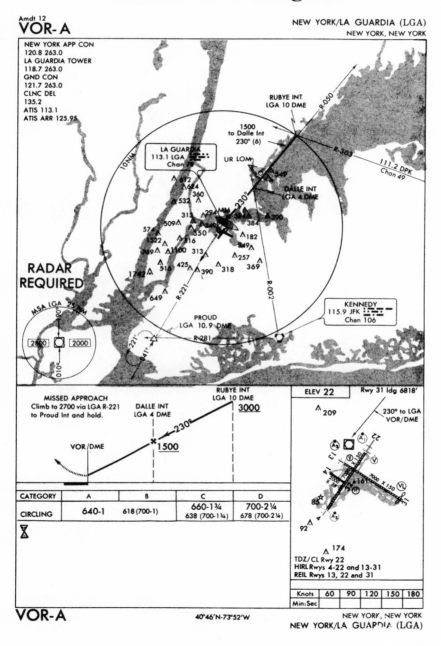

Amdt 12
VOR- A

NEW YORK/LA GUARDIA (LGA)
NEW YORK, NEW YORK

NEW YORK APP CON
120.8 263.0
LA GUARDIA TOWER
118.7 263.0
GND CON
121.7 263.0
CLNC DEL
135.2
ATIS 113.1
ATIS ARR 125.95

RUBYE INT
LGA 10 DME

1500
to Dalle Int
230° (6)

R-050

R-303

111.2 DPK
Chan 49

LA GUARDIA
113.1 LGA
Chan 78

UR LOM

349

DALLE INT
LGA 4 DME

R-390

612
624
360
532
313
294 MM
509
350
384
571
522
316
182
769
1100
313
349
1742
516
425
390
318
257
369
649
R-221
R-002

RADAR
REQUIRED

MSA LGA 25 NM

2800   2000

010°

PROUD
LGA 10.9 DME

R-281

221°
141°

KENNEDY
115.9 JFK
Chan 106

MISSED APPROACH
Climb to 2700 via LGA R-221
to Proud Int and hold.

RUBYE INT
LGA 10 DME

DALLE INT
LGA 4 DME

3000

VOR/DME

230°

1500

ELEV 22

Rwy 31 ldg 6818'

209

230° to LGA
VOR/DME

22

13

7000 X 150

191

85

92

174

TDZ/CL Rwy 22
HIRL Rwys 4-22 and 13-31
REIL Rwys 13, 22 and 31

CATEGORY	A	B	C	D
CIRCLING	640-1	618 (700-1)	660-1¾ 638 (700-1¾)	700-2¼ 678 (700-2¼)

Knots	60	90	120	150	180
Min:Sec					

VOR-A

40°46'N-73°52'W

NEW YORK, NEW YORK
NEW YORK/LA GUARDIA (LGA)

191

Not for use in Navigation

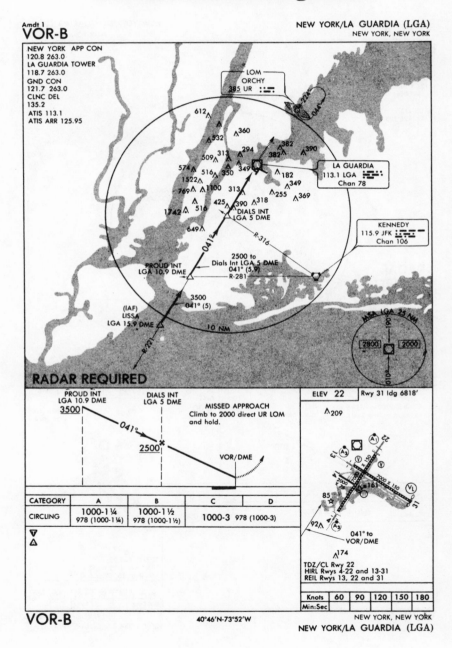

NEW YORK/LA GUARDIA (LGA)
NEW YORK, NEW YORK

NEW YORK APP CON
120.8 263.0
LA GUARDIA TOWER
118.7 263.0
GND CON
121.7 263.0
CLNC DEL
135.2
ATIS 113.1
ATIS ARR 125.95

LOM
ORCHY
385 UR

LA GUARDIA
113.1 LGA
Chan 78

KENNEDY
115.9 JFK
Chan 106

DIALS INT
LGA 5 DME

2500 to
Dials Int LGA 5 DME
041° (5.9)
R-281

PROUD INT
LGA 10.9 DME

3500
041° (5)

(IAF)
LISSA
LGA 15.9 DME

10 NM

R-316

MSA LGA 25 NM
2800   2000

RADAR REQUIRED

PROUD INT
LGA 10.9 DME
3500

DIALS INT
LGA 5 DME

MISSED APPROACH
Climb to 2000 direct UR LOM
and hold.

041°

2500

VOR/DME

ELEV 22   Rwy 31 ldg 6818'

209

041° to
VOR/DME

85

92

174

TDZ/CL Rwy 22
HIRL Rwys 4-22 and 13-31
REIL Rwys 13, 22 and 31

CATEGORY	A	B	C	D
CIRCLING	1000-1¼ 978 (1000-1¼)	1000-1½ 978 (1000-1½)	1000-3 978 (1000-3)	

Knots	60	90	120	150	180
Min:Sec					

40°46'N-73°52'W

NEW YORK, NEW YORK
NEW YORK/LA GUARDIA (LGA)

192

Not for use in Navigation

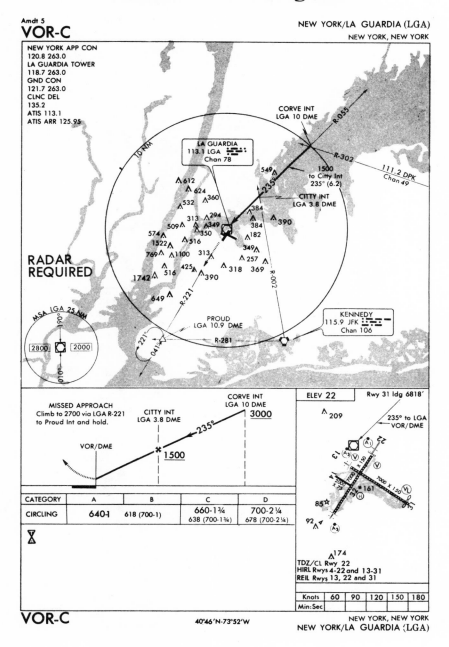

VOR-C

NEW YORK/LA GUARDIA (LGA)
NEW YORK, NEW YORK

NEW YORK APP CON
120.8 263.0
LA GUARDIA TOWER
118.7 263.0
GND CON
121.7 263.0
CLNC DEL
135.2
ATIS 113.1
ATIS ARR 125.95

10 NM

CORVE INT
LGA 10 DME

R-055

R-302

111.2 DPK
Chan 49

LA GUARDIA
113.1 LGA
Chan 78

549

1500
to Citty Int
235° (6.2)

235°

CITTY INT
LGA 3.8 DME

612
624
360
532
294
313
349
509
350
574
516
1522
769
1100
313
425
516
390

384
384
390
182
349
257
318
369

R-002

RADAR
REQUIRED

1742

649

R-221

PROUD
LGA 10.9 DME

R-281

KENNEDY
115.9 JFK
Chan 106

MSA LGA 25 NM

2800 2000

221°
041°

010°
190°

MISSED APPROACH
Climb to 2700 via LGA R-221
to Proud Int and hold.

CORVE INT
LGA 10 DME

CITTY INT
LGA 3.8 DME

3000

235°

VOR/DME

1500

CATEGORY	A	B	C	D
CIRCLING	640-1	618 (700-1)	660-1¾ 638 (700-1¾)	700-2¼ 678 (700-2¼)

ELEV 22   Rwy 31 ldg 6818'

209

235° to LGA
VOR/DME

161

85
92

174

TDZ/CL Rwy 22
HIRL Rwys 4-22 and 13-31
REIL Rwys 13, 22 and 31

Knots	60	90	120	150	180
Min:Sec					

VOR-C

40°46'N-73°52'W

NEW YORK, NEW YORK
NEW YORK/LA GUARDIA (LGA)

Not for use in Navigation

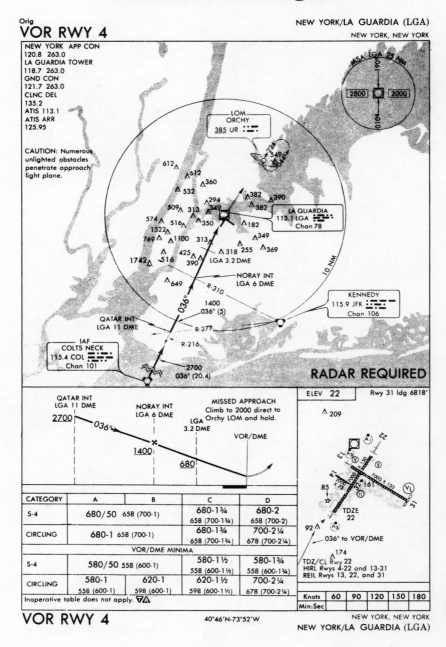

Orig
VOR RWY 4

NEW YORK/LA GUARDIA (LGA)
NEW YORK, NEW YORK

NEW YORK APP CON
120.8 263.0
LA GUARDIA TOWER
118.7 263.0
GND CON
121.7 263.0
CLNC DEL
135.2
ATIS 113.1
ATIS ARR
125.95

CAUTION: Numerous
unlighted obstacles
penetrate approach
light plane.

MSA LGA 25 NM
2800   2000

LOM
ORCHY
385 UR

LA GUARDIA
113.1 LGA
Chan 78

612   612
360
532
509   313   294   382   390
349   382
574   516   350   182
1522
769   1100   313   349
318   255   369
1742   516   425
390   LGA 3.2 DME

NORAY INT
LGA 6 DME

KENNEDY
115.9 JFK
Chan 106

036°
R-310
1400
036° (5)
R-277

QATAR INT
LGA 11 DME
R-216

IAF
COLTS NECK
115.4 COL
Chan 101

2700
036° (20.4)

10 NM

RADAR REQUIRED

QATAR INT LGA 11 DME	NORAY INT LGA 6 DME	MISSED APPROACH Climb to 2000 direct to Orchy LOM and hold.	

2700   036°   1400   680   LGA 3.2 DME   VOR/DME

ELEV 22   Rwy 31 ldg 6818'
△ 209

CATEGORY	A	B	C	D
S-4	680/50 658 (700-1)		680-1¾ 658 (700-1¾)	680-2 658 (700-2)
CIRCLING	680-1 658 (700-1)		680-1¾ 658 (700-1¾)	700-2¼ 678 (700-2¼)
VOR/DME MINIMA				
S-4	580/50 558 (600-1)		580-1½ 558 (600-1½)	580-1¾ 558 (600-1¾)
CIRCLING	580-1 558 (600-1)	620-1 598 (600-1)	620-1½ 598 (600-1½)	700-2¼ 678 (700-2¼)

Inoperative table does not apply. ▽△

TDZE 22
85
92   036° to VOR/DME
174
TDZ/CL Rwy 22
HIRL Rwys 4-22 and 13-31
REIL Rwys 13, 22, and 31

Knots	60	90	120	150	180
Min:Sec					

VOR RWY 4

40°46'N-73°52'W

NEW YORK, NEW YORK
NEW YORK/LA GUARDIA (LGA)

Not for use in Navigation

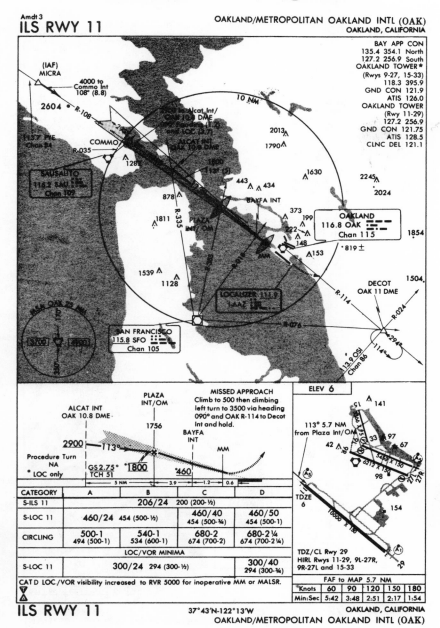

Not for use in Navigation

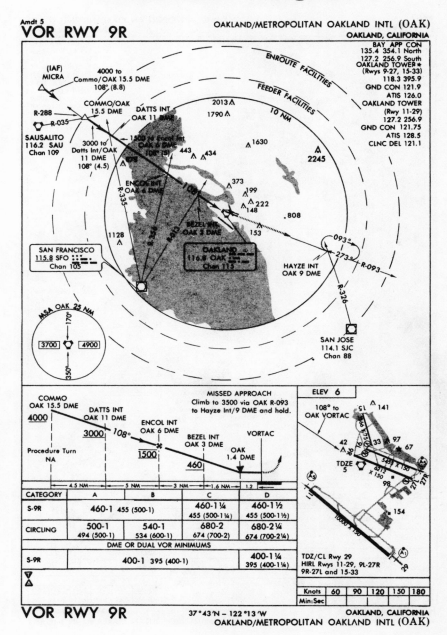

Not for use in Navigation

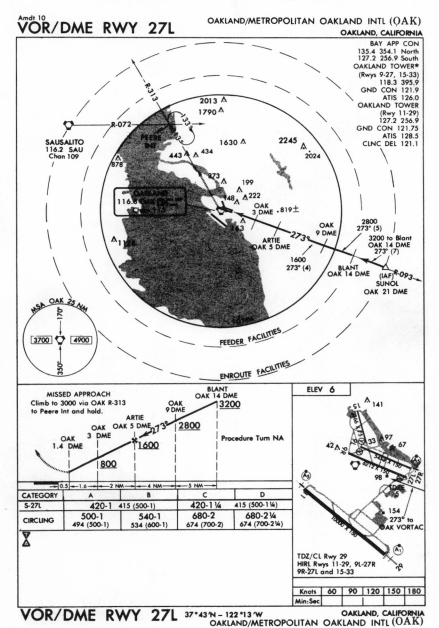

Amdt 10
VOR/DME RWY 27L

OAKLAND/METROPOLITAN OAKLAND INTL (OAK)
OAKLAND, CALIFORNIA

BAY APP CON
135.4 354.1 North
127.2 256.9 South
OAKLAND TOWER*
(Rwys 9-27, 15-33)
118.3 395.9
GND CON 121.9
ATIS 126.0
OAKLAND TOWER
(Rwy 11-29)
127.2 256.9
GND CON 121.75
ATIS 128.5
CLNC DEL 121.1

CATEGORY	A	B	C	D
S-27L	420-1	415 (500-1)	420-1¼	415 (500-1¼)
CIRCLING	500-1 494 (500-1)	540-1 534 (600-1)	680-2 674 (700-2)	680-2¼ 674 (700-2¼)

ELEV 6

TDZ/CL Rwy 29
HIRL Rwys 11-29, 9L-27R
9R-27L and 15-33

Knots	60	90	120	150	180
Min:Sec					

VOR/DME RWY 27L
37°43'N – 122°13'W

OAKLAND, CALIFORNIA
OAKLAND/METROPOLITAN OAKLAND INTL (OAK)

197

Not for use in Navigation

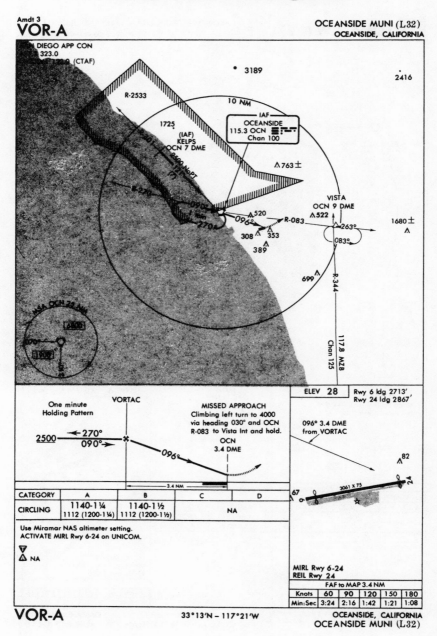

Amdt 3
VOR-A

OCEANSIDE MUNI (L32)
OCEANSIDE, CALIFORNIA

DIEGO APP CON
323.0
(CTAF)

R-2533

10 NM

3189

2416

IAF
OCEANSIDE
115.3 OCN
Chan 100

1725

(IAF)
KELPS
OCN 7 DME

∧ 763 ±

R-270

096°

270°

VISTA
OCN 9 DME
∧ 522

R-083

263°

1680 ±
∧

083°

∧ 520

308   ∧ 353

389

699

R-344

117.8 MZB
Chan 125

MSA OCN 25 NM

4000

1900

ELEV 28

Rwy 6 ldg 2713'
Rwy 24 ldg 2867'

One minute
Holding Pattern

VORTAC

MISSED APPROACH
Climbing left turn to 4000
via heading 030° and OCN
R-083 to Vista Int and hold.

096° 3.4 DME
from VORTAC

2500 ←270°
090°

096°

OCN
3.4 DME

∧ 82

3.4 NM

67

3061 X 75

CATEGORY	A	B	C	D
CIRCLING	1140-1¼ 1112 (1200-1¼)	1140-1½ 1112 (1200-1½)	NA	

Use Miramar NAS altimeter setting.
ACTIVATE MIRL Rwy 6-24 on UNICOM.

▽
△ NA

MIRL Rwy 6-24
REIL Rwy 24

FAF to MAP 3.4 NM

Knots	60	90	120	150	180
Min:Sec	3:24	2:16	1:42	1:21	1:08

VOR-A

33°13'N – 117°21'W

OCEANSIDE, CALIFORNIA
OCEANSIDE MUNI (L32)

Not for use in Navigation

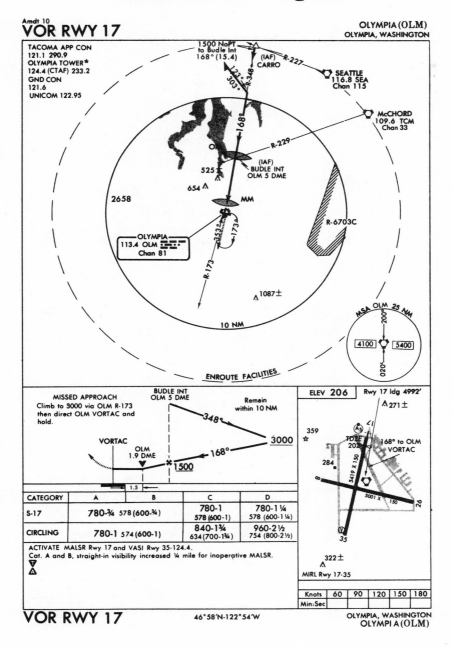

Not for use in Navigation

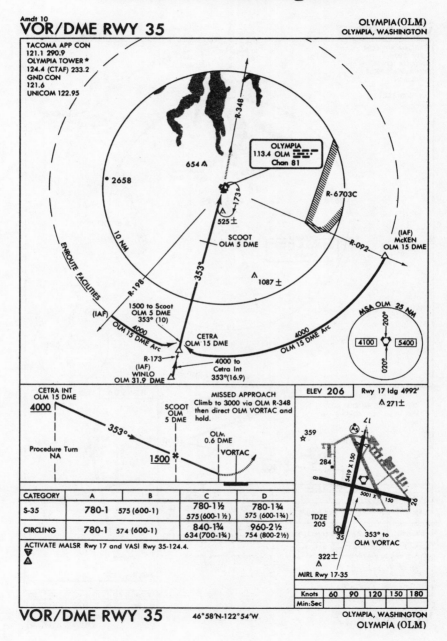

Amdt 10

VOR/DME RWY 35

OLYMPIA (OLM)
OLYMPIA, WASHINGTON

TACOMA APP CON
121.1 290.9
OLYMPIA TOWER *
124.4 (CTAF) 233.2
GND CON
121.6
UNICOM 122.95

R-348

OLYMPIA
113.4 OLM
Chan 81

654 ∧

• 2658

173 →

∧ 525 ±

R-6703C

SCOOT
OLM 5 DME

353°

R-092

(IAF)
McKEN
OLM 15 DME

10 NM

R-198

ENROUTE FACILITIES

∧ 1087 ±

MSA OLM 25 NM

(IAF)

1500 to Scoot
OLM 5 DME
353° (10)

OLM 15 DME Arc
4000

CETRA
OLM 15 DME

4000
OLM 15 DME Arc

000°
200°
4100 | 5400
020°

R-173
(IAF)
WINLO
OLM 31.9 DME

4000 to
Cetra Int
353° (16.9)

CETRA INT OLM 15 DME		MISSED APPROACH Climb to 3000 via OLM R-348 then direct OLM VORTAC and hold.	ELEV 206	Rwy 17 ldg 4992'

4000

353°

SCOOT
OLM
5 DME

OLM
0.6 DME

VORTAC

Procedure Turn
NA

1500

∧ 271 ±

359 ☆

284

5419 X 150

17

5001 X 150

8

26

TDZE
205

35

353° to
OLM VORTAC

322 ±
∧

MIRL Rwy 17-35

CATEGORY	A	B	C	D
S-35	780-1	575 (600-1)	780-1½ 575 (600-1½)	780-1¾ 575 (600-1¾)
CIRCLING	780-1	574 (600-1)	840-1¾ 634 (700-1¾)	960-2½ 754 (800-2½)

ACTIVATE MALSR Rwy 17 and VASI Rwy 35-124.4.

Knots	60	90	120	150	180
Min:Sec					

VOR/DME RWY 35

46°58'N-122°54'W

OLYMPIA, WASHINGTON
OLYMPIA (OLM)

Not for use in Navigation

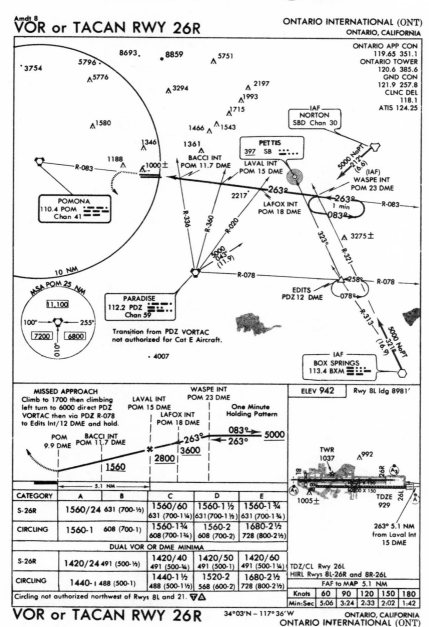

Amdt 8
VOR or TACAN RWY 26R

ONTARIO INTERNATIONAL (ONT)
ONTARIO, CALIFORNIA

ONTARIO APP CON
119.65 351.1
ONTARIO TOWER
120.6 385.6
GND CON
121.9 257.8
CLNC DEL
118.1
ATIS 124.25

Not for use in Navigation

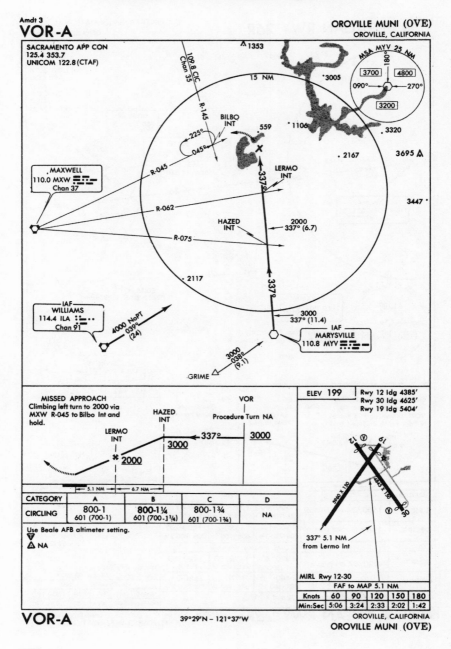

VOR-A

OROVILLE MUNI (OVE)
OROVILLE, CALIFORNIA

SACRAMENTO APP CON
125.4 353.7
UNICOM 122.8 (CTAF)

108.8 CIC
Chan 35

MSA MYV 25 NM

180°
3700 4800
090° ⊕ 270°
3200

△ 1353

• 3005

15 NM

R-145

BILBO
INT

• 559

337°

LERMO
INT

• 1106

• 3320

• 2167

3695 △

-225°
-045°

MAXWELL
110.0 MXW
Chan 37

R-045

R-062

HAZED
INT

2000
337° (6.7)

3447 •

R-075

337°

• 2117

IAF
WILLIAMS
114.4 ILA
Chan 91

4000 NoPT
039°
(24)

337°

3000
337° (11.4)

IAF
MARYSVILLE
110.8 MYV

3000
039°
(9.1)

GRIME

MISSED APPROACH
Climbing left turn to 2000 via
MXW R-045 to Bilbo Int and
hold.

VOR
Procedure Turn NA

HAZED
INT

LERMO
INT

337° 3000

3000

✳ 2000

├─ 5.1 NM ─┤├─ 6.7 NM ─┤

ELEV 199 | Rwy 12 ldg 4385'
Rwy 30 ldg 4625'
Rwy 19 ldg 5404'

337° 5.1 NM
from Lermo Int

CATEGORY	A	B	C	D
CIRCLING	800-1 601 (700-1)	800-1¼ 601 (700-1¼)	800-1¾ 601 (700-1¾)	NA

Use Beale AFB altimeter setting.
▽
△ NA

MIRL Rwy 12-30

FAF to MAP 5.1 NM

Knots	60	90	120	150	180
Min:Sec	5:06	3:24	2:33	2:02	1:42

VOR-A

39°29'N – 121°37'W

OROVILLE, CALIFORNIA
OROVILLE MUNI (OVE)

Not for use in Navigation

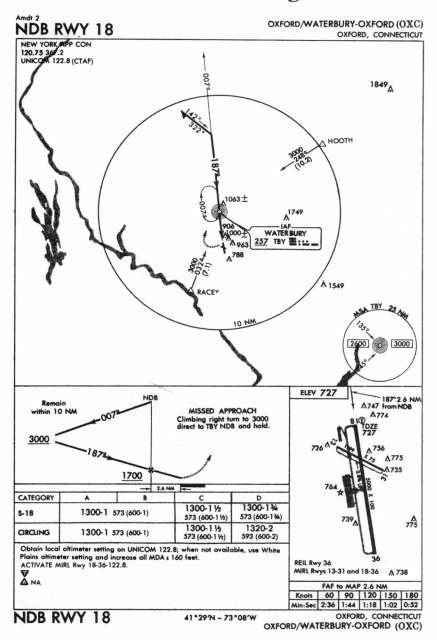

Not for use in Navigation

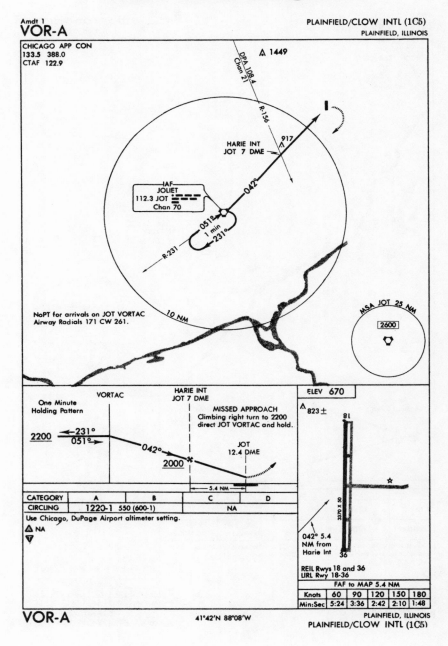

Amdt 1

VOR-A

PLAINFIELD/CLOW INTL (1C5)
PLAINFIELD, ILLINOIS

CHICAGO APP CON
133.5 388.0
CTAF 122.9

△ 1449

DPA 108.4
Chan 21

R-156

HARIE INT
JOT 7 DME

917 △

042°

IAF
JOLIET
112.3 JOT
Chan 70

051°
1 min
231°

R-231

NoPT for arrivals on JOT VORTAC
Airway Radials 171 CW 261.

10 NM

MSA JOT 25 NM

2600

VORTAC

HARIE INT
JOT 7 DME

ELEV 670

△ 823±

One Minute
Holding Pattern

MISSED APPROACH
Climbing right turn to 2200
direct JOT VORTAC and hold.

2200 ←231°
051°→

042°

JOT
12.4 DME

2000

5.4 NM

CATEGORY	A	B	C	D
CIRCLING	1220-1	550 (600-1)	NA	

Use Chicago, DuPage Airport altimeter setting.

△ NA
▽

042° 5.4
NM from
Harie Int

REIL Rwys 18 and 36
LIRL Rwy 18-36

FAF to MAP 5.4 NM					
Knots	60	90	120	150	180
Min:Sec	5:24	3:36	2:42	2:10	1:48

VOR-A

41°42'N 88°08'W

PLAINFIELD, ILLINOIS
PLAINFIELD/CLOW INTL (1C5)

Not for use in Navigation

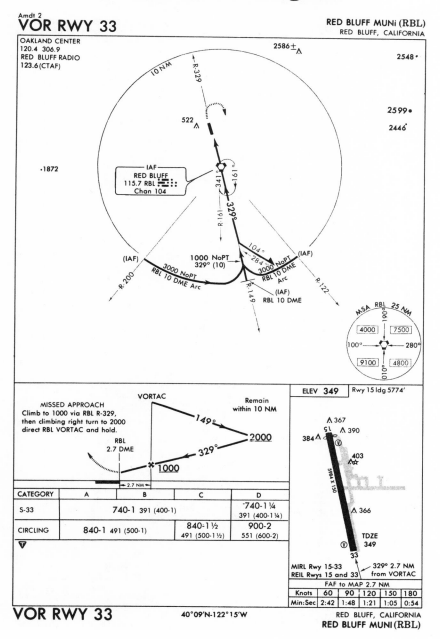

Amdt 2
VOR RWY 33

RED BLUFF MUNi (RBL)
RED BLUFF, CALIFORNIA

OAKLAND CENTER
120.4 306.9
RED BLUFF RADIO
123.6(CTAF)

2586±

2548•

10 NM
R-329

522

2599•

2446•

•1872

—— IAF ——
RED BLUFF
115.7 RBL
Chan 104

R-341°
R-191°
329°
R-161

(IAF)

R-200
3000 NoPT
RBL 10 DME Arc

1000 NoPT
329° (10)

104°
284°

3000 NoPT
RBL 10 DME
Arc

(IAF)

R-149

(IAF)
RBL 10 DME

R-122

MSA RBL 25 NM

| 4000 | 7500 |
| 9100 | 4800 |

100° — 280°

ELEV 349   Rwy 15 ldg 5774'

MISSED APPROACH
Climb to 1000 via RBL R-329,
then climbing right turn to 2000
direct RBL VORTAC and hold.

VORTAC

149°

Remain
within 10 NM

2000

329°

RBL
2.7 DME

1000

2.7 NM

∧ 367
∧ 15
∧ 390
384 ∧
403
∧☆

5984 X 150

∧ 366

TDZE
349

33

MIRL Rwy 15-33
REIL Rwys 15 and 33

329° 2.7 NM
from VORTAC

CATEGORY	A	B	C	D
S-33	740-1 391 (400-1)			740-1 ¼ 391 (400-1¼)
CIRCLING	840-1 491 (500-1)		840-1½ 491 (500-1½)	900-2 551 (600-2)

FAF to MAP 2.7 NM

Knots	60	90	120	150	180
Min:Sec	2:42	1:48	1:21	1:05	0:54

VOR RWY 33

40°09'N-122°15'W

RED BLUFF, CALIFORNIA
RED BLUFF MUNI (RBL)

Not for use in Navigation

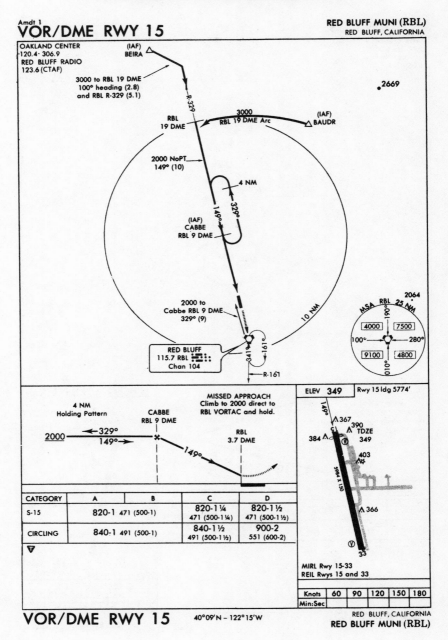

Amdt 1
VOR/DME RWY 15

RED BLUFF MUNI (RBL)
RED BLUFF, CALIFORNIA

OAKLAND CENTER
-120.4 · 306.9
RED BLUFF RADIO
123.6 (CTAF)

(IAF)
BEIRA

3000 to RBL 19 DME
100° heading (2.8)
and RBL R-329 (5.1)

R-329

•2669

RBL
19 DME

3000
RBL 19 DME Arc

(IAF)
BAUDR

2000 NoPT
149° (10)

4 NM

329°

149°

(IAF)
CABBE
RBL 9 DME

2000 to
Cabbe RBL 9 DME
329° (9)

10 NM

RED BLUFF
115.7 RBL
Chan 104

341°

161°

R-161

2064

MSA RBL 25 NM
190°
4000 | 7500
100° — 280°
9100 | 4800
010°

4 NM
Holding Pattern

CABBE
RBL 9 DME

←329°
2000
149°→

×

149°

RBL
3.7 DME

MISSED APPROACH
Climb to 2000 direct to
RBL VORTAC and hold.

ELEV 349 | Rwy 15 ldg 5774'

149°

∧367
390
TDZE
349

384 ∧

403
∧

5984 X 150

∧366

33

CATEGORY	A	B	C	D
S-15	820-1 471 (500-1)		820-1¼ 471 (500-1¼)	820-1½ 471 (500-1½)
CIRCLING	840-1 491 (500-1)		840-1½ 491 (500-1½)	900-2 551 (600-2)

MIRL Rwy 15-33
REIL Rwys 15 and 33

Knots	60	90	120	150	180
Min:Sec					

VOR/DME RWY 15

40°09'N – 122°15'W

RED BLUFF, CALIFORNIA
RED BLUFF MUNI (RBL)

Not for use in Navigation

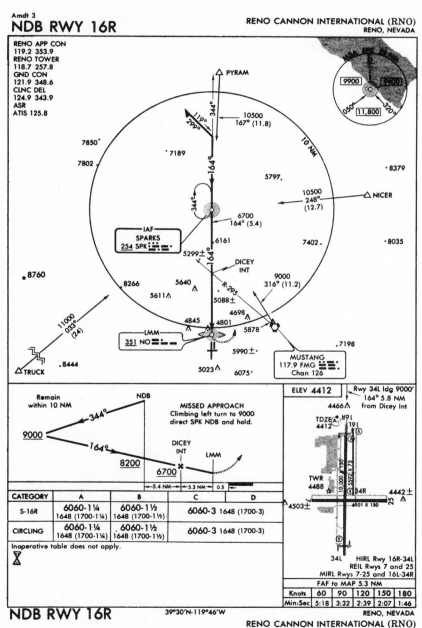

Amdt 3

NDB RWY 16R

RENO CANNON INTERNATIONAL (RNO)
RENO, NEVADA

RENO APP CON
119.2 353.9
RENO TOWER
118.7 257.8
GND CON
121.9 348.6
CLNC DEL
124.9 343.9
ASR
ATIS 125.8

NDB RWY 16R

39°30'N-119°46'W

RENO, NEVADA
RENO CANNON INTERNATIONAL (RNO)

207

Not for use in Navigation

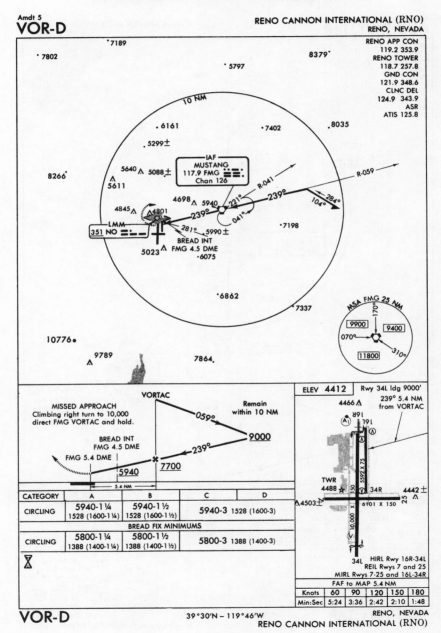

Not for use in Navigation

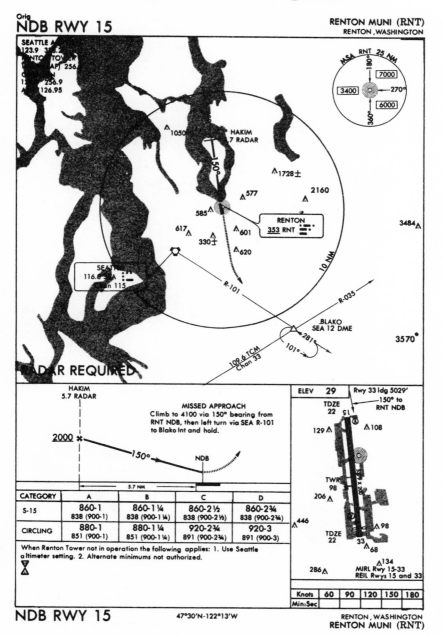

Orig
NDB RWY 15

RENTON MUNI (RNT)
RENTON, WASHINGTON

SEATTLE A
123.9
RENTON TOWER
(APP) 256.
12   256.9
A   126.95

MSA RNT 25 NM
180° 7000
3400   270°
360° 6000

1050
HAKIM
.7 RADAR
150°
1728±
577   2160
585
RENTON
353 RNT
617   601
330±   620
3484
R-101
SEA
116.   A
n 115
R-035
BLAKO
SEA 12 DME
281
3570°
109.6 TCM
Chan 33   101°

RADAR REQUIRED

HAKIM
5.7 RADAR

MISSED APPROACH
Climb to 4100 via 150° bearing from
RNT NDB, then left turn via SEA R-101
to Blako Int and hold.

2000
150°
NDB

5.7 NM

CATEGORY	A	B	C	D
S-15	860-1 838 (900-1)	860-1¼ 838 (900-1¼)	860-2½ 838 (900-2½)	860-2¾ 838 (900-2¾)
CIRCLING	880-1 851 (900-1)	880-1¼ 851 (900-1¼)	920-2¾ 891 (900-2¾)	920-3 891 (900-3)

When Renton Tower not in operation the following applies: 1. Use Seattle
altimeter setting. 2. Alternate minimums not authorized.

ELEV 29   Rwy 33 ldg 5029'
TDZE   150° to
22   RNT NDB
129   108
TWR
98
206
446
TDZE
22   33
68
134
286   MIRL Rwy 15-33
REIL Rwys 15 and 33

Knots	60	90	120	150	180
Min:Sec					

NDB RWY 15   47°30'N-122°13'W   RENTON, WASHINGTON
RENTON MUNI (RNT)

Not for use in Navigation

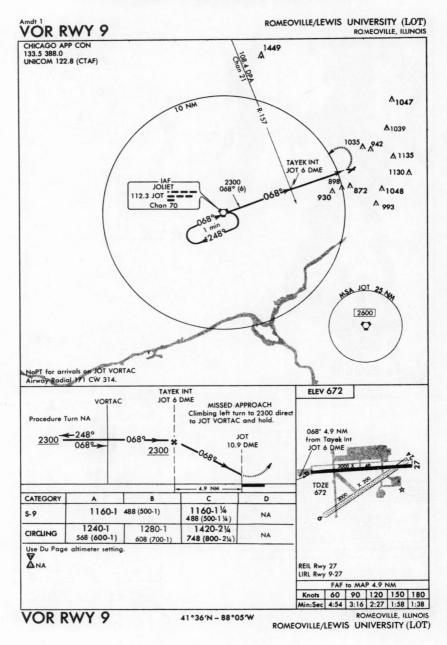

VOR RWY 9

ROMEOVILLE/LEWIS UNIVERSITY (LOT)
ROMEOVILLE, ILLINOIS

CHICAGO APP CON
133.5 388.0
UNICOM 122.8 (CTAF)

108.4 DPA
Chan 21

△ 1449

10 NM

R-157

△ 1047

△ 1039

1035 △ 942
△ △

△ 1135

1130 △

TAYEK INT
JOT 6 DME

IAF
JOLIET
112.3 JOT
Chan 70

2300
068° (6)

068°

068°
1 min
248°

898
△ △ 872 △ 1048
930 △ 993

MSA JOT 25 NM

2600

NoPT for arrivals on JOT VORTAC
Airway Radial 171 CW 314.

	VORTAC	TAYEK INT JOT 6 DME	MISSED APPROACH Climbing left turn to 2300 direct to JOT VORTAC and hold.	ELEV 672

Procedure Turn NA

2300 ←—248°
068°→

068°→

2300

JOT
10.9 DME

068°

4.9 NM

068° 4.9 NM
from Tayek Int
JOT 6 DME

3000 X 48

TDZE
672

3000 X 200

CATEGORY	A	B	C	D
S-9	1160-1 488 (500-1)		1160-1¼ 488 (500-1¼)	NA
CIRCLING	1240-1 568 (600-1)	1280-1 608 (700-1)	1420-2¼ 748 (800-2¼)	NA

Use Du Page altimeter setting.

▽ △ NA

REIL Rwy 27
LIRL Rwy 9-27

FAF to MAP 4.9 NM					
Knots	60	90	120	150	180
Min:Sec	4:54	3:16	2:27	1:58	1:38

VOR RWY 9

41°36'N – 88°05'W

ROMEOVILLE, ILLINOIS
ROMEOVILLE/LEWIS UNIVERSITY (LOT)

Not for use in Navigation

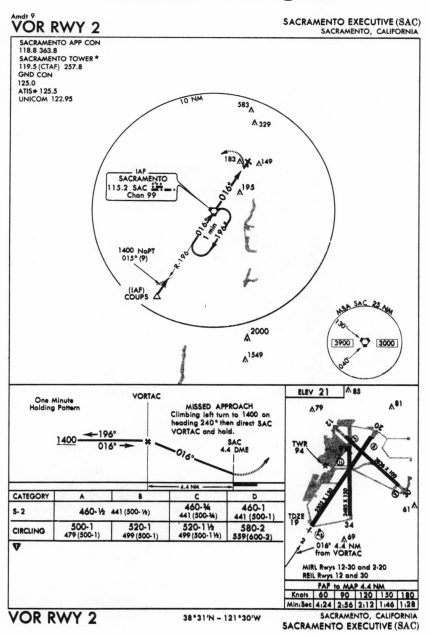

Amdt 9

VOR RWY 2

SACRAMENTO EXECUTIVE (SAC)
SACRAMENTO, CALIFORNIA

SACRAMENTO APP CON
118.8 363.8
SACRAMENTO TOWER *
119.5 (CTAF) 257.8
GND CON
125.0
ATIS * 125.5
UNICOM 122.95

10 NM

583 ∧
∧ 329

IAF
SACRAMENTO
115.2 SAC
Chan 99

183 ∧ ✕ ∧149

016°

∧195

016°
1 min
196°

1400 NoPT
015° (9)

R-196

(IAF)
COUPS △

MSA SAC 25 NM

30°

3900   3000

040°

∧ 2000

∧ 1549

One Minute
Holding Pattern

VORTAC

MISSED APPROACH
Climbing left turn to 1400 on
heading 240° then direct SAC
VORTAC and hold.

1400 ← 196°
016° →

016°

SAC
4.4 DME

4.4 NM

ELEV 21   ∧ 85

∧ 79   ∧ 81

TWR
94

TDZE
19

34

61 ∧

016° 4.4 NM
from VORTAC

∧ 69

MIRL Rwys 12-30 and 2-20
REIL Rwys 12 and 30

CATEGORY	A	B	C	D
S-2	460-½ 441 (500-½)		460-¾ 441 (500-¾)	460-1 441 (500-1)
CIRCLING	500-1 479 (500-1)	520-1 499 (500-1)	520-1½ 499 (500-1½)	580-2 559 (600-2)

FAP to MAP 4.4 NM					
Knots	60	90	120	150	180
Min:Sec	4:24	2:56	2:12	1:46	1:28

VOR RWY 2

38°31'N – 121°30'W

SACRAMENTO, CALIFORNIA
SACRAMENTO EXECUTIVE (SAC)

211

Not for use in Navigation

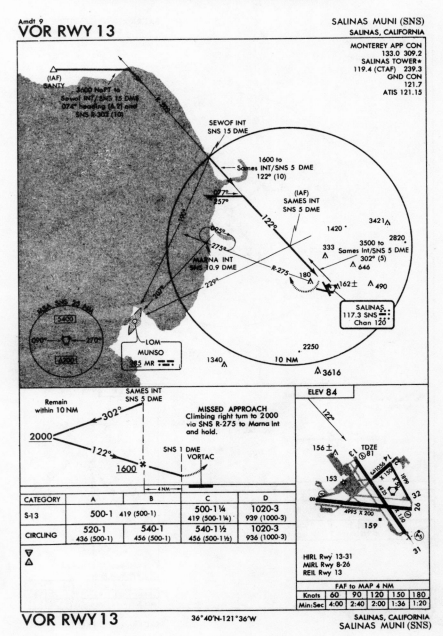

Amdt 9
VOR RWY 13

SALINAS MUNI (SNS)
SALINAS, CALIFORNIA

MONTEREY APP CON
133.0 309.2
SALINAS TOWER★
119.4 (CTAF) 239.3
GND CON
121.7
ATIS 121.15

(IAF)
SANTY

3600 NoPT to
Sewof INT/SNS 15 DME
074° heading (6.2) and
SNS R-303 (10)

SEWOF INT
SNS 15 DME

1600 to
Sames INT/SNS 5 DME
122° (10)

077°
257°

(IAF)
SAMES INT
SNS 5 DME

3421

1420

2820

333

3500 to
Sames Int/SNS 5 DME
302° (5)

646

180

162±

490

095°

275°

MARNA INT
SNS 10.9 DME

R-275

229°

MSA SNS 25 NM

5400

090°   270°

6200

LOM
MUNSO

385 MR

SALINAS
117.3 SNS
Chan 120

2250

1340

10 NM

3616

Remain
within 10 NM

SAMES INT
SNS 5 DME

302°

2000

122°

1600

SNS 1 DME
VORTAC

4 NM

MISSED APPROACH
Climbing right turn to 2000
via SNS R-275 to Marna Int
and hold.

ELEV 84

122°

156±

13

TDZE
81

153

14

1899

8

4825

32

4995 X 200

26

159

31

HIRL Rwy 13-31
MIRL Rwy 8-26
REIL Rwy 13

CATEGORY	A	B	C	D
S-13	500-1	419 (500-1)	500-1¼ 419 (500-1¼)	1020-3 939 (1000-3)
CIRCLING	520-1 436 (500-1)	540-1 456 (500-1)	540-1½ 456 (500-1½)	1020-3 936 (1000-3)

FAF to MAP 4 NM					
Knots	60	90	120	150	180
Min:Sec	4:00	2:40	2:00	1:36	1:20

VOR RWY 13

36°40'N-121°36'W

SALINAS, CALIFORNIA
SALINAS MUNI (SNS)

Not for use in Navigation

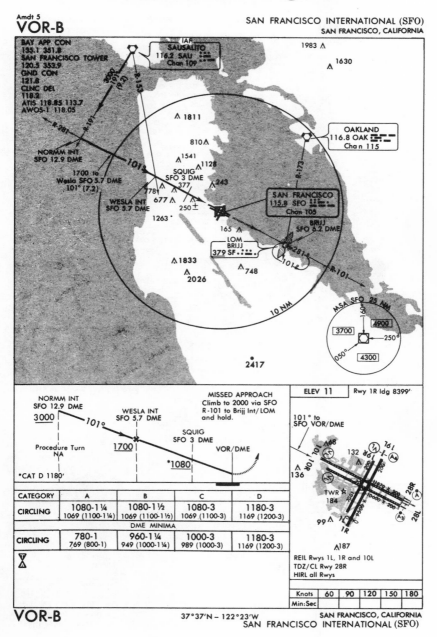

Not for use in Navigation

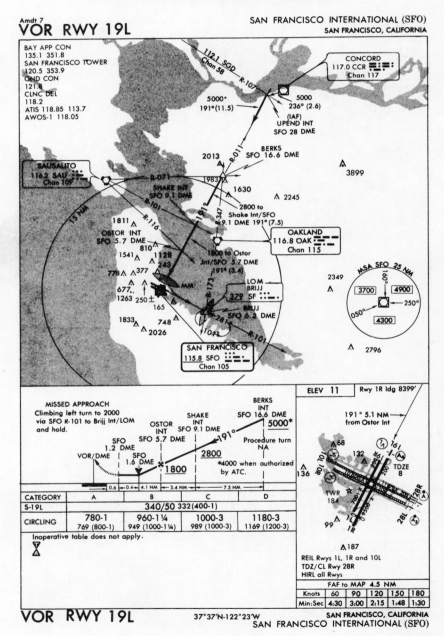

Not for use in Navigation

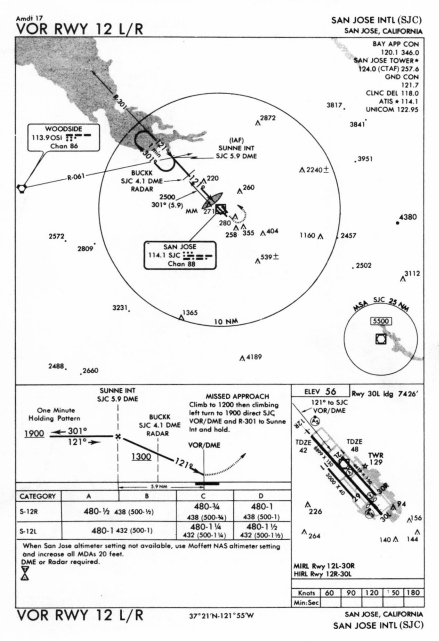

Amdt 17

VOR RWY 12 L/R

SAN JOSE INTL (SJC)
SAN JOSE, CALIFORNIA

BAY APP CON
120.1 346.0
SAN JOSE TOWER *
124.0 (CTAF) 257.6
GND CON
121.7
CLNC DEL 118.0
ATIS * 114.1
UNICOM 122.95

WOODSIDE
113.9 OSI
Chan 86

(IAF)
SUNNE INT
SJC 5.9 DME

BUCKK
SJC 4.1 DME
RADAR

2500
301° (5.9)

SAN JOSE
114.1 SJC
Chan 88

MSA SJC 25 NM

5500

10 NM

| | SUNNE INT SJC 5.9 DME | BUCKK SJC 4.1 DME RADAR | MISSED APPROACH Climb to 1200 then climbing left turn to 1900 direct SJC VOR/DME and R-301 to Sunne Int and hold. | ELEV 56 | Rwy 30L ldg 7426' |

One Minute
Holding Pattern

1900 ← 301°
121° →

1300

VOR/DME

5.9 NM

CATEGORY	A	B	C	D
S-12R	480-½ 438 (500-½)		480-¾ 438 (500-¾)	480-1 438 (500-1)
S-12L	480-1 432 (500-1)		480-1¼ 432 (500-1¼)	480-1½ 432 (500-1½)

When San Jose altimeter setting not available, use Moffett NAS altimeter setting and increase all MDAs 20 feet.
DME or Radar required.

ELEV 56   Rwy 30L ldg 7426'
121° to SJC
VOR/DME

TDZE 42
TDZE 48
TWR 129

MIRL Rwy 12L-30R
HIRL Rwy 12R-30L

Knots	60	90	120	150	180
Min:Sec					

VOR RWY 12 L/R

37°21'N-121°55'W

SAN JOSE, CALIFORNIA
SAN JOSE INTL (SJC)

Not for use in Navigation

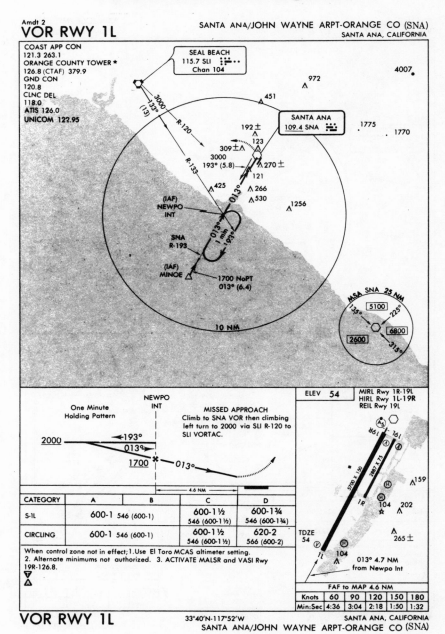

VOR RWY 1L

Amdt 2

SANTA ANA/JOHN WAYNE ARPT-ORANGE CO (SNA)
SANTA ANA, CALIFORNIA

COAST APP CON
121.3 263.1
ORANGE COUNTY TOWER *
126.8 (CTAF) 379.9
GND CON
120.8
CLNC DEL
118.0
ATIS 126.0
UNICOM 122.95

SEAL BEACH
115.7 SLI
Chan 104

SANTA ANA
109.4 SNA

4007

972

451

1775

1770

192 ±
123
309 ±
3000
193° (5.8)
270 ±
121
013°
425
266
530
1256

(IAF)
NEWPO
INT
013°
1 min
193°

SNA
R-193

(IAF)
MINOE
1700 NoPT
013° (6.4)

10 NM

MSA SNA 25 NM

135°
5100
225°
2600
6800
315°

Landing Minimums / Plan View

One Minute
Holding Pattern

NEWPO
INT

MISSED APPROACH
Climb to SNA VOR then climbing
left turn to 2000 via SLI R-120 to
SLI VORTAC.

2000
193°
013°
1700
013°

4.6 NM

ELEV 54

MIRL Rwy 1R-19L
HIRL Rwy 1L-19R
REIL Rwy 19L

570 x 150
289 x 75

159

1R
104
202

TDZE
54
265 ±

104

013° 4.7 NM
from Newpo Int

CATEGORY	A	B	C	D
S-1L	600-1 546 (600-1)		600-1½ 546 (600-1½)	600-1¾ 546 (600-1¾)
CIRCLING	600-1 546 (600-1)		600-1½ 546 (600-1½)	620-2 566 (600-2)

When control zone not in effect;1.Use El Toro MCAS altimeter setting.
2. Alternate minimums not authorized. 3. ACTIVATE MALSR and VASI Rwy
19R-126.8.

FAF to MAP 4.6 NM

Knots	60	90	120	150	180
Min:Sec	4:36	3:04	2:18	1:50	1:32

VOR RWY 1L

33°40'N-117°52'W

SANTA ANA, CALIFORNIA
SANTA ANA/JOHN WAYNE ARPT-ORANGE CO (SNA)

Not for use in Navigation

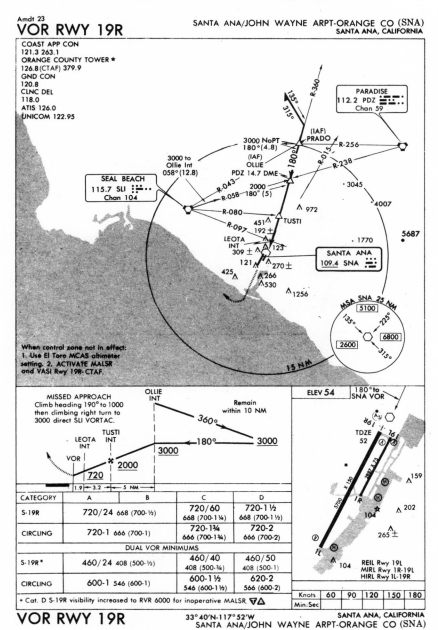

Amdt 23
VOR RWY 19R

SANTA ANA/JOHN WAYNE ARPT-ORANGE CO (SNA)
SANTA ANA, CALIFORNIA

COAST APP CON
121.3 263.1
ORANGE COUNTY TOWER ★
126.8(CTAF) 379.9
GND CON
120.8
CLNC DEL
118.0
ATIS 126.0
UNICOM 122.95

PARADISE
112.2 PDZ
Chan 59

(IAF)
PRADO

3000 NoPT
180°(4.8)

(IAF)
OLLIE

R-256
R-015
R-238

3000 to
Ollie Int
058°(12.8)

PDZ 14.7 DME

· 3045
· 4007

SEAL BEACH
115.7 SLI
Chan 104

R-043
R-058   2000
180°(5)

R-080   △ 972

TUSTI

5687
· 1770

R-097   451 △
192 △

LEOTA
INT
309 △   △ 123

SANTA ANA
109.4 SNA

121 △   △ 270

425 △   △ 266
△ 530

△ 1256

MSA SNA 25 NM
5100
135°   225°
2600   6800
315°

When control zone not in effect:
1. Use El Toro MCAS altimeter
setting. 2. ACTIVATE MALSR
and VASI Rwy 19R-CTAF.

15 NM

MISSED APPROACH
Climb heading 190° to 1000
then climbing right turn to
3000 direct SLI VORTAC.

OLLIE
INT

Remain
within 10 NM

360°

ELEV 54
180° to
SNA VOR

TUSTI
INT

LEOTA
INT

180°   3000

3000

VOR   2000

720

1.9   3.2   5 NM

TDZE
52

159 △

202 △

104 △

265 △

CATEGORY	A	B	C	D
S-19R	720/24 668 (700-½)		720/60 668 (700-1¼)	720-1½ 668 (700-1½)
CIRCLING	720-1 666 (700-1)		720-1¾ 666 (700-1¾)	720-2 666 (700-2)
DUAL VOR MINIMUMS				
S-19R *	460/24 408 (500-½)		460/40 408 (500-¾)	460/50 408 (500-1)
CIRCLING	600-1 546 (600-1)		600-1½ 546 (600-1½)	620-2 566 (600-2)

* Cat. D S-19R visibility increased to RVR 6000 for inoperative MALSR. ▽△

REIL Rwy 19L
MIRL Rwy 1R-19L
HIRL Rwy 1L-19R

Knots	60	90	120	150	180
Min:Sec					

VOR RWY 19R

33°40'N-117°52'W

SANTA ANA, CALIFORNIA
SANTA ANA/JOHN WAYNE ARPT-ORANGE CO (SNA)

217

Not for use in Navigation

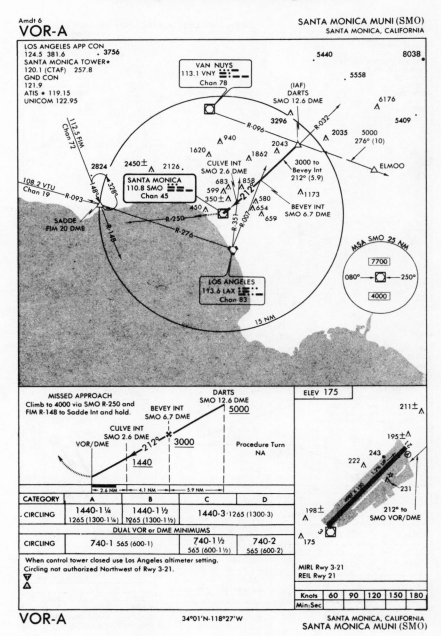

Amdt 6

VOR-A

SANTA MONICA MUNI (SMO)
SANTA MONICA, CALIFORNIA

LOS ANGELES APP CON
124.5 381.6
SANTA MONICA TOWER★
120.1 (CTAF) 257.8
GND CON
121.9
ATIS ★ 119.15
UNICOM 122.95

VAN NUYS
113.1 VNY
Chan 78

SANTA MONICA
110.8 SMO
Chan 45

LOS ANGELES
113.6 LAX
Chan 83

(IAF)
DARTS
SMO 12.6 DME

3000 to
Bevey Int
212° (5.9)

BEVEY INT
SMO 6.7 DME

CULVE INT
SMO 2.6 DME

SADDE
FIM 20 DME

5000
276° (10)

ELMOO

MSA SMO 25 NM

7700
080° ▢ 250°
4000

ELEV 175

MISSED APPROACH
Climb to 4000 via SMO R-250 and
FIM R-148 to Sadde Int and hold.

DARTS
SMO 12.6 DME
5000

BEVEY INT
SMO 6.7 DME

CULVE INT
SMO 2.6 DME
3000

VOR/DME
212°

1440

Procedure Turn
NA

2.6 NM — 4.1 NM — 5.9 NM

CATEGORY	A	B	C	D
CIRCLING	1440-1¼ 1265 (1300-1¼)	1440-1½ 1265 (1300-1½)	1440-3 1265 (1300-3)	
DUAL VOR or DME MINIMUMS				
CIRCLING	740-1 565 (600-1)		740-1½ 565 (600-1½)	740-2 565 (600-2)

When control tower closed use Los Angeles altimeter setting.
Circling not authorized Northwest of Rwy 3-21.

212° to
SMO VOR/DME

MIRL Rwy 3-21
REIL Rwy 21

Knots	60	90	120	150	180
Min:Sec					

VOR-A

34°01'N-118°27'W

SANTA MONICA, CALIFORNIA
SANTA MONICA MUNI (SMO)

Not for use in Navigation

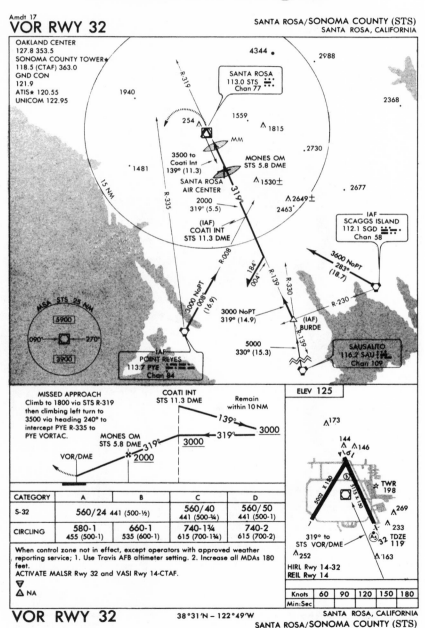

Amdt 17

VOR RWY 32

SANTA ROSA/SONOMA COUNTY (STS)
SANTA ROSA, CALIFORNIA

OAKLAND CENTER
127.8 353.5
SONOMA COUNTY TOWER★
118.5 (CTAF) 363.0
GND CON
121.9
ATIS★ 120.55
UNICOM 122.95

4344
29'88

SANTA ROSA
113.0 STS
Chan 77

1940

2368

254 △
1559
△ 1815

MM

3500 to
Coati Int
139° (11.3)

MONES OM
STS 5.8 DME

.2730

·1481

SANTA ROSA
AIR CENTER
2000
319° (5.5)

△1530±

319°

△2649±
2463°

· 2677

R-319

R-335

15 NM

(IAF)
COATI INT
STS 11.3 DME

R-008

IAF
SCAGGS ISLAND
112.1 SGD
Chan 58

184°
004°

R-139

R-330

3600 NoPT
283°
(18.7)

MSA STS 25 NM

5900

090°   270°

3900

3000 NoPT
008°
(16.9)

3000 NoPT
319° (14.9)

(IAF)
BURDE

R-230

R-139

IAF
POINT REYES
113.7 PYE
Chan 94

5000
330° (15.3)

SAUSALITO
116.2 SAU
Chan 109

MISSED APPROACH
Climb to 1800 via STS R-319
then climbing left turn to
3500 via heading 240° to
intercept PYE R-335 to
PYE VORTAC.

COATI INT
STS 11.3 DME

Remain
within 10 NM

ELEV 125

△173

139°

3000

MONES OM
STS 5.8 DME

319°

319°

3000

144
△ △146

VOR/DME

★ 2000

△252

★ TWR
198

△269

△ 233

319° to
STS VOR/DME

△163

32 TDZE
119

CATEGORY	A	B	C	D
S-32	560/24 441 (500-½)		560/40 441 (500-¾)	560/50 441 (500-1)
CIRCLING	580-1 455 (500-1)	660-1 535 (600-1)	740-1¾ 615 (700-1¾)	740-2 615 (700-2)

When control zone not in effect, except operators with approved weather
reporting service; 1. Use Travis AFB altimeter setting. 2. Increase all MDAs 180
feet.
ACTIVATE MALSR Rwy 32 and VASI Rwy 14-CTAF.

▽
△ NA

HIRL Rwy 14-32
REIL Rwy 14

Knots	60	90	120	150	180
Min:Sec					

VOR RWY 32

38°31'N – 122°49'W

SANTA ROSA, CALIFORNIA
SANTA ROSA/SONOMA COUNTY (STS)

219

Not for use in Navigation

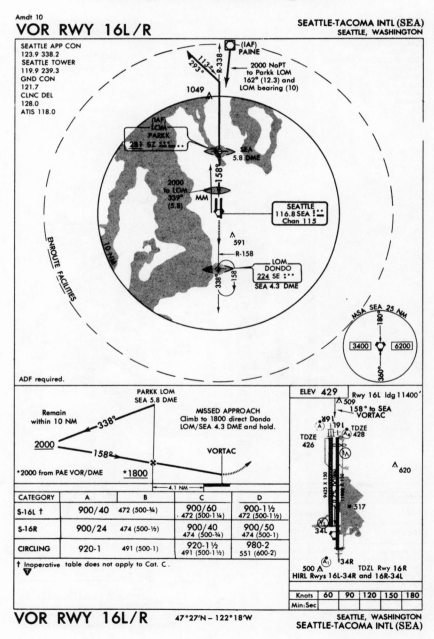

Amdt 10

VOR RWY 16L/R

SEATTLE-TACOMA INTL (SEA)
SEATTLE, WASHINGTON

SEATTLE APP CON
123.9 338.2
SEATTLE TOWER
119.9 239.3
GND CON
121.7
CLNC DEL
128.0
ATIS 118.0

(IAF)
PAINE

R-338
113°
293°

2000 NoPT
to Parkk LOM
162° (12.3) and
LOM bearing (10)

1049

(IAF)
LOM
PARKK
281 SZ 115...

SEA
5.8 DME

158°

2000
to LOM
339°
(5.8)
MM

SEATTLE
116.8 SEA
Chan 115

591

R-158

338°
158°

LOM
DONDO
224 SE
SEA 4.3 DME

ENROUTE FACILITIES
10 NM

MSA SEA 25 NM
180°
3400   6200
360°

ADF required.

PARKK LOM
SEA 5.8 DME

Remain
within 10 NM

338°

2000

158°

*2000 from PAE VOR/DME

MISSED APPROACH
Climb to 1800 direct Dondo
LOM/SEA 4.3 DME and hold.

VORTAC

*1800

4.1 NM

CATEGORY	A	B	C	D
S-16L †	900/40	472 (500-¾)	900/60 472 (500-1¼)	900-1½ 472 (500-1½)
S-16R	900/24	474 (500-½)	900/40 474 (500-¾)	900/50 474 (500-1)
CIRCLING	920-1	491 (500-1)	920-1½ 491 (500-1½)	980-2 551 (600-2)

† Inoperative table does not apply to Cat. C.

ELEV 429
Rwy 16L ldg 11400'

509
158° to SEA
VORTAC

16R
191
TDZE
428

TDZE
426

925 X 150

620

517

34L

34R

500
HIRL Rwys 16L-34R and 16R-34L

TDZL Rwy 16R

Knots	60	90	120	150	180
Min:Sec					

VOR RWY 16L/R

47°27'N – 122°18'W

SEATTLE, WASHINGTON
SEATTLE-TACOMA INTL (SEA)

Not for use in Navigation

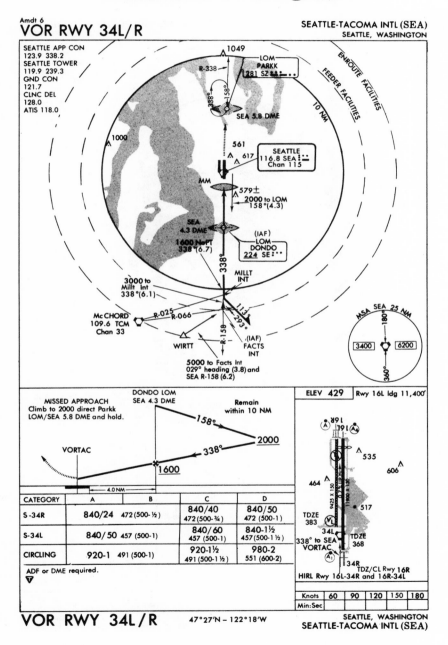

Amdt 6
VOR RWY 34L/R

SEATTLE-TACOMA INTL (SEA)
SEATTLE, WASHINGTON

SEATTLE APP CON
123.9 338.2
SEATTLE TOWER
119.9 239.3
GND CON
121.7
CLNC DEL
128.0
ATIS 118.0

ELEV 429 | Rwy 16L ldg 11,400'

VOR RWY 34L/R   47°27'N – 122°18'W

SEATTLE, WASHINGTON
SEATTLE-TACOMA INTL (SEA)

221

Not for use in Navigation

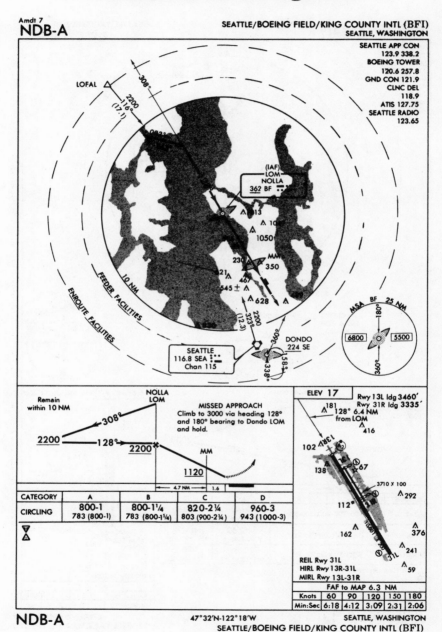

SEATTLE APP CON
123.9 338.2
BOEING TOWER
120.6 257.8
GND CON 121.9
CLNC DEL
118.9
ATIS 127.75
SEATTLE RADIO
123.65

LOFAL

308°
2200
(17.1)
116°

(IAF)
LOM
NOLLA
362 BF

FEEDER FACILITIES
ENROUTE FACILITIES
10 NM

013
10
1050
MM
230
350
321
467
545±
628

2200
323°
(12.3)

360°
338°
158°

DONDO
224 SE

SEATTLE
116.8 SEA
Chan 115

MSA BF 25 NM
180°
6800
5500
360°

Remain
within 10 NM

NOLLA
LOM

308°
2200
128°
2200

MISSED APPROACH
Climb to 3000 via heading 128°
and 180° bearing to Dondo LOM
and hold.

MM
1120

4.7 NM   1.6

ELEV 17

Rwy 13L ldg 3460'
Rwy 31R ldg 3335'
128° 6.4 NM
from LOM

181
416
102
138
67

3710 X 100
292

112°
162
376
241
59

REIL Rwy 31L
HIRL Rwy 13R-31L
MIRL Rwy 13L-31R

CATEGORY	A	B	C	D
CIRCLING	800-1	800-1¼	820-2¼	960-3
	783 (800-1)	783 (800-1¼)	803 (900-2¼)	943 (1000-3)

FAF to MAP 6.3 NM

Knots	60	90	120	150	180
Min:Sec	6:18	4:12	3:09	2:31	2:06

Not for use in Navigation

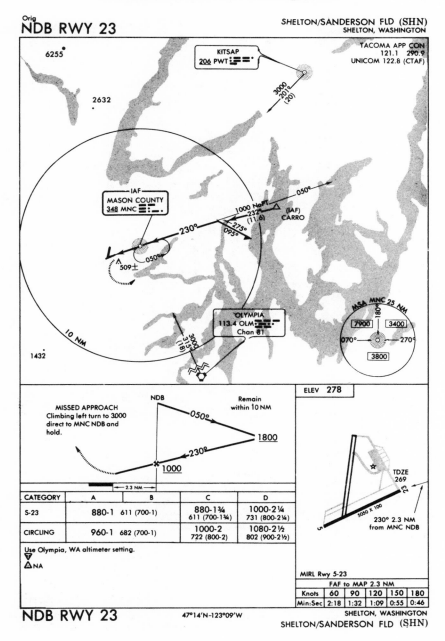

Orig
NDB RWY 23

SHELTON/SANDERSON FLD (SHN)
SHELTON, WASHINGTON

TACOMA APP CON
121.1   290.9
UNICOM 122.8 (CTAF)

KITSAP
206 PWT

6255

2632

IAF
MASON COUNTY
348 MNC

1000 NoPT
232°
(11.6)
(IAF)
CARRO

050°

230°
275°
095°

050°
509±

10 NM

1432

OLYMPIA
113.4 OLM
Chan 81

3000
315°
(18)

MSA MNC 25 NM

7900	3400
070°	270°
	3800

180°

ELEV 278

MISSED APPROACH
Climbing left turn to 3000
direct to MNC NDB and
hold.

NDB

Remain
within 10 NM

050°

1800

230°

1000

2.3 NM

TDZE
269

5050 X 100

230° 2.3 NM
from MNC NDB

CATEGORY	A		B	C	D
S-23	880-1	611 (700-1)		880-1¾ 611 (700-1¾)	1000-2¼ 731 (800-2¼)
CIRCLING	960-1	682 (700-1)		1000-2 722 (800-2)	1080-2½ 802 (900-2½)

Use Olympia, WA altimeter setting.
▽
△NA

MIRL Rwy 5-23

FAF to MAP 2.3 NM					
Knots	60	90	120	150	180
Min:Sec	2:18	1:32	1:09	0:55	0:46

NDB RWY 23

47°14'N-123°09'W

SHELTON, WASHINGTON
SHELTON/SANDERSON FLD (SHN)

223

Not for use in Navigation

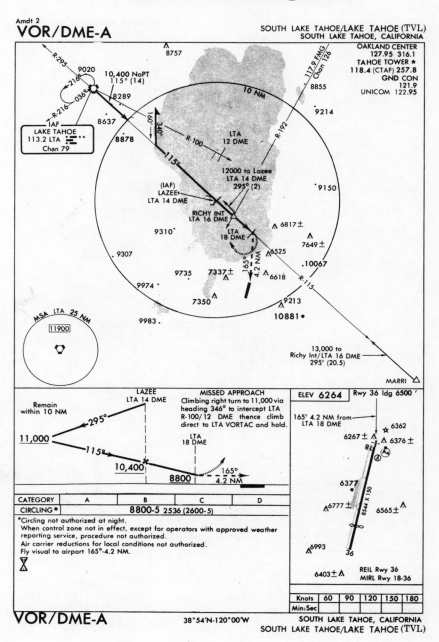

Amdt 2

VOR/DME-A

SOUTH LAKE TAHOE/LAKE TAHOE (TVL)
SOUTH LAKE TAHOE, CALIFORNIA

OAKLAND CENTER
127.95 316.1
TAHOE TOWER ★
118.4 (CTAF) 257.8
GND CON
121.9
UNICOM 122.95

IAF
LAKE TAHOE
113.2 LTA
Chan 79

10,400 NoPT
115° (14)

MSA LTA 25 NM
11900

LTA
12 DME

12000 to Lazee
LTA 14 DME
295° (2)

(IAF)
LAZEE
LTA 14 DME

RICHY INT
LTA 16 DME

LTA
18 DME

165°
4.2 NM

13,000 to
Richy Int/LTA 16 DME
295° (20.5)

MARRI

10 NM

LAZEE
LTA 14 DME

MISSED APPROACH
Climbing right turn to 11,000 via
heading 346° to intercept LTA
R-100/12 DME thence climb
direct to LTA VORTAC and hold.

ELEV 6264

Rwy 36 ldg 6500'

Remain
within 10 NM

295°

11,000

115°

10,400

8800

LTA
18 DME

165°
4.2 NM

165° 4.2 NM from
LTA 18 DME

6267 ±
6377
6777 ±
6993
36

6362
6376 ±
6565 ±
6403 ±

REIL Rwy 36
MIRL Rwy 18-36

CATEGORY	A	B	C	D
CIRCLING *	8800-5 2536 (2600-5)			

*Circling not authorized at night.
When control zone not in effect, except for operators with approved weather
reporting service, procedure not authorized.
Air carrier reductions for local conditions not authorized.
Fly visual to airport 165°-4.2 NM.

Knots	60	90	120	150	180
Min:Sec					

VOR/DME-A

38°54'N-120°00'W

SOUTH LAKE TAHOE, CALIFORNIA
SOUTH LAKE TAHOE/LAKE TAHOE (TVL)

Not for use in Navigation

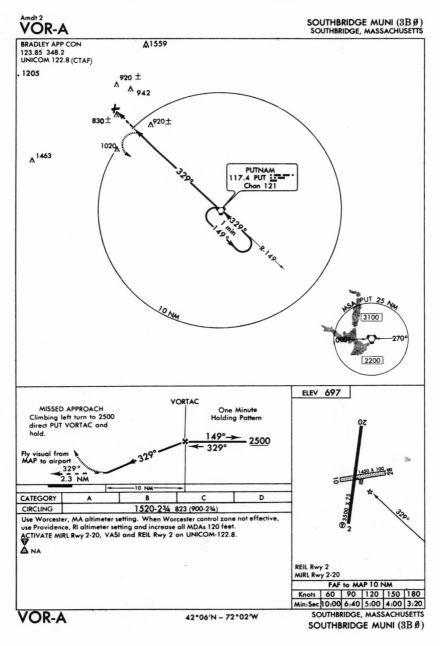

Amdt 2
VOR-A

SOUTHBRIDGE MUNI (3BØ)
SOUTHBRIDGE, MASSACHUSETTS

BRADLEY APP CON
123.85 348.2
UNICOM 122.8 (CTAF)

. 1205

△1559

920 ± △
△ 942

830± △920±

1020

△1463

329°

PUTNAM
117.4 PUT
Chan 121

329°
1 min
149°

R-149

MSA PUT 25 NM

3100

040°   270°

2200

10 NM

ELEV 697

MISSED APPROACH
Climbing left turn to 2500
direct PUT VORTAC and
hold.

VORTAC

One Minute
Holding Pattern

149°   2500
329°

329°

Fly visual from
MAP to airport
329°
2.3 NM

10 NM

CATEGORY	A	B	C	D
CIRCLING		1520-2¾ 823 (900-2¾)		

Use Worcester, MA altimeter setting. When Worcester control zone not effective,
use Providence, RI altimeter setting and increase all MDAs 120 feet.
ACTIVATE MIRL Rwy 2-20, VASI and REIL Rwy 2 on UNICOM-122.8.

▽
△ NA

20

10 1450 X 100 28

3500 X 75
2

329°

REIL Rwy 2
MIRL Rwy 2-20

FAF to MAP 10 NM					
Knots	60	90	120	150	180
Min:Sec	10:00	6:40	5:00	4:00	3:20

VOR-A

42°06'N – 72°02'W

SOUTHBRIDGE, MASSACHUSETTS
SOUTHBRIDGE MUNI (3BØ)

Not for use in Navigation

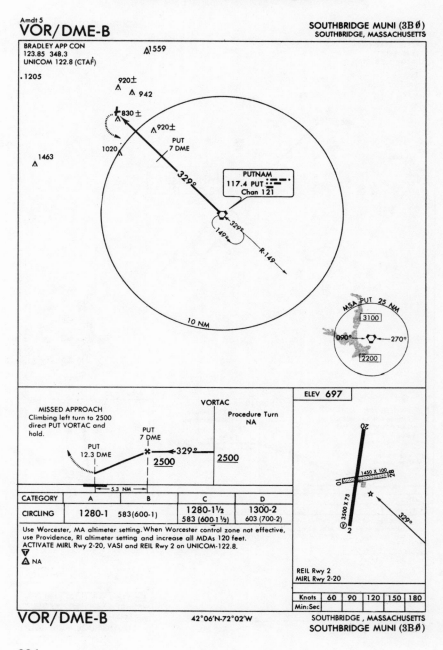

Amdt 5
VOR/DME-B

SOUTHBRIDGE MUNI (3B0)
SOUTHBRIDGE, MASSACHUSETTS

BRADLEY APP CON
123.85 348.3
UNICOM 122.8 (CTAF)

1559

.1205

920± △ 942

830±

△920±

1020

PUT
7 DME

1463

329°

PUTNAM
117.4 PUT
Chan 121

329°
149°

R-149

MSA PUT 25 NM
3100
090° — 270°
2200

10 NM

ELEV **697**

MISSED APPROACH
Climbing left turn to 2500
direct PUT VORTAC and
hold.

VORTAC

Procedure Turn
NA

PUT
7 DME

PUT
12.3 DME

←329°

2500   **2500**

5.3 NM

1450 X 100

3500 X 75

329°

CATEGORY	A	B	C	D
CIRCLING	1280-1	583(600-1)	1280-1½ 583 (600-1½)	1300-2 603 (700-2)

Use Worcester, MA altimeter setting. When Worcester control zone not effective,
use Providence, RI altimeter setting and increase all MDAs 120 feet.
ACTIVATE MIRL Rwy 2-20, VASI and REIL Rwy 2 on UNICOM-122.8.

▽
△ NA

REIL Rwy 2
MIRL Rwy 2-20

Knots	60	90	120	150	180
Min:Sec					

VOR/DME-B

42°06'N-72°02'W

SOUTHBRIDGE , MASSACHUSETTS
SOUTHBRIDGE MUNI (3B0)

Not for use in Navigation

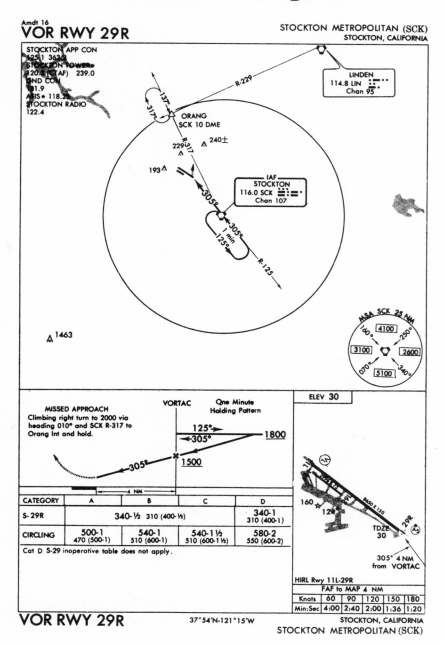

Amdt 16
VOR RWY 29R

STOCKTON METROPOLITAN (SCK)
STOCKTON, CALIFORNIA

STOCKTON APP CON
125.1 363.2
STOCKTON TOWER*
120.3 (CTAF) 239.0
GND CON
121.9
ATIS* 118.22
STOCKTON RADIO
122.4

LINDEN
114.8 LIN
Chan 95

R-229

ORANG
SCK 10 DME

240±

229°

R-317

193

305°

IAF
STOCKTON
116.0 SCK
Chan 107

305°
125°
1 min

R-125

MSA SCK 25 NM
4100
3100   2600
5100

ELEV 30

MISSED APPROACH
Climbing right turn to 2000 via
heading 010° and SCK R-317 to
Orang Int and hold.

VORTAC

One Minute
Holding Pattern

125°
305°
1800

305°
1500

4 NM

CATEGORY	A	B	C	D
S-29R	340-½ 310 (400-½)			340-1 310 (400-1)
CIRCLING	500-1 470 (500-1)	540-1 510 (600-1)	540-1½ 510 (600-1½)	580-2 550 (600-2)

Cat D S-29 inoperative table does not apply.

160

128

TDZE
30

29R

305° 4 NM
from VORTAC

HIRL Rwy 11L-29R

FAF to MAP 4 NM					
Knots	60	90	120	150	180
Min:Sec	4:00	2:40	2:00	1:36	1:20

VOR RWY 29R

37°54'N-121°15'W

STOCKTON, CALIFORNIA
STOCKTON METROPOLITAN (SCK)

Not for use in Navigation

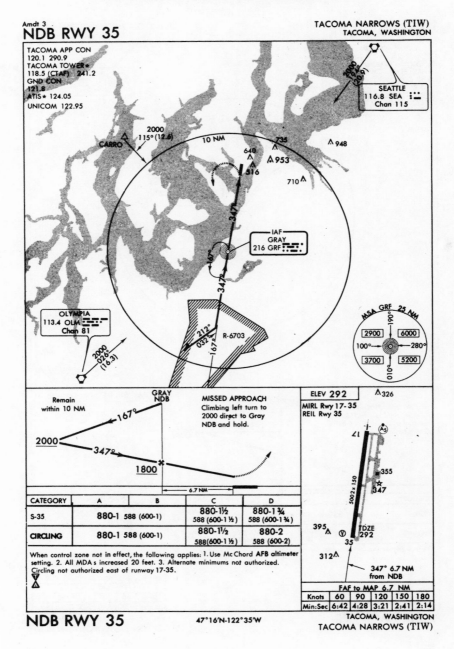

Amdt 3
NDB RWY 35

TACOMA NARROWS (TIW)
TACOMA, WASHINGTON

TACOMA APP CON
120.1 290.9
TACOMA TOWER★
118.5 (CTAF) 241.2
GND CON
121.8
ATIS★ 124.05
UNICOM 122.95

SEATTLE
116.8 SEA
Chan 115

2000
115° (12.6)
CARRO

10 NM

735
640
516
953
948
710

IAF
GRAY
216 GRF

OLYMPIA
113.4 OLM
Chan 81

2000
026°
(16.3)

212°
032°
167°
347°

R-6703

MSA GRF 25 NM

| 2900 | 6000 |
| 3700 | 5200 |

100° ... 280°

GRAY
NDB

Remain
within 10 NM

167°

2000

347°

1800

6.7 NM

MISSED APPROACH
Climbing left turn to
2000 direct to Gray
NDB and hold.

ELEV 292   326

MIRL Rwy 17-35
REIL Rwy 35

17
355
347
5002 x 150

395
TDZE
292
35

312

347° 6.7 NM
from NDB

CATEGORY	A	B	C	D
S-35	880-1 588 (600-1)		880-1½ 588 (600-1½)	880-1¾ 588 (600-1¾)
CIRCLING	880-1 588 (600-1)		880-1½ 588(600-1½)	880-2 588 (600-2)

When control zone not in effect, the following applies: 1. Use Mc Chord **AFB** altimeter
setting. 2. All MDA s increased 20 feet. 3. Alternate minimums not authorized.
Circling not authorized east of runway 17-35.

FAF to MAP 6.7 NM

Knots	60	90	120	150	180
Min:Sec	6:42	4:28	3:21	2:41	2:14

NDB RWY 35

47°16'N-122°35'W

TACOMA, WASHINGTON
TACOMA NARROWS (TIW)

Not for use in Navigation

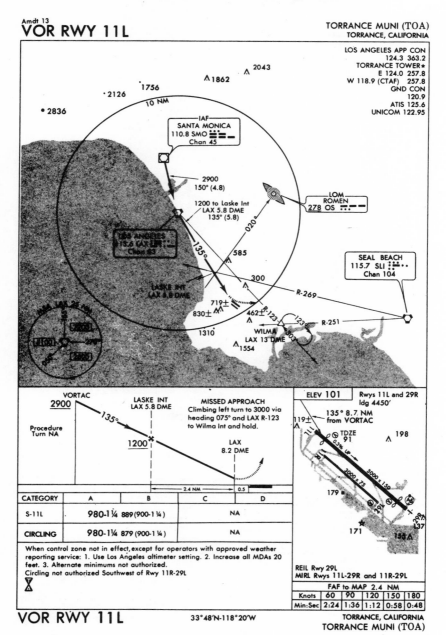

Amdt 13

VOR RWY 11L

TORRANCE MUNI (TOA)
TORRANCE, CALIFORNIA

LOS ANGELES APP CON
124.3 363.2
TORRANCE TOWER★
E 124.0 257.8
W 118.9 (CTAF) 257.8
GND CON
120.9
ATIS 125.6
UNICOM 122.95

2043

△1862

1756

·2126

10 NM

· 2836

IAF
SANTA MONICA
110.8 SMO
Chan 45

2900
150° (4.8)

1200 to Laske Int
LAX 5.8 DME
135° (5.8)

LOM
ROMEN
278 OS

LOS ANGELES
115.6 (LAX LIM)
Chan 83

135°

585

LASKE INT
LAX 5.8 DME

300

R-269

SEAL BEACH
115.7 SLI
Chan 104

719±

830±

462±

R-123

123

R-251

1310

WILMA
LAX 13 DME

△1554

VORTAC
2900

LASKE INT
LAX 5.8 DME

MISSED APPROACH
Climbing left turn to 3000 via
heading 075° and LAX R-123
to Wilma Int and hold.

ELEV 101

Rwys 11L and 29R
ldg 4450'

135°

Procedure
Turn NA

1200

LAX
8.2 DME

135° 8.7 NM
from VORTAC

119±

TDZE
91

0.3% UP

△ 198

2.4 NM

0.5

179

3000 x 75

5000 x 150

171

155

137

CATEGORY	A	B	C	D
S-11L	980-1¼ 889 (900-1¼)		NA	
CIRCLING	980-1¼ 879 (900-1¼)		NA	

When control zone not in effect, except for operators with approved weather
reporting service: 1. Use Los Angeles altimeter setting. 2. Increase all MDAs 20
feet. 3. Alternate minimums not authorized.
Circling not authorized Southwest of Rwy 11R-29L

REIL Rwy 29L
MIRL Rwys 11L-29R and 11R-29L

FAF to MAP 2.4 NM				
Knots	60	90	120	150	180
Min:Sec	2:24	1:36	1:12	0:58	0:48

VOR RWY 11L

33°48'N-118°20'W

TORRANCE, CALIFORNIA
TORRANCE MUNI (TOA)

229

Not for use in Navigation

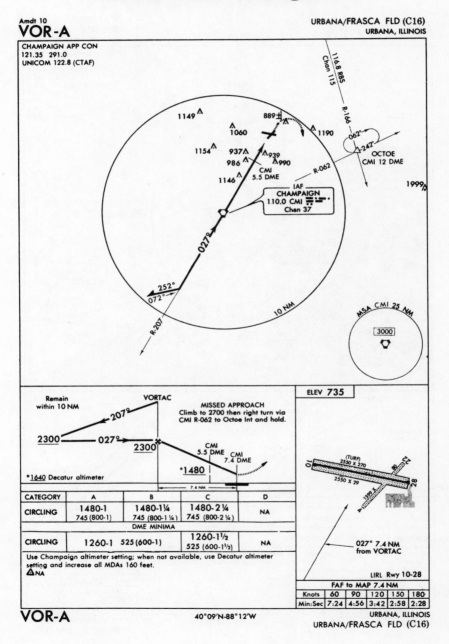

VOR-A

URBANA/FRASCA FLD (C16)
URBANA, ILLINOIS

CHAMPAIGN APP CON
121.35 291.0
UNICOM 122.8 (CTAF)

116.8 RBS
Chan 115

R-168

062°

247°

OCTOE
CMI 12 DME

R-062

1999

1190

889

1149

1060

1154

937

939

990

986

CMI
5.5 DME

1146

IAF
CHAMPAIGN
1.10.0 CMI
Chan 37

027°

252°
072°

R-207

10 NM

MSA CMI 25 NM

3000

Remain within 10 NM

VORTAC

207°

MISSED APPROACH
Climb to 2700 then right turn via
CMI R-062 to Octoe Int and hold.

ELEV 735

2300

027°

2300

CMI
5.5 DME

CMI
7.4 DME

*1640 Decatur altimeter

*1480

7.4 NM

(TURF)
2550 X 270

2550 X 29

10

28

1999

027° 7.4 NM
from VORTAC

CATEGORY	A	B	C	D
CIRCLING	1480-1 745 (800-1)	1480-1¼ 745 (800-1¼)	1480-2¼ 745 (800-2¼)	NA

DME MINIMA

CIRCLING	1260-1 525(600-1)		1260-1½ 525 (600-1½)	NA

Use Champaign altimeter setting; when not available, use Decatur altimeter
setting and increase all MDAs 160 feet.
△NA

LIRL Rwy 10-28

FAF to MAP 7.4 NM					
Knots	60	90	120	150	180
Min:Sec	7:24	4:56	3:42	2:58	2:28

VOR-A

40°09′N-88°12′W

URBANA, ILLINOIS
URBANA/FRASCA FLD (C16)

Not for use in Navigation

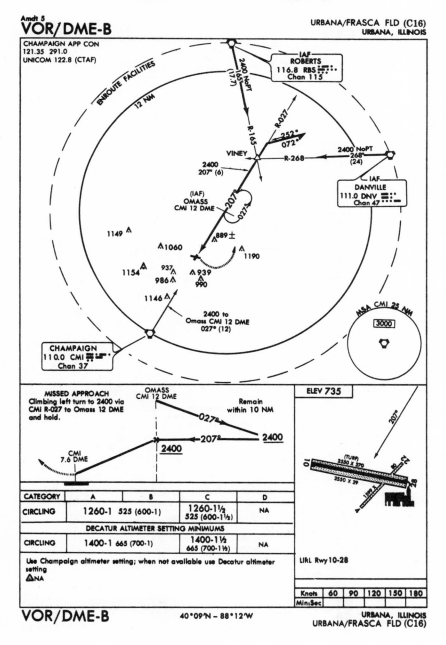

Not for use in Navigation

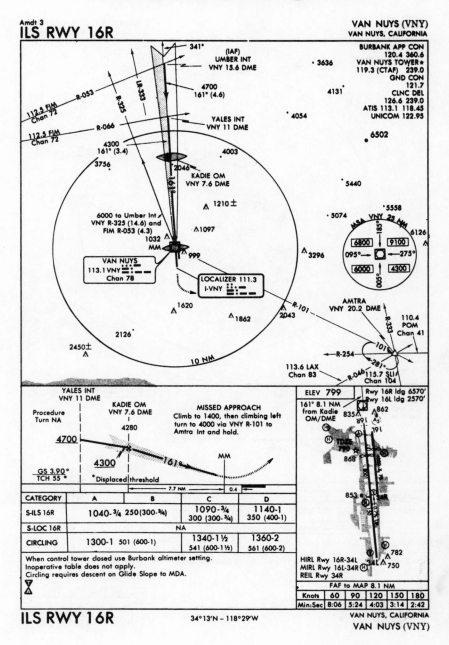

Amdt 3

ILS RWY 16R

VAN NUYS (VNY)
VAN NUYS, CALIFORNIA

341°
(IAF)
UMBER INT
VNY 15.6 DME

• 3636

BURBANK APP CON
120.4 360.6
VAN NUYS TOWER ★
119.3 (CTAF) 239.0
GND CON
121.7
CLNC DEL
126.6 239.0
ATIS 113.1 118.45
UNICOM 122.95

4700
161° (4.6)

4131 •

R-053
R-325
LR-333

112.5 FIM
Chan 72

112.5 FIM
Chan 72

R-066

YALES INT
VNY 11 DME

• 4054

4300
161° (3.4)

• 4003

• 6502

3756 •

2046

KADIE OM
VNY 7.6 DME

• 5440

⋏ 1210±

• 5558

6000 to Umber Int
VNY R-325 (14.6) and
FIM R-053 (4.3)

⋏ 1097

1032
MM

• 5074

⋏ 3296

MSA VNY 25 NM
185°
6126 ⋏
6800 | 9100
095° ◻ 275°
6000 | 4300
005°

999

VAN NUYS
113.1 VNY ▪▪▪ ━ ━
Chan 78

LOCALIZER 111.3
I-VNY ▪▪ ▪▪ ━ ━

R-101

AMTRA
VNY 20.2 DME

110.4
POM
Chan 41

R-333

⋏ 1620

⋏ 1862

2043

101°

281°

R-254

⋏

2126 •

113.6 LAX
Chan 83

R-046
115.7 SLI
Chan 104

2450±
⋏

10 NM

ELEV 799

161° 8.1 NM
from Kadie
OM/DME

Rwy 16R ldg 6570'
Rwy 16L ldg 2570'

835

862

16R

868

191

720

782

853

161°

16L
34L

750

HIRL Rwy 16R-34L
MIRL Rwy 16L-34R
REIL Rwy 34R

Missed Approach / Profile

YALES INT
VNY 11 DME

KADIE OM
VNY 7.6 DME

Procedure
Turn NA

4280

MISSED APPROACH
Climb to 1400, then climbing left
turn to 4000 via VNY R-101 to
Amtra Int and hold.

MM

4700

4300
161°

GS 3.90°
TCH 55 °

*Displaced threshold

7.7 NM   0.4

FAF to MAP 8.1 NM

CATEGORY	A	B	C	D
S-ILS 16R	1040-¾ 250 (300-¾)		1090-¾ 300 (300-¾)	1140-1 350 (400-1)
S-LOC 16R	NA			
CIRCLING	1300-1 501 (600-1)		1340-1½ 541 (600-1½)	1360-2 561 (600-2)

When control tower closed use Burbank altimeter setting.
Inoperative table does not apply.
Circling requires descent on Glide Slope to MDA.

Knots	60	90	120	150	180
Min:Sec	8:06	5:24	4:03	3:14	2:42

ILS RWY 16R

34°13'N – 118°29'W

VAN NUYS, CALIFORNIA
VAN NUYS (VNY)

Not for use in Navigation

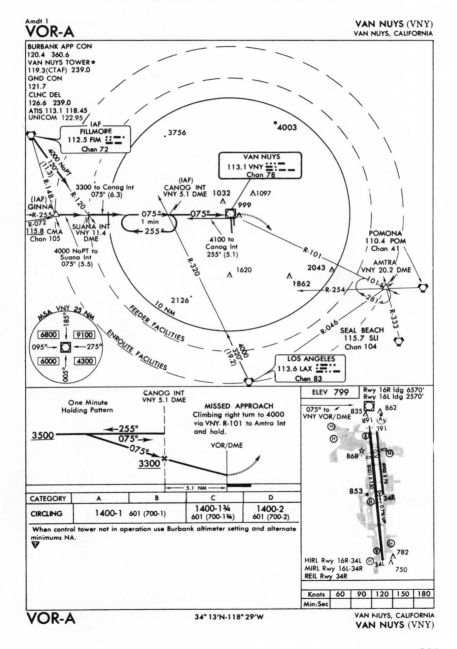

Amdt 1
VOR-A

VAN NUYS (VNY)
VAN NUYS, CALIFORNIA

BURBANK APP CON
120.4 360.6
VAN NUYS TOWER ★
119.3(CTAF) 239.0
GND CON
121.7
CLNC DEL
126.6 239.0
ATIS 113.1 118.45
UNICOM 122.95

IAF
FILLMORE
112.5 FIM
Chan 72

.3756

•4003

VAN NUYS
113.1 VNY
Chan 78

4000 NoPT
(11.5)

R-148

R-120

3300 to Canog Int
075° (6.3)

(IAF)
CANOG INT
VNY 5.1 DME 1032

Λ1097

Λ 999

(IAF)
GINNA
R-255
R-072
115.8 CMA
Chan 105

SUANA INT
VNY 11.4
DME

075°
1 min
255°

075°

4100 to
Canog Int
255° (5.1)

POMONA
110.4 POM
Chan 41

4000 NoPT to
Suana Int
075° (5.5)

R-320

Λ 1620

R-101

2043 Λ

Λ
1862

R-254

AMTRA
VNY 20.2 DME

101.8

281°

R-333

2126•

10 NM

FEEDER FACILITIES

MSA VNY 25 NM

185°
6800 9100
095° 275°
6000 4300
005°

ENROUTE FACILITIES

4000
320°
(19.2)

R-046

SEAL BEACH
115.7 SLI
Chan 104

LOS ANGELES
113.6 LAX
Chan 83

CANOG INT
VNY 5.1 DME

One Minute
Holding Pattern

←255°
3500
075°
075°
3300 ✕

MISSED APPROACH
Climbing right turn to 4000
via VNY. R-101 to Amtra Int
and hold.

VOR/DME

ELEV 799

Rwy 16R ldg 6570'
Rwy 16L ldg 2570'

075° to
VNY VOR/DME

835
16R

Λ 862

191

868

853

34R

5.1 NM

CATEGORY	A	B	C	D
CIRCLING	1400-1	601 (700-1)	1400-1¾ 601 (700-1¾)	1400-2 601 (700-2)

When control tower not in operation use Burbank altimeter setting and alternate
minimums NA.

782
34L
750

HIRL Rwy 16R-34L
MIRL Rwy 16L-34R
REIL Rwy 34R

Knots	60	90	120	150	180
Min:Sec					

VOR-A

34°13'N-118°29'W

VAN NUYS, CALIFORNIA
VAN NUYS (VNY)

Not for use in Navigation

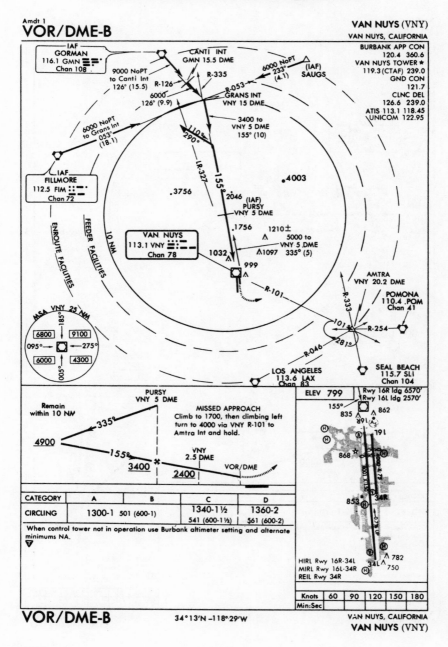

Not for use in Navigation

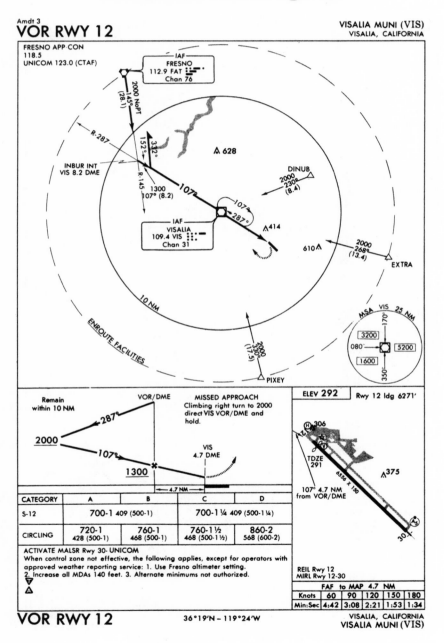

FRESNO APP·CON
118.5
UNICOM 123.0 (CTAF)

IAF
FRESNO
112.9 FAT
Chan 76

2000 NoPT
145°
(28.1)

R-287

152°

312°

INBUR INT
VIS 8.2 DME

R-145

1300
107° (8.2)

107°

A 628

DINUB
2000
230°
(8.4)

107°
287°

A 414

IAF
VISALIA
109.4 VIS
Chan 31

610 A

2000
268°
(13.4)

EXTRA

10 NM

ENROUTE FACILITIES

2000
330°
(17.5)

PIXEY

MSA   VIS   25 NM

3200

170°

080°   5200

1600

350°

Remain
within 10 NM

VOR/DME

287°

2000

107°

1300

4.7 NM

MISSED APPROACH
Climbing right turn to 2000
direct VIS VOR/DME and
hold.

VIS
4.7 DME

ELEV 292   Rwy 12 ldg 6271'

306

TDZE
291

A 375

6556 x 150

107° 4.7 NM
from VOR/DME

CATEGORY	A	B	C	D
S-12	700-1 409 (500-1)		700-1¼ 409 (500-1¼)	
CIRCLING	720-1 428 (500-1)	760-1 468 (500-1)	760-1½ 468 (500-1½)	860-2 568 (600-2)

ACTIVATE MALSR Rwy 30- UNICOM
When control zone not effective, the following applies, except for operators with
approved weather reporting service: 1. Use Fresno altimeter setting.
2. Increase all MDAs 140 feet. 3. Alternate minimums not authorized.

REIL Rwy 12
MIRL Rwy 12-30

FAF to MAP 4.7 NM				
Knots	60	90	120	150	180
Min:Sec	4:42	3:08	2:21	1:53	1:34

VOR RWY 12   36°19'N – 119°24'W   VISALIA, CALIFORNIA
VISALIA MUNI (VIS)

Not for use in Navigation

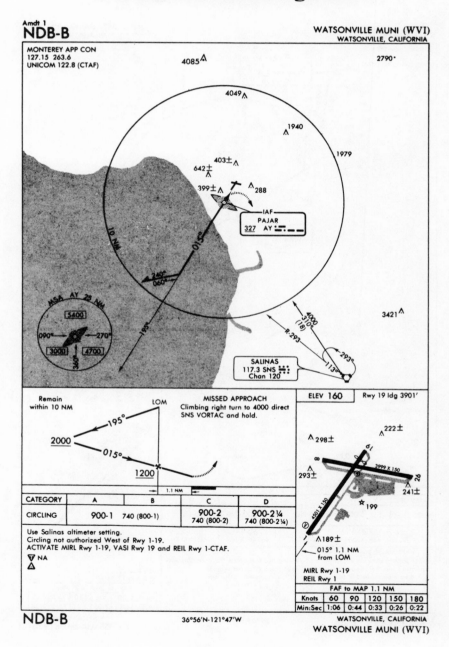

MONTEREY APP CON
127.15 263.6
UNICOM 122.8 (CTAF)

4085

2790'

4049

1940

1979

403±

642±

399±

288

IAF
PAJAR
327 AY

240°
060°

MSA AY 25 NM

5400

090°   270°

3000   4700

360

3421

R-293

4000
310°
(16)

293°

113°

SALINAS
117.3 SNS
Chan 120

Remain
within 10 NM

LOM

MISSED APPROACH
Climbing right turn to 4000 direct
SNS VORTAC and hold.

ELEV 160

Rwy 19 ldg 3901'

195°

2000

015°

1200

1.1 NM

298±

222±

293±

3999 X 150

241±

150 X 150

199

189±

015° 1.1 NM
from LOM

MIRL Rwy 1-19
REIL Rwy 1

CATEGORY	A	B	C	D
CIRCLING	900-1	740 (800-1)	900-2 740 (800-2)	900-2¼ 740 (800-2¼)

Use Salinas altimeter setting.
Circling not authorized West of Rwy 1-19.
ACTIVATE MIRL Rwy 1-19, VASI Rwy 19 and REIL Rwy 1-CTAF.

▽ NA
△

FAF to MAP 1.1 NM					
Knots	60	90	120	150	180
Min:Sec	1:06	0:44	0:33	0:26	0:22

Not for use in Navigation

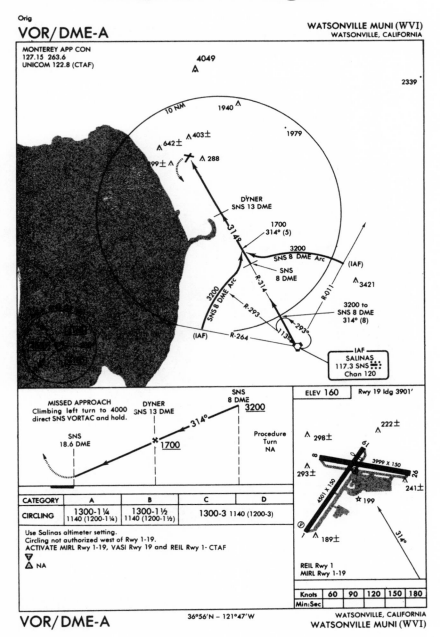

Orig

VOR/DME-A

WATSONVILLE MUNI (WVI)
WATSONVILLE, CALIFORNIA

MONTEREY APP CON
127.15 263.6
UNICOM 122.8 (CTAF)

4049
⋀

2339

10 NM
1940 ⋀

1979

⋀642± ⋀403±
⋀ 288
599± ⋀

DYNER
SNS 13 DME

1700
314° (5)

3200
SNS 8 DME Arc
(IAF)

SNS
8 DME
⋀ 3421

R-314

3200
SNS 8 DME Arc
R-293
R-011

3200 to
SNS 8 DME
314° (8)

293°
(IAF)
R-264
113°

IAF
SALINAS
117.3 SNS
Chan 120

Missed Approach / Profile

MISSED APPROACH
Climbing left turn to 4000
direct SNS VORTAC and hold.

DYNER
SNS 13 DME

SNS
8 DME
3200

314°

SNS
18.6 DME
1700

Procedure
Turn
NA

ELEV 160   Rwy 19 ldg 3901'

222±
⋀

⋀ 298±

3999 X 150

⋀
293±

450 X 150

241±

☆ 199

⋀ 189±

314°

CATEGORY	A	B	C	D
CIRCLING	1300-1¼ 1140 (1200-1¼)	1300-1½ 1140 (1200-1½)	1300-3 1140 (1200-3)	

Use Salinas altimeter setting.
Circling not authorized west of Rwy 1-19.
ACTIVATE MIRL Rwy 1-19, VASI Rwy 19 and REIL Rwy 1- CTAF
▽
⋀ NA

REIL Rwy 1
MIRL Rwy 1-19

Knots	60	90	120	150	180
Min:Sec					

VOR/DME-A

36°56'N – 121°47'W

WATSONVILLE, CALIFORNIA
WATSONVILLE MUNI (WVI)

Not for use in Navigation

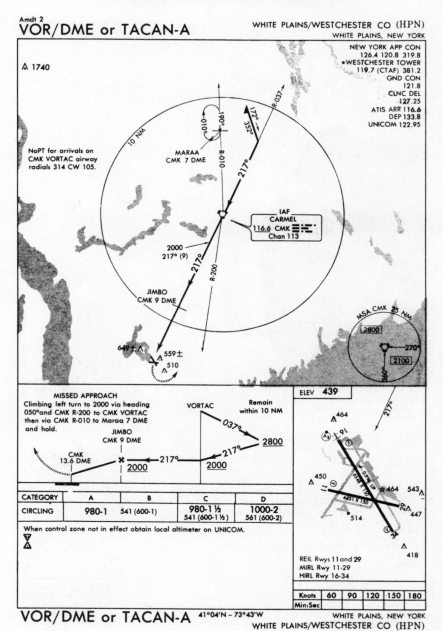

Amdt 2

VOR/DME or TACAN-A

WHITE PLAINS/WESTCHESTER CO (HPN)
WHITE PLAINS, NEW YORK

NEW YORK APP CON
126.4 120.8 319.8
*WESTCHESTER TOWER
119.7 (CTAF) 381.2
GND CON
121.8
CLNC DEL
127.25
ATIS ARR 116.6
DEP 133.8
UNICOM 122.95

Λ 1740

NoPT for arrivals on
CMK VORTAC airway
radials 314 CW 105.

10 NM

010°
190°
352°
172°

R-037
R-010
217°

MARAA
CMK 7 DME

IAF
CARMEL
116.6 CMK ⚏⚏ ⚏⚏ *
Chan 113

2000
217° (9)

217°
R-200

JIMBO
CMK 9 DME

649±Λ
559±
510

MSA CMK 25 NM
2800
270°
2100

MISSED APPROACH
Climbing left turn to 2000 via heading
050°and CMK R-200 to CMK VORTAC
then via CMK R-010 to Maraa 7 DME
and hold.

VORTAC
Remain
within 10 NM

037°
2800

JIMBO
CMK 9 DME

217°
2000

CMK
13.6 DME
217°
2000

ELEV 439

Λ464
16-31
Λ450
*464 543Λ
4851 X 150
447
29
514

418

REIL Rwys 11 and 29
MIRL Rwy 11-29
HIRL Rwy 16-34

CATEGORY	A	B	C	D
CIRCLING	980-1	541 (600-1)	980-1 ½ 541 (600-1½)	1000-2 561 (600-2)

When control zone not in effect obtain local altimeter on UNICOM.

Knots	60	90	120	150	180
Min:Sec					

VOR/DME or TACAN-A
41°04'N – 73°43'W

WHITE PLAINS, NEW YORK
WHITE PLAINS/WESTCHESTER CO (HPN)

Not for use in Navigation

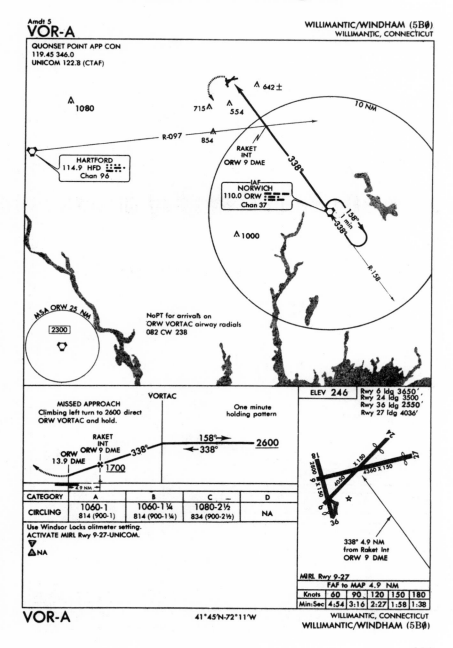

Not for use in Navigation

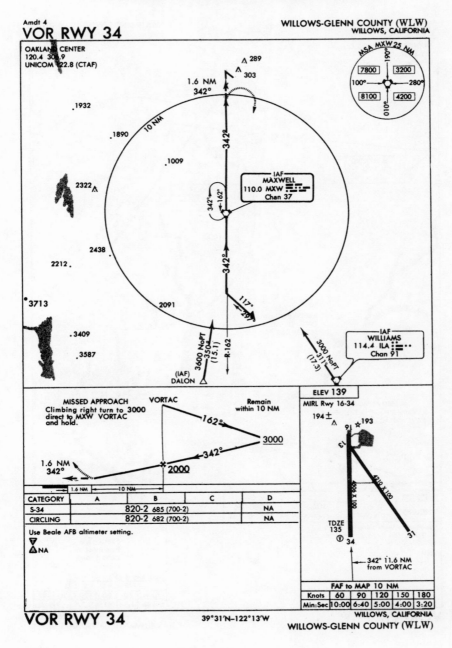

Amdt 4

VOR RWY 34

WILLOWS-GLENN COUNTY (WLW)
WILLOWS, CALIFORNIA

OAKLAND CENTER
120.4 30?.9
UNICOM 22.8 (CTAF)

MSA MXW 25 NM

| 7800 | 3200 |
| 8100 | 4200 |

100° — 280°

289
303

1.6 NM
342°

.1932

10 NM

.1890

342°

.1009

2322

IAF
MAXWELL
110.0 MXW
Chan 37

342°—162°

2438

342°

2212.

2091

117°
29?

3713

3000 NoPT
31?° (17.3)

IAF
WILLIAMS
114.4 ILA
Chan 91

.3409

.3587

3600 NoPT
3504 (15.1)
R-162

(IAF)
DALON

ELEV 139

MIRL Rwy 16-34

194±

91 ★193

MISSED APPROACH
Climbing right turn to 3000
direct to MXW VORTAC
and hold.

VORTAC

Remain
within 10 NM

162°

3000

342°

1.6 NM
342°

✕ 2000

1.6 NM ⟷ 10 NM

TDZE
135
34

342° 11.6 NM
from VORTAC

CATEGORY	A	B	C	D
S-34	820-2 685 (700-2)			NA
CIRCLING	820-2 682 (700-2)			NA

Use Beale AFB altimeter setting.

NA

FAF to MAP 10 NM

Knots	60	90	120	150	180
Min:Sec	10:00	6:40	5:00	4:00	3:20

VOR RWY 34

39°31'N–122°13'W

WILLOWS, CALIFORNIA
WILLOWS-GLENN COUNTY (WLW)

Not for use in Navigation

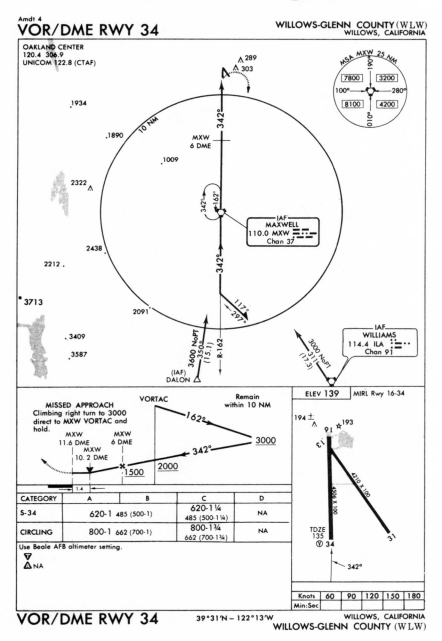

Amdt 4
VOR/DME RWY 34

WILLOWS-GLENN COUNTY (WLW)
WILLOWS, CALIFORNIA

OAKLAND CENTER
120.4 306.9
UNICOM 122.8 (CTAF)

MSA MXW 25 NM

7800	3200
100°	280°
8100	4200

.1934

.1890

.1009

10 NM

342°

289
303

MXW
6 DME

2322

342°

162°
342°

IAF
MAXWELL
110.0 MXW
Chan 37

2438

2212 .

342°

• 3713

2091 •

117°
297°

.3409

.3587

R-162

IAF
WILLIAMS
114.4 ILA
Chan 91

3000 NoPT
(17.3)

3600 NoPT
350°
(15.1)

(IAF)
DALON

ELEV 139 | MIRL Rwy 16-34

MISSED APPROACH
Climbing right turn to 3000
direct to MXW VORTAC and
hold.

VORTAC

Remain
within 10 NM

162°

194 ±
91 ☆193
13

MXW
11.6 DME

MXW
6 DME

3000

4210 X 100

342°

MXW
10. 2 DME

1500   2000

2000

4500 X 100

1.4

TDZE
135
① 34

31

CATEGORY	A	B	C	D
S-34	620-1 485 (500-1)		620-1¼ 485 (500-1¼)	NA
CIRCLING	800-1 662 (700-1)		800-1¾ 662 (700-1¾)	NA

342°

Use Beale AFB altimeter setting.
▽
△NA

Knots	60	90	120	150	180
Min:Sec					

VOR/DME RWY 34

39°31'N – 122°13'W

WILLOWS, CALIFORNIA
WILLOWS-GLENN COUNTY (WLW)

Amdt 24
NDB RWY 6

WINDSOR LOCKS/BRADLEY INTERNATIONAL (BDL)
WINDSOR LOCKS, CONNECTICUT

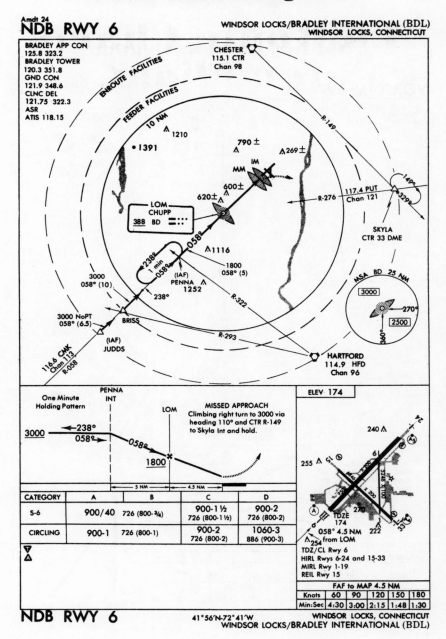

BRADLEY APP CON
125.8 323.2
BRADLEY TOWER
120.3 351.8
GND CON
121.9 348.6
CLNC DEL
121.75 322.3
ASR
ATIS 118.15

ENROUTE FACILITIES

FEEDER FACILITIES

CHESTER
115.1 CTR
Chan 98

10 NM
△1210

•1391

790 ±
△

△269±

MM   IM

LOM
CHUPP
388 BD ▬▬ •••

R-149

620± △   600± △

R-276   117.4 PUT
Chan 121

SKYLA
CTR 33 DME

058°

△1116

238° 1 min
058°

1800
058° (5)

(IAF)
PENNA △
1252

NSA BD 25 NM

3000

3000
058° (10)

238°

R-322

270°

2500

360°

3000 NoPT
058° (6.5)

BRISS

R-293

116.6 CMK
Chan 113
R-058

(IAF)
JUDDS

HARTFORD
114.9 HFD
Chan 96

One Minute Holding Pattern

PENNA INT

LOM

MISSED APPROACH
Climbing right turn to 3000 via heading 110° and CTR R-149 to Skyla Int and hold.

ELEV 174

3000 ──238°──
058°──

058°

1800

5 NM   4.5 NM

240 △

255 △

270

TDZE 174

058° 4.5 NM from LOM
△254

TDZ/CL Rwy 6
HIRL Rwys 6-24 and 15-33
MIRL Rwy 1-19
REIL Rwy 15

CATEGORY	A	B	C	D
S-6	900/40	726 (800-¾)	900-1½ 726 (800-1½)	900-2 726 (800-2)
CIRCLING	900-1	726 (800-1)	900-2 726 (800-2)	1060-3 886 (900-3)

FAF to MAP 4.5 NM					
Knots	60	90	120	150	180
Min:Sec	4:30	3:00	2:15	1:48	1:30

NDB RWY 6

41°56'N-72°41'W

WINDSOR LOCKS, CONNECTICUT
WINDSOR LOCKS/BRADLEY INTERNATIONAL (BDL)

Appendix C

En Route Charts for *Flight Simulator*

NEW YORK AND BOSTON AREA CHART

FLIGHT SIMULATOR II REFERENCE CHART
NOT TO BE USED FOR REAL WORLD AERIAL NAVIGATION

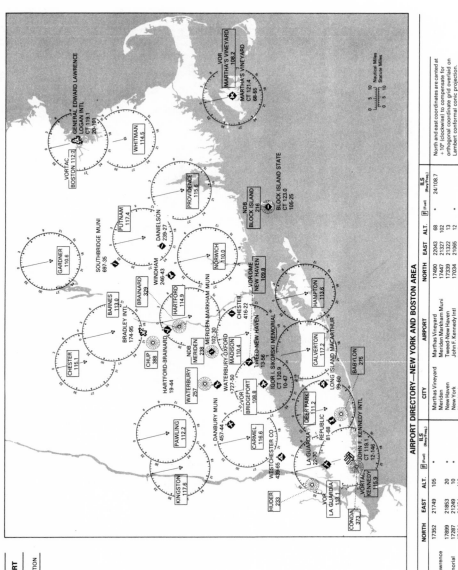

North and east coordinates are canted at +10° (clockwise) to compensate for orthogonal coordinate grid overlaid on Lambert conformal conic projection.

AIRPORT DIRECTORY—NEW YORK AND BOSTON AREA

CITY	AIRPORT	NORTH	EAST	ALT.	ILS (Rwy/Freq.)
Block Island	Block Island State	17352	21749	105	*
Boston	General Edward Lawrence	17899	21853	20	
	Logan Intl.	17287	21249	10	
Bridgeport	Igor I. Sikorski Memorial	17404	21434	416	
Chester	Chester	17360	21120	457	
Danbury	Danbury Muni	17617	21607	239	
Danielson	Danielson	17069	21177	81	
Farmingdale	Republic	17551	21371	19	
Hartford	Hartford-Brainard	17132	21278	99	
Islip	Long Island MacArthur				

CITY	AIRPORT	NORTH	EAST	ALT.	ILS (Rwy/Freq.)
Marthas Vineyard	Marthas Vineyard	17490	2043	68	
Meriden	Meriden-Markham Muni	17447	21327	102	
New Haven	Tweed-New Haven	17339	21322	13	
New York	John F. Kennedy Intl	17034	21065	12	24/108.7
New York	La Guardia	17091	21026	22	
Oxford	Waterbury-Oxford	17422	21229	727	
Southbridge	Southbridge Muni	17733	21543	697	
White Plains	Westchester Co	17226	21065	439	
Willimantic	Windham	17573	21521	246	
Windsor Locks	Bradley Intl	17638	21351	174	

Reprinted courtesy of SubLOGIC Corporation. Copyright 1986.

FLIGHT SIMULATOR II REFERENCE CHART.   NOT TO BE USED FOR REAL WORLD AERIAL NAVIGATION

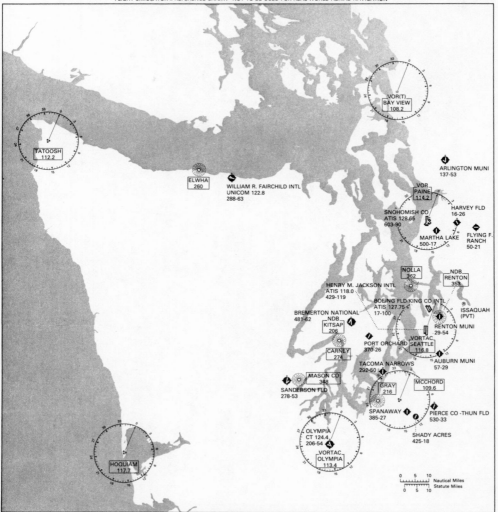

AIRPORT DIRECTORY—SEATTLE AREA

CITY	AIRPORT	NORTH	EAST	ALT.	F (Fuel)	ILS (Rwy/Freq.)	
Alderwood Manor	Martha Lake	21502	6670	500			North and east coordinates are canted at −21° counterclockwise to compensate for orthogonal coordinate grid overlaid on Lambert conformal conic projection.
Arlington	Arlington Muni	21616	6737	137			
Auburn	Auburn Muni	21290	6586	57			
Bremerton	Bremerton National	21407	6470	481			
Everett	Snohomish Co	21525	6665	603	•	16/109.3	
Issaquah	Issaquah	21362	6668	500	•		
Monroe	Flying F. Ranch	21481	6738	50			
Olympia	Olympia	21218	6343	206	•		
Puyallup	Pierce Co.-Thun Fld	21206	6534	530			
Port Angeles	William R. Fairchild Intl.	21740	6375	288	•		
Port Orchard	Port Orchard	21373	6483	370			
Renton	Renton Muni	21351	6612	29			
Seattle	Boeing Fld/King Co Intl	21376	6596	17	•		
Seattle	Henry M. Jackson Intl. (Seattle-Tacoma Intl)	21343	6584	429			
Shelton	Sanderson Fld.	21353	6316	278			
Snohomish Co. (Paine Field) see Everett							
Snohomish	Harvey Fld	21505	6711	16			
Spanaway	Shady Acres	21201	6501	425			
Spanaway	Spanaway	21215	6491	385			
Tacoma	Tacoma Narrows	21300	6480	292			

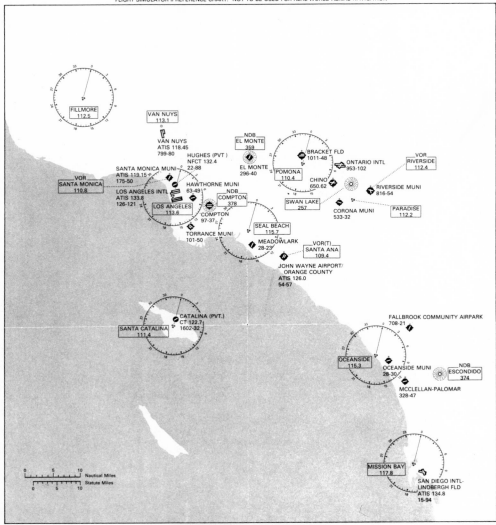

AIRPORT DIRECTORY—LOS ANGELES AREA

CITY	AIRPORT	NORTH	EAST	ALT.	F (Fuel)	ILS (Rwy/Freq.)	
Carlsbad	McClennan-Palomar	14931	6112	328			North and east coordinates are canted at
	Catalina (PVT)	15149	5744	1602			−19° (counterclockwise) to compensate
Chino	Chino	15319	6079	650			for orthogonal coordinate grid overlaid
Compton	Compton	15,334	5859	97			on Lambert conformal conic projection.
Corona	Corona Muni	15280	6083	533			
El Monte	El Monte	15397	5952	296			
Fallbrook	Fallbrook Community Airpark	15023	6144	708			
Hawthorne	Hawthorne Muni	15358	5831	63			
Huntington Beach	Meadowlark	15244	5911	28			
LaVerne	Brackett Fld	15378	6038	1011			
Los Angeles	Hughes (PVT)	15386	5808	22	*		
Los Angeles	Los Angeles Intl	15374	5805	126	*		
Oceanside	Oceanside Muni	14974	6095	28			
Ontario	Ontario Intl	15347	6099	952			
Riverside	Riverside Muni	15288	6141	816			
San Diego	San Diego Intl–Lingbergh Fld	14761	6102	15	*		
Santa Ana	John Wayne Airport/ Orange County	15211	5961	54			
Santa Monica	Santa Monica Muni	15402	5799	175	*		
Torrance	Torrance Muni	15308	5815	101			
Van Nuys	Van Nuys	15498	5811	799	*	16R/111.3	

Reprinted courtesy of SubLOGIC Corporation. Copyright 1986.

AIRPORT DIRECTORY—CHICAGO AREA

CITY	AIRPORT	NORTH	EAST	ALT.	⚡(feet)	ILS (freq/freq)
Aurora	Aurora Muni	17152	16393	706		
Bloomington	Bloomington-Normal	16593	16246	875		
Champaign (Urbana)	University of Illinois Willard	16400	16465	754	*	31/109.1
Chicago	Chicago Midway	17156	16628	619	*	
Chicago	Chicago-O'Hare Intl	17243	16578	667	*	
Chicago	Lansing Muni	17049	16697	614		
Chicago	Merrill C. Meigs	17189	16671	592	*	
Chicago/Blue Island	Howell	17100	16627	600		
Chicago/Schaumburg	Schaumburg Air Park	17247	16515	795		
Chicago/West Chicago	DuPage	17213	16466	757		
Danville	Vermilion Co	16471	16685	695		
Dwight	Dwight	16874	16404	630		
Frankfort	Frankfort	17025	16596	775		
Gibson City	Gibson City Muni	16594	16461	759		
Joliet	Joliet Park District	17038	16490	582		
Kankakee	Greater Kankakee	16846	16597	625		
Monee	Sanger	16980	16646	786		
Morris	Morris Muni	17004	16413	588		
New Lenox	New Lenox-Howell	17025	16571	745		
Paxton	Paxton	16578	16507	780		
Plainfield	Clow Intl	17116	16502	670		
Romeoville	Lewis University	17081	16518	672		
Urbana	Frasca Field	16448	16482	735		

North and east coordinates align with orthogonal coordinate grid overlaid on Lambert conformal conic projection.

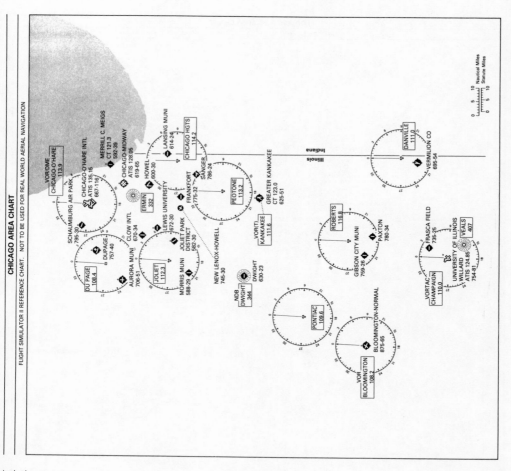

CHICAGO AREA CHART

FLIGHT SIMULATOR II REFERENCE CHART.   NOT TO BE USED FOR REAL WORLD AERIAL NAVIGATION

LEGEND

Civil-Public use airport

Restricted/Private-Nonpublic use airport, having emergency use or landmark value

Rotating light in operation, sunset to sunrise

Airport Name
Advisory Frequency (if available)
Elevation (feet) — Length (hundreds of feet)

SANTA MONICA
ATIS 119.15
175-50

VOR

VORTAC (Distance Measuring Equipment Able)

VOR/DME

Non Directional Beacon

If VOR falls directly on an airport, only the airport symbol will be shown. The VOR facility type is shown at the top of the box.

VOR/DME
NAME
FREQUENCY

NAME
FREQUENCY

NAME
FREQUENCY

NAME
FREQUENCY

AIRPORT NAME ABBREVIATIONS
CO   County
FLD   Field
INTL   International
MUNI   Municipal
(PVT)   Private Airport (prior permission before landing)

AIRPORT DIRECTORY—SAN FRANCISCO AREA

CITY	AIRPORT	NORTH	EAST	ALT.		ILS (Rwy/Freq.)
Alameda NAS	Nimitz Field	17402	5102	13		
Antioch	Antioch	17407	5295	185		
Concord	Buchanan Field	17449	5214	23	*	
Fremont	Fremont	17226	5177	4		
Half Moon Bay	Half Moon Bay	17312	5004	67		
Hayward	Hayward Air Terminal	17329	5145	47		
Livermore	Livermore Muni	17304	5247	397	*	25/110.5
Mountain View	Moffett Field NAS	17220	5134	34	*	
Oakland	Oakland Intl	17365	5124	7		11/111.9
						29/108.7
Palo Alto	Palo Alto	17245	5119	5		
San Carlos	San Carlos	17281	5084	2		
San Francisco	San Francisco Intl	17340	5060	10	*	28L/109.5
San Jose	San Jose Intl	17185	5164	56		12R/111.1
San Jose	Reid-Hillview	17160	5194	133		
San Rafael	Hamilton Army	17534	5082	3		
Tracy	Tracy Muni	17258	5366	192	*	

North and east coordinates are canted at −20° (clockwise) to compensate for orthogonal coordinate grid overlaid on Lambert conformal conic projection.

ENLARGED SECTION SAN FRANCISCO AREA CHART

FLIGHT SIMULATOR II REFERENCE CHART.   NOT TO BE USED FOR REAL WORLD AERIAL NAVIGATION.

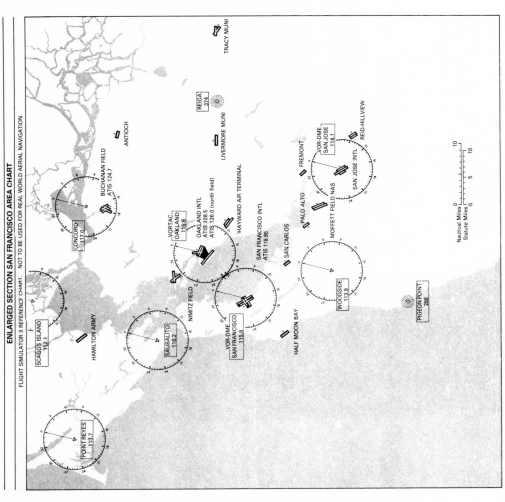

LEGEND

Civil-Public use airport	
®	Restricted-Private Nonpublic use airport, having emergency use or landmark value
☆	Rotating light in operation, sunset to sunrise
SANTA MONICA ATIS 119.15 175-50	Airport Name Advisory Frequency (if available) Elevation (feet) — Length (hundreds of feet)
⬦	VOR
⬦	VORTAC (Distance Measuring Equipment Able)
◉	VOR-DME
◎	Non Directional Beacon
NAME FREQUENCY	
NAME FREQUENCY	
NAME FREQUENCY	
NAME FREQUENCY	
VOR-DME NAME FREQUENCY	If VOR falls directly on an airport, only the airport symbol will be shown. The VOR facility type is shown at the top of the box.

AIRPORT NAME ABBREVIATIONS

CO	County
FLD	Field
INTL	International
MUNI	Municipal
(PVT)	Private Airport (prior permission before landing)

AIRPORT DIRECTORY - SAN FRANCISCO AREA

CITY	AIRPORT	NORTH	EAST	ALT.	F (Fuel)	ILS (Rwy/Frq)
Alameda NAS	Nimitz Field	17402	5102	13		
Antioch	Antioch	17407	5296	185		
Chico	Chico	18158	5567	239		
Columbia	Columbia	17289	5753	2116		
Concord	Buchanan Field	17449	5214	23	*	
Fremont	Fremont	17226	5177	4		
Fresno	Chandler Downtown	16671	5752	279		
Fresno	Fresno Air Terminal	16679	5795	331		
Garberville	Garberville	18514	5010	544		
Half Moon Bay	Half Moon Bay	17312	5145	67		
Hayward	Hayward Air Terminal	17329	5145	47		
Little River	Mendocino Co	18174	4895	571		
Livermore	Livermore Muni	17304	5247	397	*	25/110.5
Lodi	Kingdon	17408	5460	16		
Lodi	Lodi	17447	5503	59		
Marysville	Yuba Co	17840	5608	62		
Merced	Merced	16980	5608	154		
Minden	Douglas Co	17594	6104	4717		
Modesto	Modesto City	17172	5518	98		
Monterey	Monterey Peninsula	16862	5069	243	*	11/111.9
Mountain View	Moffett Field NAS	17220	5134	34		29/108.7
Napa Co	Napa Co	17571	5187	33		
Oakland	Oakland Intl	17365	5124	7	*	
Oroville	Oroville	18003	5592	200		
Palo Alto	Palo Alto	17245	5119	5		
Placerville	Placerville	17591	5748	2585		
Porterville	Porterville	16294	5898	443		
Red Bluff	Red Bluff	18347	5500	348		
Reno	Reno Cannon Intl	17788	6176	4412		
Reno-Stead	Reno-Stead	17875	6169	5046		
Sacramento	Sacramento Metro	17581	5477	23		
Sacramento	Sacramento Exec	17595	5482	23		
Salinas	Salinas	16856	5161	85		
San Carlos	San Carlos	17281	5084	2		
San Francisco	San Francisco Intl	17340	5060	10	*	28J/109.5
San Jose	San Jose Intl	17185	5164	56		12R/111.1
San Rafael	Reid-Hillview	17160	5194	133		
San Rafael	Hamilton Army	17534	5082	3		
Santa Rosa	Sonoma Co	17756	5066	125		
Santa Rosa	Santa Rosa Air Center	17711	5066	98		
South Lake Tahoe	Lake Tahoe	17570	6016	6265		
Stockton	Stockton Metro	17312	5467	30		
Tracy	Tracy Muni	17258	5366	192	*	
Truckee	Truckee-Tahoe	17761	6031	5901		
Visalia	Visalia	16454	5831	292		
Watsonville	Watsonville	16895	5138	161		
Willows	Willows-Glenn Co	18087	5409	138		

North and east coordinates are canted at
−20° (clockwise) to compensate for
orthogonal coordinate grid overlaid on
Lambert conformal conic projection.

SAN FRANCISCO AREA CHART

FLIGHT SIMULATOR II REFERENCE CHART. NOT TO BE USED FOR REAL WORLD AERIAL NAVIGATION.

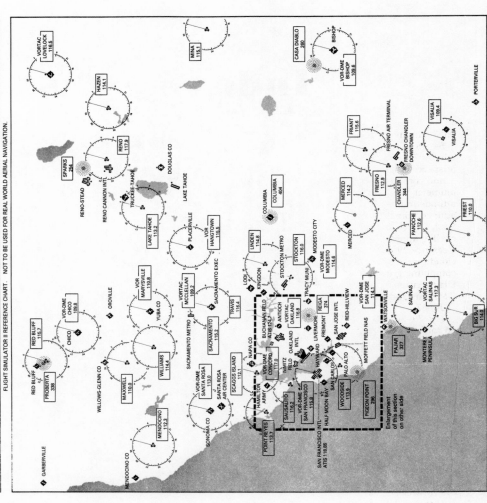

Nautical Miles 0 10 20 30 40 50
Statute Miles 0 10 20 30 40 50

Reprinted courtesy of SubLOGIC Corporation. Copyright 1986.

250

Index